Guide to Mauritius

First published in 1988 by Bradt Publications, 41 Nortoft Road, Chalfont St Peter, Bucks, SL9 0LA, England. Published in the USA by the Globe Pequot Press, 6 Business Park Road, PO Box 833, Old Saybrook, CT 06475-0833

This edition published in 1994

Copyright © 1994 Royston Ellis

British Library Cataloguing in Publication Data
A catalogue record for this book is available from the British Library

ISBN 1 898323 06 2

US Library of Congress
A catalogue record for this book is available from the Library of Congress.

US ISBN 1-56440-536-2

Maps: *Inside covers* by Carte Blanche
      Others by Caroline Crump

Cover photographs by Gemunu Amarasinghe
Illustrations by Rebecca Vanes (from photographs by Gemunu Amarasinghe)

Typeset by Acorn Bookwork, Salisbury, Wiltshire
Printed by BPC Wheatons Ltd, Exeter

THE AUTHOR

Royston Ellis is a travel writer based in Sri Lanka from where he contributes features on Asian and African destinations to major British newspapers and magazines. He is the author of the Bradt guides *India By Rail* and *Sri Lanka by Rail*.

ACKNOWLEDGEMENTS

My desire to write this guide grew out of my own enjoyment at visiting Mauritius. To all those who helped with the first edition, now completely rewritten, I am grateful for their continued advice and assistance, especially to Roselyne Hauchler, the charming and dedicated publicity officer of the Mauritius Government Tourist Office, to Marcello Giobbe, and to my old friend in Mauritius, Lindsay Genave. New friends Alain O'Reilly and Alain Maderbocus were extraordinarily kind and helpful. My thanks also to the Sri Lankan photographer, Gemunu Amarasinghe, who accompanied me on two recent visits to Mauritius and assisted me in preparing this new edition.

Royston Ellis
Bentota, Sri Lanka
1994

Trochetia, *Trochetia boutoniana*, the national flower of Mauritius

Guide to Mauritius

For tourists, business visitors and independent travellers

Royston Ellis

BRADT PUBLICATIONS, UK
THE GLOBE PEQUOT PRESS INC, USA

MAURITIUS

Photo: Gemunu Amarasinghe

It isn't just another tropical island,
It is a very unique, very special place.
Beautiful of course,
But so much more than that.
It is a hundred miles of soft
Golden coral beaches, clear calm
Coastal lagoons, spectacular scenery
That ranges from mountains to forests,
To gorges to craters;
and, it is sophistication itself.
Its cosmopolitan nature means one has the pick of the world's cuisine.
The Indian Ocean which surrounds the island offers up the finest seafoods.
The hotels believe in only the ultimate in luxury.

For more information please contact:

**The Mauritius Government
Tourist Office**
Emmanuel Anquetil Building
Sir Seewoosagur Ramgoolam Street
Port Louis
Mauritius
Tel: (+230) 201 1703
Fax: (+230) 212 5142

**The Mauritius Government
Tourist Office**
32/33 Elvaston Place
London SW7 5NW
United Kingdom
Tel: (+44 71) 584 3666
Fax: (+44 71) 225 1135

Contents

PART ONE

BRIEFING

INTRODUCTION

Mauritius, people say, is expensive. It is – but only if you want it to be. You can eat well in one of the luxury beach hotels and pay as much as in a top class restaurant in London, or you can enjoy local cuisine in a Port Louis eatery for less than a pound.

Mauritius is like that: a country for all seasons, and all budgets. For me, the marvel of Mauritius is how quickly one feels at home there. Everything is familiar and yet satisfyingly exotic. There is very little culture shock since Mauritius is a blend of people and religions from all continents. Strangers can soon find the Mauritius they want.

The 'exclusivity' of Mauritius has been preserved by a policy that prohibits charter flights and by a strategy that woos the well-to-do tourist. Perhaps this has given rise to the myth that it is an expensive place to visit. In this guide I hope to show that it isn't necessarily so.

Any visitor in a strange land for the first time will feel nervous about venturing beyond the hotel compound. In Mauritius, you need not feel apprehensive. There is an aura of middle class respectability about the country; the people are courteous and helpful: it seems *safe*. Yet the island is not dull, despite its towns and suburbs being apparently lifeless after 9pm. Its rugged mountain scenery dramatically dominates the cement boxes in which people live as defence against cyclones. Its volcanic origins set the tone of the country, giving Mauritius a vibrancy that is exciting. There is so much to do and see, and an atmosphere that encourages visitors to please themselves.

The nature lover will be overwhelmed by the haunting beauty of the island, from the starkness of the mountains to the flower-bedecked glades of the wildlife parks and nature reserves. The energetic and adventurous can go hunting, deepsea fishing, and climbing or spend less energy and more money in the island's casinos. The gourmet can track down dishes unique to Mauritius, such as smoked marlin, while the shopper can drool over duty-free diamonds.

Sooner or later someone in Mauritius will tell you that after God made Mauritius he liked it so much he fashioned paradise in its image. Mark Twain is responsible for perpetuating that idea and I am grateful to the label on a bottle of the local Green Island rum for the complete quotation:

'You gather the idea that Mauritius was made first and then heaven, and that heaven was copied after Mauritius.'

Where to go to enjoy your own particular piece of heaven? Tourists who want action and an afterbeach disco lifestyle should head for Grand Bay in the northwest. The deepsea fishermen will be better served by hotels in the Black River district on the west coast. Those who want to relax within the privacy of garden resorts by the beach will enjoy hotels in the south or on the east coast.

Business visitors will need to be centrally and comfortably located which means staying in Quatre Bornes or Curepipe. The independent traveller will find places to fit a limited budget in the capital, Port Louis, or Mahebourg, near the airport in the southeast. Anywhere you stay, you will be treated with a welcome that is genuine and warm.

Visitors to Mauritius, someone claimed, come first as tourists and stay in a beach hotel. On their second visit they rent selfcatering accommodation. On their third visit they stay with a Mauritian family. They feel at home.

If you are a first time visitor, this guide will help you to feel at home too. If you are visiting Mauritius on business, you will find hints to save the legwork of tracing information. And if you are an independent traveller on a limited budget, you will have the best time of all: discovering that Mauritius can be inexpensive and lots of fun.

Mauritius is a land of contrasting scenes and moods. Isolated from other land masses, at a crossroads between Africa, Australia and Asia, and with no land between it and the Antarctic, it is unique.

Profile

FACTS & FIGURES

Country

An independent state in the Indian Ocean, south of the Equator and just north of the Tropic of Capricorn, consisting of the islands of Mauritius, Rodrigues and dependencies. The island is known as Maurice in French.

Size

Mauritius is 1,864km^2 (720 square miles) in area, Rodrigues is 104km^2. The total area with dependencies is 2,045km^2.

History

Discovered by Arabs, then Portuguese, Mauritius was first settled by the Dutch. It was claimed by the French in 1715 as the Ile de France and captured by the British in 1810. It was a British colony until 1968 when it became an independent member of the Commonweath grouping of countries. It became a Republic in 1992.

Government

A parliamentary democracy with elections every five years, the most recent being in July 1991.

Population

1,100,000 of Indian, African, European and Chinese origin.

Language

The official language is English but Creole is the most widely used. Most people speak (and read) French, with Hindi, Tamil and Chinese as the main alternatives.

Religions

Hinduism, Islam, Christianity and also Confucianism and Buddhism.

Economy

Based on industrial and agricultural exports, tourism and financial services, with low unemployment and inflation.

Currency	The rupee (abbreviated to Rs), which is divided into 100 cents. The international exchange rate fluctuates daily, linked to a basket of currencies. The rate of exchange in February 1994 was Rs26 for £1, and Rs18.65 for US$1.
Weights & Measures	The metric system was officially introduced in 1985. However distances shown on sign posts are still in miles and weights in shops and markets are in pounds.
Climate	Hot summers (November to April) with average coastal temperature of 30°C (86°F) and warm winters (May to October), averaging 24°C (75°F). Interior temperatures are 5°C lower. The rainy season is January to May with the possibility of a stray cyclone in January and February.
Nature	Mountainous with plateaux; flowers, forests and crops; rare wildlife and nothing dangerous; fine beaches within coral reefs.
Visitors	Tourists come all the year round with November to January and August being the most popular months. May and October are most pleasant. In 1993, there were almost 400,000 visitors.
Hotels	At the end of 1992 there were 84 hotels (not including boarding houses) offering 5,271 rooms.

GEOGRAPHY

Its isolated location kept Mauritius from being settled until 400 years ago and even today, most people don't know where it is, or even of its existence. On a world map, it is an insignificant dot in that vast expanse of ocean between southern Africa and Australia, at longitude 57½° east, latitude 20° south, overshadowed by its much larger neighbour, Madagascar, 855kms (550 miles) to the west.

Africa is the nearest continent, with Mombasa some 1,800kms (1,200 miles) away. It is also 3,370kms (2,900 miles) southwest of Sri Lanka and 6,000kms (3,728 miles) from Perth. London, by air, is 9,755kms (6,060 miles) away.

Mauritius is part of the Mascarene Archipelago, together with its closest neighbour, the French island of Réunion (161km/100 miles away), and its own territory, Rodrigues, which lies 563km (350 miles) to the east, a mountainous, barren island only 103km^2 (40ml^2) in size. The Cargados Garayos Archipelago, also known as the St Brandon Islands, 395kms (245 miles) northeast of Mauritius, and the two Agalega Islands, 1200kms (745 miles) to the north are Mauritian dependencies.

Mauritius also claims Tromelin Island, although this is occupied by France, and would like to reclaim the Six Islands, Peros Banhos, Salomon, Trois Frères and Diega Garcia, which have, since 1965, been the British Indian Ocean Territory.

The Island of Mauritius is 65km (40 miles) long, at its longest, and 45km (28 miles) across at its widest. There are 160km (100 miles) of coastline, almost entirely surrounded by coral reefs, while the centre is a great plateau punctuated by impressive mountains. The whole state, including its dependencies, has a land area of only 2,045km^2 (790ml^2), although, because the islands are so spread out, its sea area is vast.

Around Mauritius itself there are more than 15 islets lying in their own lagoons, and north of the island, uninhabited except for wildlife, are five small islands: Serpent, Round, Flat, Gabriel and Gunner's Quoin.

Whether arriving by air or approaching from the sea, the mountains are awesome, incredible: volcanic spires thrown up by eruptions millions of years ago. These jagged peaks of basalt dominate the landscape and skyline wherever one looks.

The island's origins go back 13 million years when masses of molten lava bubbled up beneath the ocean floor. It took five million years to surface through the activity of two volcanic craters. The weathered crater rims of these once enormous peaks still remain as the mountain ranges of Black River, Grand Port and Moka.

Further volcanic activity followed four million years later, opening up the craters of Trou-aux-Cerfs, Bassin Blanc and Trou Kanaka. The island's volcanoes have now been extinct for 200,000 years, although odd lava flows may have occurred 10,000 years ago. The first colonisers were marine plants and the larvae of sedentary marine animals. Lichens encrusted the bare rocks and as a powdery soil was formed, plants brought by winds, sea and birds began to take root.

The island's rugged profile is a constant reminder of these cataclysms. Coastal plains smothered in sugarcane, leaves waving like long green ribbons in the wind, soar without the warning of foothills into stark peaks. The broad plain of the north rises to an extensive, fertile plateau, itself broken by more volcanic steeples and gorges. This tableland (600m/1,970ft high) is also bordered by mountains which roll down to the crags of the southern coastline.

It is not the height of the mountains which is impressive, but the sheer oddity of their shape. The highest is Piton de la Rivière Noire at 826m (2,711ft). Pieter Both is next at 820m (2,690ft) with Pouce – the thumb-shaped mountain looming behind Port Louis – at 812m (2,664ft).

Despite the mountains and a rainfall on the windward slopes of the central plateau that can amount to five metres (197ins) a year, Mauritius is not an island of great rivers. There are some 60 small rivers and streams, many degenerating as they reach the coast into rubbish-clogged trickles through cement ditches and culverts. The Grand River South East is the largest, 39.4kms (24.5 miles) long. The Rivière du Poste is 24.1kms (15 miles) long.

The main harbour is at Port Louis, the capital, on the west coast. The airport is at the opposite side of the island to the capital, at Plaisance, not far from the old east coast harbour of Grand Port, 45km (28 miles) from Port Louis, and 21.7kms (13.5 miles) from Curepipe, the residential town in the tableland of the interior.

The island is divided into the same nine districts as it was when the British captured it in 1810. In a clockwise direction from the capital, these districts are: Port Louis, Pamplemousses, Rivière du Rempart, Flacq, Grand Port, Savanne and Black River with Plaines Wilhems and Moka in the centre. Rodrigues is a district by itself.

The eccentric terrain of Mauritius means that the island is blessed with a diversity of scenery not usually found in such a small area, and since there are good roads, travel only takes a matter of minutes. For instance, relief from the humid heat of Port Louis can be found in 25 minutes in Curepipe, 22km (13.5 miles) away. When the brashness of the northwest coast is too much, there is the tranquility of the southwest, or the dramatic coastline of the south.

POPULATION

There are probably 1,100,000 inhabitants now although the population is rising rapidly. Over 150,000 of them now live in Port Louis, but the most populous area is the central district of Plaine Wilhems where 30% of the population live in the towns of Curepipe, Beau Bassin/Rose Hill, Quatre Bornes and Vacoas/Phoenix. Approximately 35,000 people live in Rodrigues.

Despite the high population density (about 570 people per km^2), there is no impression of an island teeming with humanity. Town streets are uncrowded (even if the roads are jammed with cars) and deserted areas of beach and forest are easy to find.

In 1835, when the British abolished slavery, there were just over 100,000 inhabitants. By 1901, this had grown to 371,023 and at the time of independence in 1968 the population had swelled to 700,000.

The population is overwhelmingly young with a natural increase of

11.6 per 1,000 inhabitants in 1986. Life expectancy is around 65 years
for a male and 71 years for a female.

PEOPLE

Intoxicating mixture

In the enthusiastic prose of the Government Tourist Office 'the people
are unique for their sheer diversity: Indians, Creoles, Muslims,
French, Chinese and an intoxicating range of mixtures'.

It is potentially an explosive mixture too although here the tensions
are relaxed, replaced by a verve for living and a lifestyle that inspired
another slogan of the Tourist Office: 'the most cosmopolitan island in
the sun'.

Mauritians are delighted to speak to visitors, although the stranger
may have to start up the conversation first. The ethnic diversity
means that, unless dressed like a typical tourist, you won't stand out
and can wander around without being the object of curiosity. If
people approach to talk to you, it will probably be a genuine offer of
help or hospitality and not a sales ploy.

Since all Mauritians are descended from immigrants, (many elders
have grandparents who actually lived in another country) the ethnic
groups are distinctive in appearance, religion and language, although
the distinctions are getting blurred and the many ethnic labels have
now been whittled down to The General Population, The Indo-
Mauritians and The Sino-Mauritians.

General population

All those who can't be tagged as being of Indian or Chinese descent,
the General Population makes up about 30% of the islanders. They
are the whites, the Creoles and the Mixed Breeds, with European
influences of culture and religion, although Creoles and the mixed
races have African ancestors.

The whites are descended from French settlers. Curiously, despite
158 years of British presence, only a handful of families think of
themselves as 'English'. These Franco-Mauritians make up only 2 to
3% of the population, but hold much of the island's private wealth
and dominate the professions and management.

Mauritian Creoles are *hybrids* of any kind, whether with white
ancestry or African or Malagasy origins.

Creoles of varying hue are the result of inter-marriage that cut
across class and ethnic considerations. They form about a quarter of
the total population, part of every strata of society as well as forming
a large working class. Their influence is a unifying one and their
language, Creole, is the *lingua franca* of the entire population, spoken
by all races.

Indo-Mauritians

Indian immigrants began to arrive after the emancipation of slaves in 1835, although some came later from the Indian subcontinent. By 1861 the Indian population outnumbered the whites and Creoles by 192,634 to 117,416, forming the ethnic and cultural majority. They now make up two thirds of the population.

There are two major groups by religious definition: Hindus (some of whom are actually Tamils) and Muslims. Many of the Muslims migrated independently from India and Pakistan as traders. The Hindus form over 52% of the population and the Muslims about 16%. To confuse the situation, inter-marriage has resulted in an Indo-Mauritian element being introduced into the (Christian) General Population as well.

As well as forming the backbone of the labouring and agricultural communities, the Indo-Mauritians have developed through a history of industrial and political agitation to take vital roles in the economic and political life of the island.

Sino-Mauritians

Mauritians of Chinese origin are a small but ubiquitous ethnic community forming about 2% of the population. The first Chinese migrants came from Canton in the 19th century but the largest group is the Hakkas, from the province of Honan in northeast China.

There is a large Chinese quarter in Port Louis but Sino-Mauritians are to be found throughout the island, mostly as retailers or traders.

Their contribution to the development and unification of Mauritius is Chinese cuisine, which is found in private homes, as well as in restaurants and food stalls.

In spite of this wide variety of peoples, one of the attractions of Mauritius is its ethnic *mix*, not its ethnic *division*.

The Prime Minister of Mauritius, Sir Aneerood Jugnauth, summed up his people aptly when he said: 'The single great wealth of this island nation is its people, a multi-national group with an amazing blend of cultures, a political maturity admired by friend and foe alike and a jealously guarded freedom ... The hospitality of Mauritians is legendary and spontaneous'.

RELIGION

There were 87 different religious denominations represented in Mauritius according to the 1983 census figures. Since there is complete freedom of religion, new sects or groupings have emerged within the main religions of Hinduism, Christianity and Islam. Mauritians enjoy the festivals of other religions as well as their own.

Christianity

Christianity was the first religion in Mauritius and is now the religion of both the General Population and of more than 80% of the Sino-Mauritians. Roman Catholicism became the official religion of the Ile de France in 1721, spreading with the Franch conversion of their slaves and still permitted to flourish after the British arrived.

There are at least a quarter of a million Roman Catholics and a cathedral – St Louis – in Port Louis.

Anglicans, Presbyterians, and the evangelical Christian religions such as the Assembly of God and Adventists all play a part in the society, as do at least a dozen other denominations including Jehovah Witnesses, Methodists and Swedenborgians. With its various sects, Christianity is the second largest faith in the country, and about 30% of the population are Christians of some kind.

Hinduism

Over 52% of Mauritians are followers of one of the many Hindu sects, the majority being Sanatanists, or orthodox Hindus.

Local Tamils however have their own religion which has evolved since 1771 when the French granted permission for a Tamil temple in Port Louis, and the reformist movement of Arya Samaj in which worship is of spirit Brahma and not of statues or idols, took hold from 1910, when the first 'Samaj' was opened in Port Louis.

Devout Hindus proclaim their faith with small shrines and red or white pennants fluttering outside their homes. Several villages have Hindu temples, the largest being at Triolet.

Tamils sometimes indulge in spectacular forms of worship in honour of different deities, such as fire walking and piercing their flesh with enormous needles. Saints of other religions, especially Père Laval whose shrine is at Sainte Croix, are also worshipped by Hindus.

As with Christianity, there are a variety of sects including Kabir Panthis, a reformist group, Rabidass, and the Hare Rama Krishna sect.

Islam

The Muslims of Mauritius form about 16% of the total population. The vast majority (95%) of them are Sunni Muslims and are divided into three subgroups.

The Sunni Hanafites number over 150,000; the Meimons, are a much smaller (about 3,000) aristocracy, with responsibility for the best-known mosque in Mauritius, the Jummah (Friday) Mosque in Port Louis; while the Sunni Surtis number about 5,000.

The Shi'ite Muslims are very few and are subdivided into groups. One is the Cocknies from Cochin in the south east of India who came as boat builders to Mauritius. Since inter-marrying with Creoles they have created a people known as Creole Lascars.

Chinese religions

The Chinese religions are almost dying out since the majority of Sino-Mauritians have embraced Roman Catholicism. The 1983 census revealed 3,657 Buddhists and 76 believers in Confucianism.

The first Chinese temple was opened in Port Louis in 1846. Other temples have since been opened by the Cantonese Nam Shun Fooye Koon society and the Hakka Heeh Foh society. There is a temple for Buddhist nuns in Volcy Pougnet Street in Port Louis.

Other religions

There are about 600 Baha'is in Mauritius and about three dozen Jews. According to the 1983 census, 338 Mauritians followed 56 other religions. Only 0.2% of the population claimed to have no religion.

Throughout Mauritius there are gothic-style churches, high-domed temples, minareted mosques and ornate pagodas in the most unlikely places – the middle of a sugar canefield, by the race course – testifying to the strong Mauritian belief in religion. It is not fanaticism but an enduring way of life which Mauritians relish.

LANGUAGE

The official language of Mauritius is English; the real language of the people is Creole.

The English-speaking visitor should not count on being understood everywhere in Mauritius. Although English is the medium of teaching in schools and the working language of government and business, out of school and work it is rarely used with ease. Less than 3,000 Mauritians speak English at home.

French is sometimes seen as the language of the elite and is used in polite and formal circumstances, although not at government level. The daily newspapers are in French with only the occasional paragraph in English. It is the home tongue of about 35,000 Mauritians but has lost popularity over the years.

Creole is the *lingua franca* of Mauritius, understood and spoken by all Mauritians, whatever their mother tongue. It is the home language of about 52% of the population but incredibly, is neither taught in schools nor officially recognized as a language, and has no popular written form. It is a *patois*, structurally distinct from French but borrowing most of its vocabulary from that tongue, although pronunciation is different. It evolved from the pidgin used by the French masters of the 18th century to communicate with their slaves, also borrowing words from African and Malagasy dialects.

Its popularity stems from the ease with which it can be learnt. Since the African population was disinclined to learn Indian or Chinese languages, the new immigrants of the 19th century took to

Creole as an easy means of communicating. It requires little intellectual effort to speak and English, French and Indian words can be adapted by 'creolising' them. There are no rules, it can be pronounced according to whim and foreigners settling in Mauritius soon speak it without embarrassment at making grammatical errors (it has no grammar) or pronouncing words wrongly.

Creole's lowly origins have caused the language to be treated with contempt in the past but its unifying value as the one language that all Mauritians speak and understand has now been recognised. While it shares characteristics with the Creole spoken in the Caribbean and the Bayous of Louisiana, a Mauritian would not immediately understand, for example, the Creole of Dominica.

The main mother tongue of the country's largest ethnic group is Hindi. Tamil was actually the first Indian language spoken in Mauritius and today about the same number speak Tamil as their home language as speak French.

While Hindi is the medium for religious ceremonies and is looked on as a sign of education and prestige (spoken as a home language by over 100,000 people), the Indian equivalent of Creole is Bhojpuri, spoken by more than 200,000. Other Indian languages used as mother tongues are Urdu, Telegu, Marathi and Gujarathi.

Arabic is also spoken, although most of the preaching in the mosques is in Creole. Less than a third of the Chinese community (about 6,000) speak Chinese languages, including Hakka, Mandarin and Cantonese. There are 22 languages actually spoken in Mauritius, an extraordinary number for just over a million people.

For the visitor wanting to speak Creole, there are several locally-printed Creole phrase books on sale in Mauritius. The language is written phonetically and the hardest part seems to be to understand the odd spelling used, such as *ahn-kohr* (meaning *more*). Although it sounds an aggressive language it is very colourful, rich in clichés and ribaldry.

Jummah Mosque, Port Louis

The Past

HISTORY

The delightful *mélange* that is Mauritius has its origins in a mixed-up history. It was Dutch ... French ... and finally British until the country's independence in 1968.

When the British invaded in 1810 their aim was to neutralise the island so it wouldn't be used as a base for French attacks on British vessels bound for India, not colonisation. Although the British remained longer than anyone else (158 years) the settlers – who were French speaking traditionalists – were allowed to keep their religion, customs, laws and language, and the predominant remaining European influence is French.

The first recorded discovery of Mauritius was by Islamic colonisers, when, in 975 AD, Hasan ibn Ali, a mercurial leader from Shiraz, Iran, left his homeland with a fleet of seven ships and a band of followers.

Most of them eventually settled in Mombasa and Pemba although one of their ships went as far as the Comoros, a name derived from the Arabic *Komr*. From there they reached Madagascar and the islands to the east of it. In 15th century maps, these were shown as *Dina Arobi* (Mauritius), *Dina Margabim* (Réunion) and *Dina Moraze* (Rodrigues).

It is unlikely that the colonisers actually settled in *Dina Arobi*. The island was uninhabited then and no evidence of Arab settlements has ever been found. Its neighbour, Madagascar, known to the Arabs as *Qanbalu*, was inhabited but according to a 12th century observer, Idrisi, its inhabitants had no boats capable of crossing the sea.

In the wake of Vasco de Gama's penetration of the Indian Ocean via the Cape of Good Hope, came the Portuguese *conquistadores*. While they progressed along the African and Indian coasts, they never tried to establish themselves properly in Madagascar and neighbouring islands. Pero Mascarenhas (after whom the Mascarenes were named) is credited with the European discovery of Réunion in 1512 and Mauritius is said to have been discovered by navigator Domingo Fernandez about 1511, although there is some doubt that he ever saw the island. No Portuguese settlement was started despite the island's ideal situation on the route from the Cape to India.

Mauritius became known on Portuguese maps as *Ilha do Cirne*,

Island of the Swan, possibly after the 'land swan' which then inhabited the island: the dodo. A more prosaic theory is that the name was
derived from that of a Portuguese vessel.

In 1538 Diego Rodriguez gave his name to the island still known as
Rodrigues. Portuguese names have also survived on other neighbouring islands including Diego Garcia in the Chagos Archipelago, which
was named after another Portuguese navigator.

If the Portuguese did visit Mauritius, it was infrequently. On their
way to and from India they preferred to use the Mozambique Channel, staying close to the African coast rather than risking the open
sea. Mauritius remained uninhabited except by bats and tropical
birds, many of which, like the dodo, are now extinct.

The great bay on the southeast corner of the island, now known as
Grand Port, was a natural haven for ships. During the latter part of
the 16th century, Swan Island was probably used by pirates who
preyed on the pilgrim route between India and Jeddah. Vessels from a
Dutch fleet on its way from Amsterdam to Java sailed in during a
violent storm in September 1598. Many of the crew were suffering
from scurvy and the landfall was seen as a godsend.

Admiral Wybrandt van Warwyck was in command of the fleet and
he arrogantly named the bay after himself, calling it Warwyck Haven,
a name immediately forgotten. His choice of a name for the island
had a catchier ring to it. He claimed possession for the Stadthouder
of the Netherlands, Prince Mauritius van Nassau.

The Dutch were fascinated by the island, especially by the trusting
curiosity of the birds which had yet to learn fear and allowed themselves to be knocked down with a club. In Grant's *History of Mauritius* published in London in 1801 the dodo is described as 'a
feathered tortoise' whose sluggish movements made it an easy target
for the laziest hunter. But although the Dutch called occasionally for
shelter, food and fresh water, sharing their victualling visits with
pirates, they took little interest in developing the island.

In 1622, Danish adventurers arrived, hoping to exploit the ebony
with which the island abounded. The French and British, too, began
to see possibilities both for trade and strategy in the Mascarenes and
sent out expeditions in 1638. Their ships arrived too late.

In May 1638, Cornelius Simonsz Gooyer had set up the first perma-
nent Dutch settlement in Mauritius. He was sent by the Netherlands
East India Company and became the first governor, over a population
of 25 colonists who planned to exploit the island's resources of fine
ebony and ambergris, as well as rearing cattle and growing tobacco.

Over the next few years, a hundred slaves were imported from
Madagascar and convicts sent over from Batavia. The convicts were
Europeans, Indonesians and Indians and were employed in cutting
ebony. The free colonists came from Baltic and North Sea ports, har-
dened men who were settlers out of desperation and coercion rather

than through brave ideals. From its very first settlement, Mauritius had a mixed of races that was to set a pattern for its future.

The settlers supported themselves by raising vegetables and live-stock which they sold to the Company or, for more profit, to the crews of visiting French, English and pirate ships. Yet although the settlement grew to 500, it did not prosper.

The slaves from Madagascar escaped to the forest and began to exact revenge for Dutch cruelties by destroying their crops and slaughtering their cattle. Invasions by hungry rats added to the pro-blems of the settlement. The lack of interest by the Dutch East India Company in its fledgeling colony finally demoralised the colonists.

A few years after the Dutch founded the Cape of Good Hope in 1652, the island was abandoned completely, the European market for ebony being glutted.Only the sugar cane that had been introduced from Batavia and the runaway Malagasy slaves in the forests remained.

The Dutch tried again in 1664, starting a settlement under the aegis of the Cape colony. They were more ambitious this time with attempts at agriculture on a commercial scale, including tobacco, sugar cane, indigo and maize. Deer, introduced from Java, thrived in the forests and were hunted for food and pelts. Forts were built on the eastern coast, forests cleared and domestic animals raised.

Legend has it that the Dutch were driven off for a second time in 1710 by the rats they had themselves accidently introduced. Pique at colonial bureaucracy also played its part since the superior (although junior) colony at the Cape received preferential treatment from the Dutch authorities. The settlers were ill-suited to be colonists; they suf-fered from the heat, were undisciplined, lazy and prone to drunkenness.

Meanwhile, a new state was forming in Madagascar. Called Liber-talia, it was a pirate republic founded by a French adventurer and a defrocked Italian monk. There was no shortage of tough men, mostly pirates from every nation, who made Libertalia their home. From there they successfully plundered shipping throughout the Indian Ocean and their community thrived. These men were to contribute to the new colonisation of Mauritius.

The French East India Company had already occupied Bourbon (now Réunion) as a trading centre, but although the island had fertile soil and attracted as settlers a great number of pirates and their off-spring by Malagasy women, it lacked harbours. The attraction of a vacant Mauritius with its well-protected bays was irresistible.

A preliminary expedition led by Guillaume Dufresne D'Arsel took possession of Mauritius in the name of King Louis XV of France in September 1715, naming it the Ile de France so its ownership would be in no doubt. D'Arsel placed the French flag near what is now Port Louis, drew up a document witnessed by his officers declaring the island French and, after three days, sailed away.

Nearly seven years passed before the French East India Company actually occupied the island. In 1721 a motley crew of Company officials, settlers, and slaves from Madagascar, Mozambique and West Africa were landed. Swiss mercenaries made up the garrison. Pirates and their women accompanied them.

More women were rounded up on the waterfronts of St Malo and Bordeaux and shipped out to swell the island's population. It was hoped that a grant of land, a sum of money and the prospect of an imported wife would be enough to tempt men to settle.

For the first 14 years, the French colony followed the dismal experience of the Dutch. Only the most desperate and toughest of settlers survived, eking out a living from the pittance they earned from the Company. Their appallingly treated slaves also escaped to become *marrons*, living in the forest and sabotaging the plantations.

A forlorn settlement of palm thatched cabins sprung up near the west coast harbour of Port Louis, where the French East India Company decided to build the capital. The Company, however, maintained its headquarters in Bourbon, despairing of ever controlling their reluctant settlers or making a profit on their investment in the Ile de France.

The solution was an inspired one. As the new Governor of the Ile de France and Bourbon, the French East India Company appointed an aristocratic sea captain, Bertrand François Mahé de Labourdonnais. He was 38 and full of ambition when he sailed into the Port Louis harbour in 1735.

The wretched conditions of the settlers dismayed Labourdonnais. There were 190 whites in the island and 648 blacks, most of them African or Malagasy slaves, together with a few Indians from the Coromandel and Malabar coasts.

Labourdonnais transformed the island from a colony of malcontents into 'the star and key of the Indian Ocean'. He was a born leader and as a naval man understood the lusty spirit of men with pirate blood flowing in their veins. Despite – or was it because of? – his own blue blood, he had an affinity for the struggling colonisers. He began his task by giving them self-respect and ambition.

He ordered that the seat of government of the two colonies be transferred from Bourbon, which was better established, to the Ile de France, and set up a council to administer the islands. He channelled the seafaring abilities of his settlers back to the sea, deliberately creating a navy of buccaneers.

The thatched hovels were demolished and in their place rose forts, barracks, warehouses, hospitals and houses, many of which survive in part of Port Louis today. Government House was built of coral blocks, roads were opened throughout the island and a ship building industry commenced.

Although he had to import slaves, Labourdonnais made their lot easier by also importing ox-carts so slaves could be utilised for more skilled tasks. He turned many of them into artisans, to make up for the lack of skilled men among the settlers.

He also pushed through an agriculture programme that concentrated on feeding the islanders and on marketable produce. On his own estates he grew sugar cane, encouraging new settlers to start plantations of cotton, indigo, coffee and manioc. The first sugar factory was opened at Villebague in 1744. A salt pan was started and he even tried to rear silkworms.

Gradually a civilised life evolved in Port Louis, attracting colonisers from Bourbon, and even from good French families. Labourdonnais is known today as the father of the colony.

In 1746, with England and France at war, Labourdonnais led an expedition of nine ships from the Ile de France to India. There they defeated a British squadron and captured Madras, the most important British outpost.

Labourdonnais' actions resulted in a conflict with Dupleix, his superior in India, and to his own downfall. Dupleix wanted Madras razed to the ground but Labourdonnais refused because he knew the British would pay a ransom to get Madras back.

He was accused of accepting a bribe to preserve Madras and was replaced as Governor of the Ile de France. On his return to France he was thrown into the Bastille. Although in 1751 he was found innocent, he died a broken man two years later, aged 54. His statue stands in Port Louis facing out across the harbour. The town of Mahebourg (started in 1805) is named after him. So, too, is Mahé, capital of the Seychelles.

In 1764, the French East India Company, brought to bankruptcy by the Seven Years War, made over its assets, including the Ile de France, to the French king. In 1767, the Royal Government was established on the island. At that time there was a population of 18,773 which included 3,163 Europeans and 587 free blacks, mostly Hindus. The rest were slaves.

The appositely named Pierre Poivre (Peter Pepper) was picked as administrator. He introduced varieties of plants from South America, including pepper, and even offered tax incentives to planters to grow them. Under his influence, the colony developed as an agricultural and trading centre. He improved the harbour facilities and the accommodation for both colonists and slaves, and secured the cooperation of the planters in exploiting the island's natural resources.

When the French East India Company was wound up, and their monopoly broken, private enterprise became the fashion. Everyone was trying to make profits, usually unethically. Privateering flourished, especially during the American Revolutionary War when the Ile de France was the base for 29 privateer expeditions from 1779 to 1782, as well as several others fitted out for 'war and trade'.

In 1785 the Ile de France was declared the seat of government of all French possessions east of the Cape. A French nobleman, Vicomte de Souillac, was made governor (from 1779 to 1787) bringing an era of extravagance to the colony. Port Louis became renowned for its bright social life with dancing parties for the young and old, duelling, gambling, drinking and hunting. There was privateers' booty aplenty to pay for it.

At the same time, public affairs were neglected; fraud, corruption and dishonesty were commonplace and land speculation and scandals were rife.

On the last Sunday in January 1790, a packet-boat arrived in the Port Louis harbour from France, flying a new flag, the Tricolour. It brought news of the revolution in France. An elected assembly and municipal councils were set up and tribunals replaced courts of justice. A National Guard was formed, streets were renamed and revolutionary clubs started. Church property was confiscated and white, red and blue cockades were sported with delight. A guillotine was even erected in the Champ de Mars but its only victim was a dog (some historians say a goat) decapitated to try it out.

The colonists' enthusiasm for the revolutionary principles of liberty, equality and fraternity faltered when in 1796 two agents of the Directoire, wearing splendid orange cloaks, arrived from France and informed the startled colonists that slavery was abolished. The news was received with anger and the agents had to flee for their lives.

The last French governor of the Ile de France was appointed by Napoleon Bonaparte in 1803 to bring the colony back to order after 13 years of autonomy. With such a task, it was inevitable that the governor, General Charles Decaen, would be unpopular.

He dissolved all the elected councils and adopted a dictatorial attitude to administration. But since planters were allowed to keep their slaves and privateers their hugely profitable (and patriotic) calling of attacking British vessels, the people accepted his rule.

Decaen founded primary schools and the Lycée Coloniale which became Royal College. He extended Government House, created Mahebourg near Grand Port, and encouraged intellectual societies and agricultural development. He also codified the Napoleonic laws which are still in force.

Yet Decaen found himself increasingly isolated from France. The British were expanding their influence in the Indian Ocean and he expected retribution for the attacks of the Port Louis based privateers on their shipping.

When the British captured the Cape of Good Hope in 1806, and France failed to provide him with adequate forces, Decaen was driven to desperate measures and requisitioned the privateers' vessels, including that of the notorious Robert Surcouf.

Robert Surcouf was a rough yet witty man, renowned as the 'King of the Corsairs', who attacked English vessels with great success during the so-called *guerre de course* which lasted from 1793 to the Peace of Amiens in 1802.

An Englishman once remonstrated with Surcouf saying: 'The French only fight for profit whilst the English fight for honour and glory'.

'That only proves', replied Surcouf, 'that each of us fights to acquire something that he does not possess.'

The British, incensed by the harassment of their shipping routes to India, began to close in, blockading the Ile de France, and preventing ships from entering or leaving Port Louis.

In 1809, British forces from both the Cape and India occupied the neighbouring island of Rodrigues from which they prepared their attack on all the Mascarenes. Bourbon, which had been renamed Réunion during the revolutionary years, was taken. A major battle was fought between the French and British fleets off Grand Port in August 1810. After prolonged fighting, the French won a victory that no one expected.

In December, 70 vessels and 11,500 soldiers set sail from Rodrigues for the north of the Ile de France. British spies and reconnaisance had found a passage near Gunner's Quoin through the shoals of the northern coast at Cap Malheureux. Decaen was taken by surprise as he awaited the invasion closer in Port Louis. The British forces under General Abercrombie marched on the capital, meeting only token resistance.

Faced with the might of the British forces and the indifference of the settlers to remaining French, Decaen surrendered.

Soldiers were to be treated as civilians, not as prisoners of war, and were allowed to leave the island. Settlers who did not want to stay under a British administrator were permitted to return to France with all their possessions. These generous capitulation terms also included British pledges to preserve the island's laws, customs, language, religion and property.

The majority of settlers remained. The island, not France, was their home. Perhaps some expected the colony to be restored to France in peace time. The Treaty of Paris did restore Bourbon/Réunion in 1814 but the Ile de France, by now with its former name of Mauritius, was confirmed as a British possession.

A dashing, unorthodox personality in the Labourdonnais mould, Robert Farquhar, became the first British governor in 1810, aged 34.

He soon revealed himself as remarkably independent of the British government in London, taking advantage of the long time it took for despatches from London to reach Mauritius to act as he thought best.

Farquhar was skilful in winning the French settlers to his side, particularly through his scrupulous interpretation of the capitulation terms. Since the settlers were allowed their customs, he permitted them to continue with the slave trade despite the British law of 1807 which prohibited trading in slaves in the British Empire.

Nor was there an influx of British settlers. The few who arrived to trade were not popular, although the British officials who stayed for years did become liked.

Farquhar had to contend with many calamities during his administration, including an outbreak of smallpox in 1811 and of rabies in 1813.

There was a disastrous fire in Port Louis in 1816 when 700 houses, mostly wooden, were destroyed which resulted in new ones being built of stone. A cholera epidemic broke out in 1819, and there were fierce cyclones in 1818 and 1819.

Farquhar campaigned for reliance on sugar cane because it was the only money-making crop able to withstand cyclones, encouraging the planters to abandon coffee, cotton and their other crops. He also established Port Louis as a free port open to ships of all nations to compensate for the absence of booty from privateering, and stimulated food production and road building. He proved to the inhabitants that there were distinct economic advantages in being British instead of French.

He mixed with everyone, encouraging the younger generation and opening dialogue with coloured leaders. Although his stance on slavery seemed ambivalent, he believed in attacking the slave trade at its source (in this case Madagascar) and worked for its elimination there as a way of ending the trade to Mauritius. He set up an office for the registration of slaves and tried to ameliorate the condition of slavery in the face of hostility from their owners.

Yet like Labourdonnais before him, Farquhar ran foul of his home government and was recalled to England in 1817. He returned to Mauritius, though, in 1820 as Sir Robert and governed for a further three years.

The attempts by the British government to abolish slavery in Mauritius met with resistance from the planters who, having been persuaded to concentrate on sugar as an income-earning export crop, relied on slave labour to produce it. The arrival of Attorney General John Jeremy in 1832 to force through emancipation led to clashes and Jeremy was obliged to flee the island.

This time the planters' triumph was short lived, and slavery was abolished on February 1 1835. The planters were however paid over two million pounds compensation. They considered this to be half the total value of their 68,613 registered slaves.

For the slaves the pleasure of emancipation was dulled by the imposition of a four year period of apprenticeship during which they were supposed to work for their former masters in return for meagre wages. Not surprisingly, the scheme failed and slaves took up residence in unpopulated coastal areas where they suffered years of neglect. The wily planters turned to an alternative source of compliant labour: Indian migrants, known in Mauritius as 'the coolie trade'.

Indian migrants had been in Mauritius since 1736 when Labourdonnais brought in 40 artisans from Pondicherry. They were followed by others who worked as messengers, servants and even as merchants. In 1834, the planters began actively to recruit workers in India to replace the labour lost to them by emancipation. By 1838, there were 24,000 Indians in Mauritius and over 200,000 were brought in between 1840 and 1870 to meet the insatiable demands of the rapidly expanding sugar industry.

While the British administration introduced parliamentary elections and limited franchise in 1886 in response to demands for reform, the Indians continued to arrive until they constituted the majority of the population, no longer easily assimilated.

Recruitment ended in 1907 by which time the impact of Indian immigration had changed the course of the island's history. The new majority came to wield influence in all spheres, not only by their contribution of an efficient workforce that sustained the economy, but also by a vigorous intellectual force in politics.

The political reforms of 1886, however, excluded the Indian population although they launched the beginning of a parliamentary democracy. Universal franchise was finally granted only in 1959.

In 1901 Mohandas Gandhi (later Mahatma Gandhi) visited Mauritius and as a result sent Manillal Doctor, an Indian lawyer, to Port Louis in 1907 to organise the indentured labourers who had no say in politics and no civil rights. A Royal Commission from Britain visited in 1907 and made wide-ranging recommendations for the reorganization of agriculture, the civil service, education and the constitution under which only 2% of the population were then qualified to register as electors.

Party politics followed the constitutional reforms of 1886 with the 'Oligarques' of the conservative Parti de l'Ordre dominant over the 'democrats' of Action Libérale until the early 1920s. The socialist Mauritius Labour Party (MLP) founded in 1936 represented one side of the traditional two-party system with the Railliement Mauricien on the right. A multi-party system based on ethnic as well as political appeal evolved after 1950.

The First World War brought suffering to the island with drastic cuts in shipping bringing food shortages and consequent price rises. There was a local campaign after the war for Mauritius to be returned to France but the so called 'retrocessionist' candidates were heavily defeated in the 1921 general election.

The Second World War brought infrastructural development. The British based their fleet at Port Louis and Grand Port, as well as building an airport at Plaisance and a sea plane base at Baie du Tombeau (an unfortunate name). A large telecommunication station was built at Vacoas, although the first underwater telephone cable, linking South Africa to Australia, had been laid to Mauritius in 1901.

In the election held after the war, the MLP won the majority of seats in the Legislative Council set up under the 1948 constitution. This success was repeated in 1953. After the 1959 election (the first held following the introduction of universal adult franchise), Hindu doctor (later Sir) Seewoosagur Ramgoolam, leader of the MLP, became Chief Minister, then Premier in 1965, holding the post until 1982.

Mauritius became an independent country within the Commonwealth of Nations in 1968, with Queen Elizabeth II as Head of State represented by a Governor General.

In 1971 social and industrial unrest led by the Mouvement Militant Mauricien (MMM) resulted in a state of emergency. The party's leaders, including Paul Berenger, a Franco-Mauritian born in 1945, were jailed for a year.

In the election of 1982, the MMM, with Paul Berenger as General Secretary and a 53-year-old Hindu British-trained lawyer, Aneerood Jugnauth, as President, captured all 62 directly elected seats. Aneerood Jugnauth became Prime Minister with Berenger as his Finance Minister.

Tensions among the ministers resulted in a break when Berenger resigned with ten of his cabinet colleagues. Mr Jugnauth formed a new party, the Mouvement Socialiste Militant (MSM) drawing on defectors from other parties and allying himself with Sir Seewoosagur's MLP and the Parti Mauricien Social Democrate (PMSD) of the flamboyant right wing figure, Sir Gaetan Duval.

The new alliance scored a victory that gave them 41 of the directly elected seats and five of the eight 'best loser' seats. (The 'best loser' system was devised by the British to ensure that every ethnic group has adequate representation.) Sir Seewoosagur became Governor General.

Following the defection of some party members and the resignation of six parliamentarians because of a drug smuggling scandal, the next general election was held a year early, on August 30 1987. This resulted in a win for the Alliance of parties led by Prime Minister Aneerood Jugnauth (MSM), Sir Satcam Boolell (PTR) and Sir Gaetan Duval (PMSD).

Knighted in 1988, Sir Aneerood Jugnauth became Prime Minister again after a general election in 1991 when he led the alliance of the MSM and MMM. In 1992, Mauritius became a republic and M Cassam Uteem, a former minister, was nominated as President in July 1992.

The Present

ADMINISTRATION

Parliamentary democracy

Mauritius is now a parliamentary democracy with universal adult franchise. General elections are held at least every five years. The role of the President, although important, is limited in powers to official and ceremonial procedures. Authority is delegated by him to the Council of Ministers, a body of ministers headed by the Prime Minister.

The Prime Minister is the member of the National Assembly (parliament) who appears to the President to command the support of the majority of its members. Based on the Westminster model, the Assembly has a speaker and members representing 21 electoral constituencies.

Government by coalition is a common feature of Mauritian politics and reflects the way of life of the people. The class divisions and communal differences of the postwar period are gradually crumbling as the economic situation improves. Education, industrialisation and the improving prosperity have also helped people attain better status and heightened their aspirations.

This (or it could be due to religious restraint) seems to have created a willingness to avoid disruptive influences to the national and political wellbeing, thereby allowing for the compromises of coalition.

Local government elections are held every three years on a party political basis. The municipalities are the urban areas of Port Louis, Curepipe, Beau Bassin/Rose Hill, Quatre Bornes and Vacoas/Phoenix. There are also District Councils in the rural areas of Grand Port/Savanne, Moka/Flacq, Pamplemousses/Rivière du Rempart.

The Judiciary is divided into the Supreme Court, the Court of Criminal Appeal, the Intermediate Court, the Court of Civil Appeal, the Industrial Court and ten District Courts. Final appeal is to the Judicial Committee of the Privy Council in the UK.

National flag

The flag of Mauritius consists of four equal width horizontal stripes. In descending order these are red, blue, yellow and green so when the flag is flying, red is at the top. Its size is in the proportion of six to four.

The colours have been interpreted as red for freedom and independence; blue for the Indian Ocean; yellow represents the light of independence shining over the nation; while green is for the agriculture of Mauritius and shows the country's colour throughout the twelve months of the year.

Crest
The crest of Mauritius reflects its past more than its present, flanked by a dodo and a stag, both clutching shoots of sugar cane. The shield portrays a medieval ship, presumably representing the island's discoverers, and three stylistic trees.

There are also a key and a shining star, depicting the country's motto which appears below it:

STELLA CLAVISQUE MARIS INDICI

EDUCATION

Education up to university level is free but not compulsory. Nevertheless, the literacy rate among the younger generation is high and 95% of all children attend school. There are about 300 primary schools and a small number of pre-primary schools.

The education boom began in the 1960s, with the opening of scores of private colleges. Free education at secondary level was introduced in 1977 with an immediate doubling of the number of students enrolled, and with new schools being opened by government.

The University of Mauritius (at Le Réduit) was opened in 1965, originally to train civil servants in preparation for Independence. It now runs schools of Administration, Agriculture and Technology. The Mauritius Institute of Education trains the country's school teachers and is responsible for the national certificate of primary education. The Mahatma Gandhi Institute (at Moka) concentrates on African and Asian studies.

ECONOMY

The influence on the economy of Sir Robert Farquhar, the first British governor, is only now waning, 171 years after his departure from Mauritius. Farquhar realised the value of an export oriented economy but encouraged a reliance on one export only: sugar. It was not until 1985 that sugar was displaced as the country's main foreign exchange earner by industrial products.

The reliance on a one-crop economy meant that the prosperity of Mauritius depended on the world demand for sugar and on home climatic conditions. When both were favourable, Mauritius benefited.

This is what happened in the early 1970s when economic growth averaged 9% per year. The standard of living improved visibly; new houses were built of concrete blocks and electricity served 90% of the island's dwellings. However, the pace of economic advance slowed as the sugar boom fizzled out.

The salvation was the Export Processing Zone (EPZ) set up in 1970 to attract foreign, as well as to encourage local, investment.

Inflation, which was 14.5% in 1981, dropped to 6.7% in 1985 and continues to run in low single figures. Unemployment, which reached over 25% of the registered work force in 1983, is low. By 1993 labour from abroad for both the textile and construction industries was being hired from Sri Lanka and Taiwan. Wages in 1993 started at the equivalent of US$125 per month for a floor worker, with clerks and typists earning about US$215 and mechanics and electricians in the US$250 to US$315 bracket. Engineers and other professionals started at US$750 to US$900 per month. In addition to these basic wages, employers pay an additional 40% in statutory social costs, including an end of the year bonus.

The government provides medical care and social security benefits and there is a national pension scheme to which both employer and employee contribute.

INDUSTRY

When industrialisation began in the 1960s the emphasis was to produce locally the goods that were being imported, creating jobs and saving on foreign exchange. Small industries were set up by local entrepreneurs, encouraged by fiscal incentives. Scope for profitable expansion was limited, however, by the size and buying power of the local market.

The Yaoundé Convention, allowing African countries associated with the European Economic Community (EEC) to have access to European markets for their goods, provided the fillip Mauritius needed. An Export Processing Zone (the EPZ) was set up in 1970 and policy switched to the labour intensive production of goods for export.

A package of fiscal incentives including exemption from certain taxes and duties, freedom to repatriate capital and profits, and a guarantee against State takeovers was offered. Investors saw other advantages in the adaptability of an amenable work force and in the network of sophisticated Mauritian entrepreneurs with whom to associate.

The scheme attracted investors from several countries, including the UK, France, West Germany, Holland, India, South Africa, Hong Kong, Singapore, Taiwan and Australia.

In actual fact, more than half the companies (and 50% of the capital invested) set up under the EPZ legislation are under Mauritian, not foreign, control. New factories have opened up throughout the island with the benefits of employment in industry spreading to all areas.

The EPZ produces 95% of all Mauritius's industrial exports. Nearly 560 enterprises have been established under its banner and about 90,000 new jobs have been created. An unexpected outcome has been the number of jobs for women, who comprise as much as 75% of the workforce. Nearly half the workforce are engaged in the knitwear industry.

The manufacturing sector is the largest employer in the country and the main foreign exchange earner. It registered an annual growth rate of 15% over the period 1982–85, rising to 30% from 1986–89, and then stabilised at approximately 12% between 1990–92. At the same time per capita income shot up from US$900 in 1982 to above US$3,000 in 1992.

The manufacturing sector produces a variety of goods which are exported to Europe, the USA, the Nordic countries, the eastern and southern African markets, Japan, etc. Products include woven garments, sportswear, woollen knitwear (in fact, Mauritius is the third largest exporter of woollen knitwear in the world), watches, watch-straps, leather goods, plush toys, carnival masks, sunglasses, lenses, spectacle frames, ship models, plastic products, engineering products, electronic items, printing of books and magazines, etc. However, the industrial set up is largely dominated by textiles and textile products and the textile industry accounts for 80% of the total earning of the manufacturing sector.

After the success of the EPZ, concern was expressed that the concentration on textiles could be as risky as the reliance on sugar had been. So diversification became the name of the game in industry as well as in the cane fields. In preparation for the 21st century, the industrial development strategy is directed towards other areas. These include electronics (the production of parts like printed circuit boards, PABX systems, etc), printing and publishing, involving the printing of books, magazines, desktop publishing, colour separation, etc, informatics (software development, computer aided publications, etc), engineering (supporting metal industries, coachworks, dies and moulds, assembly of concrete mixers, dumpers, etc), and jewellery.

Meanwhile Mauritius has become world famous as a reliable supplier of manufactured goods. The 'made in Mauritius' label is familiar and much sought after as the country gains a reputation for high quality standards.

The Mauritius Export Development and Investment Authority (MEDIA) was opened in 1985 by government and private sector officials to promote the industrialisation process of the country, help industries find new markets for their products, and attract the right type of entrepreneur to the EPZ. MEDIA's office is in the new build-ing next to the old National Hotel, at 25 Pope Hennessy Street (Level 2, BAI building), PO Box 1184, Port Louis, tel: (230) 208 7750/(230) 212 8047, fax: (230) 208 5965, telex: 4597 MEDIA IW.

The success in displacing sugar's importance to the economic base of Mauritius was crucial. The industrialisation of sugar itself is also taking place with such by-products as molasses, rum, ethyl alcohol and acetic acid. A fertiliser plant is also now in operation.

Industries targeted to the limited home market are also flourishing. Goods manufactured locally include food and beverages (rum, wine, beer and soft drinks), cigarettes, packaging, stationery, furniture, building blocks, various plastic pipes and fittings, shipbuilding and mechanical engineering as well as handicrafts. Export quality EPZ products are also available in local shops, particularly clothes and shoes.

AGRICULTURE AND FISHING

Sugar

When the sugar cane is fully grown, the roads of the flat lands in the north of Mauritius are like tunnels through the canefields. With noth-ing to be seen except the blue sky above and the green ribbons of cane waving in the wind, it is easy to imagine that the whole of the island is one vast sugar plantation.

As recently as 1980 over 90% of the cultivable land of Mauritius was devoted to sugar production. By 1985 this had dropped to 80%, and it is decreasing annually as agricultural diversification gathers momentum. In the last century there were 250 sugar factories. Now tall, crumbling chimney stacks are all that remain – monuments to the early days of the industry that made Mauritius.

Sugar cane was introduced from Batavia (Jakarta) by the Dutch in 1639. A plaque recording the date can be seen set into a portion of stone wall standing in a palm grove on the Ferney Sugar Estate near Vieux Grand Port, the Dutch landing place.

It was the French governor, Labourdonnais, who began sugar pro-duction in earnest. He set up the first sugar factory at Villebague in the centre of the island in 1744, using slave labour. By the time the British arrived in 1810 there were 10,000 acres under cultivation.

The British governor, Farquhar, persuaded the settlers to expand their cane cultivation because of the crop's ability to withstand cyclones. Coffee, the main crop under the French, was not so resi-lient.

The first stream mill was introduced by Adrien d'Epernay in 1822 on his estate at Quatre Cocos in Flacq. However only after the abolition of duties on Mauritius-grown sugar in 1825, which allowed it to be imported into Britain on the same terms as sugar from the Caribbean, did the industry thrive.

The early sugar mills relied on slaves and oxen to turn the rollers to crush the cane. The juice was extracted and collected in cauldrons where foreign matter was skimmed off. Then it was boiled, using the *bagasse* (the crushed cane) as fuel and the syrup was cooled until it crystallised into sugar. An old sugar factory has been re-created in the Royal Botanic Gardens at Pamplemousses, and a copy of an early sugar mill showing how sugar was produced in 1770 can be seen in action at Domaine les Pailles, ten minutes drive from Port Louis.

Animal-driven mills were gradually replaced by machinery, with the last one closing in 1853. The last sugar windmill was decommissioned in 1862, by which time production had risen to 130,000 tonnes.

Due to the island's volcanic beginnings, which caused the soil to be strewn with boulders and stones, every inch of the land used for cane growing has had to be cleared by hand. The gaunt piles of rock in the midst of the canefields are a forceful reminder of the toil of the men and women who worked in the blisteringly hot sun to clean these patches in the volcanic blanket.

The stony nature of the soil still restricts mechanical harvesting although tractors and forklifts are used to transport the cut cane for processing. The ox carts which can be seen on country lanes are carrying cane for smallholders.

The success of the sugar industry is the reason for the complicated network of roads in the island, in which strangers invariably get lost. Originally, sugar was shipped around the coast to Port Louis by boat. Trails were opened up so the inland estates could send their sugar for shipment by cart. These trails became makeshift roads and then gave way to railways.

The first railway line was between Port Louis and the north, opened in 1864. Six branch lines were in operation by 1904. Smaller railways ran between the rows of cane to link with the main lines.

The main railway system operated for a hundred years, until 1964, when it was closed down as being uneconomic, since its use for profitable freight was confined to the crop season. The complex pattern of roads which replaced it was developed under the initiative of the planters, and according to their needs.

There have been advances in recent years in the methods of cultivating sugar. Irrigation has been improved and now overhead sprinklers are often seen rotating over the canefields. Fertilisers are used to greater effect and weeds and pests are more easily controlled by chemicals.

New cane is planted in cycles to be harvested after 14 to 18 months. The ratoons (shoots) appear from the second year onward.

They are harvested every 12 months during the June to December cropping period.

The number of sugar estates is dwindling as part of a centralisation policy, and in 1987 there were only 19 estates, each with a processing factory. Only one, Rose Belle near Mahebourg, is government owned. The rest are owned by the major companies which form the Mauritius Sugar Producers Association. They account for 55% of the sugar producing land leaving the rest to some 40,000 smallholding planters.

When cane is cut, it is transported as soon as possible to the nearest factory where it is bulk fed into mechanical crushers. A constant supply of cane is needed to maintain production so the pace is frenetic. On one occasion a load of cane was fed into the crushers so quickly a labourer's bicycle was gobbled up by the machinery too, causing considerable damage to the plant.

The factories are self powered, as they were in the 19th century, but now it is more scientific. The fibrous residue from the cane, the *bagasse*, is used to produce electricity, not only for the factories but to augment the national supply.

The factories that remain have become ultra efficient in sugar production, worker welfare management and diversification. They are also required to cultivate other crops, such as potatoes and tomatoes, which are planted between the rows of cane. Some estates have branched out into growing flowers, particularly the red, waxlike anthuriums (*Anthurium andraeanum*) for export, and into pineapple and watercress cultivation, hotel development and other projects.

The soil and climate of Mauritius are first rate for sugar production and even the rains that fringe the cyclones are beneficial. The sight of cane labourers wearing enormous floppy hats, their arms and legs swathed in protective clothing as they patiently tend the fields, reveals their extreme dedication. This is supported by management's research and experiments to produce the best quality cane.

The Chamber of Agriculture, the first of its kind in the world, was founded in 1853 and a Station Agronomique opened in 1893. In 1925 the College of Agriculture, which concentrated on training people for the factory side of production, came into existence.

The Sugar Cane Research Station opened in 1930 followed in 1947 by the Sugar Research Institute funded by a tax levied on sugar production. In 1984 a Sugar Authority was established to provide for the industry's financial needs and to monitor its performance as well as plan for its future.

Not surprisingly, a typical Mauritian has a sweet tooth. From childhood, sugar has been an accepted part of the daily diet. Brightly coloured sugar confections shaped like the mountains of Mauritius are sold by hawkers in every town and village. Tea is always served with sugar. While its importance to the economy may be diminishing, sugar's popularity with Mauritians is unlikely to turn sour.

Tea

The tea you drink in Mauritius is locally produced too, distinctive because of the vanilla used to flavour it or, with the plain black tea, its lack of flavour.

Teas with the best flavour are grown at heights greater than the altitude of the tea plantations in Mauritius. However, the Mauritius tea is popular for blending and it is the island's second major crop.

The central highlands around Curepipe are the main plantation area. The cooler temperatures and the greater rainfall of the highland plateau suit tea. Being a plant that grows as a sturdy bush with deep roots and a long life, it can withstand winds of cyclonic force.

Tea's roots in Mauritius actually go back to the 18th century when it was grown by settlers for their own use. One governor, Sir James Pope Hennessy, whose statue in the Place D'Armes faces Government House, tried, during his term of office (1883 to 1889), to encourage the growing of tea as an industry. From the early 1960s extensive planting was pursued until, 25 years later, there were 40km^2 land under tea.

The crewcut tops of the bushes have a uniform appearance from the nimble fingers of tea pluckers, and from an electric shearer. The plucking is done with incredible dexterity early in the morning by men as well as by sari-clad women. Only the top two or three young leaves are removed from the branches. The green leaf is then bagged and transported to a factory where it dries, ferments and is sorted and prepared for packing.

There are eight tea factories operated by the Tea Development Authority, which was set up in 1971 as the state producer of tea. Tea grown by private companies, cooperatives and individuals contributes about 20% of the total population. Over 80% of Mauritius's tea is exported, mainly to the UK and Pakistan, although some also goes to the USSR.

In recent years the fortunes of the tea industry have fluctuated, with its demise seeming likely in the late 1970s. Then the Tea Development Authority was reconstructed, factories expanded with new processing equipment, tea plantation land was rehabilitated and inducements offered for improved cultivation methods. The production target was set at 8,000 tonnes of made tea by 1986 but this was reached by 1984 when export earnings were a record Rs247 million.

Tea is not seasonal like sugar and, since it grows where sugar can't and is labour intensive in the field, it is an ideal crop. However, Mauritius has to compete with traditional tea growing countries like Ceylon (Sri Lanka) and with its price not guaranteed its value to the economy can fall as well as rise.

Tobacco

Tobacco has been grown in Mauritius since the days of the Dutch and for the past 60 years has been a major local industry. In 1926, the British American Tobacco Company established itself in Mauritius and today their factory is on the outskirts of Port Louis just north of Camp Yoloff.

Although it is a major crop, tobacco is not exported and often falls short of local demand. Production has risen steadily in recent years reaching around 800 tonnes annually, with 841.75 tonnes in 1985-86. In 1960 when production was 566 tonnes it was calculated that 1,100 cigarettes were smoked per head of population per year.

Most of the tobacco is Virginia flue-cured although Amarello air-cured is also produced. It is grown on small plantations by private planters under the supervision of the state controlled Tobacco Board. The main areas are in the northern districts of the island: Pamplemousses, Rivière du Rempart and Flacq.

More tobacco is being grown each year and it is seen as a potential export crop, if it can first supply the growing domestic market and improve in quality to compete on the world market.

Other crops

Diversification of crops is nothing new for Mauritius, although previously different crops have been grown on a random basis because the island's volcanic terrain means there is a shortage of cultivatable land. Water too can be a problem since rainfall varies according to whether a farm is on the coast with 1,016 millimetres of rain a year, or on the central plateau with 5,080 millimetres.

The staple diet of Mauritians is rice, which has to be imported. However, enough potatoes for local demand are now grown, in excess of 20,000 tons a year. Maize production is increasing, although a substantial proportion has to be imported.

Ground nuts, onions, garlic, manioc, various leaf vegetables and spices are grown locally, as well as the tiny, round Mauritian tomato known quaintly as *pomme d'amour*. The growing of pulses such as peas and beans is being encouraged.

Fruits abound, especially pineapples which are offered, already peeled in spirals, for sale at every major street corner and bus station. Banana, papayas and traditional tropical fruit such as mangoes, litchis, watermelons, coconuts and citrus thrive and are of commercial importance.

Coffee is only grown on a small scale because it is in flower during the risky cyclone season. It can be found in the Chamarel area of the south, growing sheltered by the ridges of the hillsides.

Enough poultry and eggs are produced for domestic needs. Cattle rearing has been developed on some sugar estates as part of the

diversification policy but meat is still important. Goat meat is popular
and is produced commercially. Pigs and sheep are also raised, but in
smaller numbers than cattle or goats.

Fisheries

The romantic sight of a small rowing boat, bobbing peacefully in a
sun-drenched lagoon while its crew pull up a net full of fish, is a
glimpse of the tradition behind an expanding fishing industry. Mauritius has 1.7 million km^2 of marine surface area, known as its Exclusive Economic Zone (EEZ), which it is intent on developing.

Since the first settlers came to Mauritius, fishing has been confined
to the lagoon and offshore lagoon areas. Most fishermen, being
Creoles of small means, do not have the equipment or the inclination
for fishing far beyond the reefs. They use traditional methods, with
wooden (or sometimes fibreglass) boats of six to seven metres in
length. The crew fish with handlines, basket traps, seines, gill nets and
harpoons. These artisanal fishing grounds, the only source of fresh
fish supply, spread over an area of 1,020km^2 for Mauritius and
1,380km^2 for Rodrigues.

Banks fishery is conducted by motherships using small dories with
outboard motors, operated by a crew of three. The mother vessel
remains at sea for 35 to 55 days with the dories bringing in their
catch for gutting and freezing twice a day.

The mothership's load is landed at the new (1985) fishing port of
Trou Fanfaron in Port Louis as frozen fish. A total of 4,627 tonnes
was landed in 1986, more than 90% of it *Lethrinus mahsena* (*or
Sanguineus*), known locally as Dame Berri.

The areas fished are the St Brandon, Nazareth and Saya de Malha
banks on the Mauritius/Seychelles ridge, and the Chagos bank
around the Chagos Archipelago, submarine plateaus which lie 20 to
25 metres below the surface.

Tuna fishing for mainly skipjack (oceanic bonito: *Katsuwonus
pelamis*) and yellowfin tuna (*Thunnus albacares*), is a major industrial
activity. Tuna canning started in 1972 when most of the fish had to
be imported from the Maldives.

International big game fishing competitions are held frequently and
are popular with tourists who pay high fees to participate. The catch
is mainly marlin (*makaira*) and swordfish (*Xiphias gladius*) which is
usually sold to one of the enterprises producing smoked marlin. This
is a delicacy comparable to smoked salmon and can be tasted in
luxury hotels and restaurants.

Sea salt, incidently, is produced in Mauritius, with salt pans along
the coast in the Black River district, in the area known as Les Salines.
The salt is used for local consumption only.

If you like eating fish, look out for Mama Rouge (orange rock cod:
Cephalopholis aurantius), a grouper. It is much in demand, with a

flesh that tastes like crab. Mauritian cooks complain that it is priced beyond their pockets or exported to Réunion where people pay more for it. A fish frequently to be found on menus is Capitaine (*Lethrinus nebulosos*), a snapper sold frozen as *poisson la Perle*.

Fish farming is an old tradition, using *barachois*, artificial sea ponds, which breed finfish, crabs and oysters.

The local oyster (*Crassostrea cuculata*) lives in brackish water on rocks and mangrove roots. Efforts to introduce faster growing species from the USA were tried without success.

A few species of seaweed with commercial importance for the food, cosmetic and medical industries have been identified, as have four marine shrimp species with potential for commercial aquaculture.

The cultivating of freshwater fish is another possibility. Mauritius, being an oceanic island remote from continental land masses, is limited in endemic freshwater fauna and does not have any freshwater fish or crustaceans suitable for culture, but researchers are experimenting with introducing a wide variety of species for commercial cultivation.

Development of the EEZ is at present confined to the expansion of all sections of the fishing industry. For the future, however, studies have revealed a wealth of minerals on the ocean floor and there is also the possibility of ocean thermal energy conversion. It all seems a long way from the tranquil sight, beloved by tourists, of a fisherman casting his net in a picturesque lagoon.

TOURISM

The first tourists to arrive in Mauritius by air were 50 passengers and crew on a Qantas flight from Australia to South Africa, who landed in 1952. The airline agents were asked in advance to find overnight accommodation for them and, seeing the possibilities, bought a colonial mansion in Curepipe. This became the Park Hotel and is now the administrative offices of the island's Beachcomber group of hotels.

It was followed with a small beach hut hotel built where the Beachcomber's Brabant and Paradise Hotels now stand on the Morne in the south. Another hotel was built five miles from the airport, at Le Chaland, in 1962 when BOAC (now British Airways) started flying to the island. This became the Beachcomber Club which has now been pulled down and rebuilt as the splendid Shandrani.

By 1966 earnings from tourism had reached Rs15 million a year. Ten years later this had risen to 184 million rupees and in that year, 1976, 92,561 tourists arrived. In 1986, there was a total of 165,310 arrivals and the gross earnings from tourism topped the thousand million rupees mark for the first time at Rs1,187 million.

The number of arrivals more than doubled the 1986 figure by 1992

when 335,400 visitors flew in. Tourist receipts were estimated at
Rs4,655 million in 1992. The provisional figure for 1993 arrivals was
close to 400,000.

Tourism is the island's third largest foreign exchange earner after
the EPZ and sugar. The industry provides employment, although not
necessarily directly, for over 12,000 people. Since earnings from tourism circulate very quickly into the economy, the impact of the industry is considerable. However, tourism has also been a factor in the
increase in imports, especially foodstuffs.

Extensive promotion campaigns in the 1970s and huge investments
in hotels resulted in rapid growth. The 22 hotels offering 1,600 beds
at the beginning of the last decade had risen to 56 hotels with nearly
6,000 beds by 1986. At the end of 1992, there were 84 hotels with
5,271 rooms. Studies have been made on the careful development of
tourism in the future and the prospects are, given the concern of the
Mauritius Government Tourist Office (MGTO), that tourism will
continue to be an asset and not a blight on the island.

The MGTO runs an enquiry desk on the ground floor of the
Emmanuel Anquetil building, across the road from the town hall in
Port Louis, where a collection of charming young ladies answer ques-
tions and supply armfuls of literature about the island's attractions.

The main tourist generating country used to be Réunion, contribut-
ing around 24% of all tourist arrivals annually, but in 1987 France
topped the list with 51,300 visitors. Réunion contributed 49,400 and
South Africa 29,400 out of a total of 213,360. Germany was next with
13,350 arrivals while the United Kingdom increased its 1986 figure by
3,000 to 11,250 visitors. Australians accounted for 3,200 arrivals in
1987 and the USA 1,750.

A comparison in trends can be seen from the figures six years later
when residents of Réunion again made up the largest number of visitors (81,260). France came second with 74,300, South Africa third
with 39,790, then Germany (29,800) and the UK (24,150). Italy discovered Mauritius with 14,980 visitors, but Australia (5,100), Japan
(3,520) and the USA (1,830) remained unimpressed.

With 'the aim of achieving a coordinated and concerted approach
to promoting the long term and sustainable development of the tourism industry', a National Forum was held at the Maritim Hotel (near
Port Louis) in May 1992. Among the conclusions was to 'emphasise
the need to maintain the current tourism policy which aims at cultivating the high-spending segments of the major tourist-generating
markets', and to be 'conscious of the necessity to ensure that our
tourism product meets the expectations of the more informed and
demanding tourists'.

A somewhat prosaic but vital conclusion was a vow to 'improve
further the infrastructural services associated with tourism development (such as toilets, international telephone booths and parking

space at the airport, at the harbour and in towns and villages)'. It's happened.

A fascinating outcome of the forum was the development of three Codes of Ethics, for Tourism Professionals, for Mauritians, and for Tourists. Professionals, among other things, were urged to 'protect the interests of Mauritians so as to make them feel in no way inferior to tourists'.

Mauritians were themselves encouraged to be open-minded and generous. 'Tourists bring you a whole world to discover. You, for your part, will share with them the real values of your country'. Another suggestion: "Be true to yourself and be simple in your manner: do not ape another behaviour pattern which will make you lose your identity'.

Reproduced here (translated from French by the MGTO) is the Code of Ethics for Tourists, since it shows how great is the concern of Mauritians for the right approach to visitors to their country.

FOR TOURISTS

You are already most welcome in Mauritius. You'll be even more so if you will readily appreciate that our island...

> ...considers its most important asset is its people. They are well worth meeting and enjoying a friendly chat with;
> ...possesses a rich capital of cultures, needs and values which it cherishes more than anything else;
> ...is ready to give you value for money, but is not prepared to sell its soul for it;
> ...has wealth of its own, which deserves to be preserved;
> ...treats all its visitors like VIPs, but does not take kindly to those who overact the part;
> ...is not all lagoon and languor, and boasts a host of many splendoured sights;
> ...considers, without being prude, that nude when flaunted can be provocative and offensive;
> ...is not a faraway paradise of unlimited licence;
> ...takes pride in serving you with a smile and would be grateful for a smile in return;
> ...and will bare its soul willingly if you will handle it with care.

The future of the tourist industry looks bright in view of the attractions of Mauritius itself. Many of the hotels are expanding their capacity and there seems to be a natural limit on new hotels being built because of the shortage of sites. By maximising the use of hotels with a year round season, the industry can still grow without becoming a monster that swallows the very attractions which make Mauritius worth visiting.

Getting There

BY AIR

The biggest expense of a visit to Mauritius is getting there. Because it is so far from the main air and sea routes, this is neither cheap nor easy. And there are no holiday charter flights offering cut price, seat only fares: the government won't allow them.

The closest mainland gateways are those in Africa. From Johannesburg and Durban there are flights by Air Mauritius (airline code: MK) and South African Airways (SA) on most days of the week. Advance purchase (APEX) and excursion fares are available.

Other African cities linked to Mauritius by air are Harare, with a direct weekly flight by Air Zimbabwe (and also by MK), and Lusaka, which has an occasional service by Zambia Airways. In addition, Air Mauritius operates twice weekly between Nairobi and Mauritius via Madagascar with excursion fares available in first class as well as economy.

Getting to Mauritius can be cheaper if you stop over on the way to another destination, as long as it is included in a ticket calculated on a mileage based fare. A free stopover from the USA or UK can be included on the promotional Round the World (RTW) tickets sold at special fares by South African Airways in conjunction with Northwest Airlines (NW). Mauritius is a stopover on the SA flight between Johannesburg and Taipei on an RTW itinerary with SA linking up with NW in Taipei or in London.

The fare in 1994 for an SA/NW RTW originating in London either via South Africa or the USA and the Orient to Mauritius, and onward, was £3,179 in first class, £2,416 in business class and £1,172 in economy class (source: WEXAS).

From London, there are direct flights, via the Seychelles, by British Airways (BA), and some non-stop or direct flights by Air Mauritius. The regular return fares applicable in 1994 from London to Mauritius were £4,236 in first class, £2,876 in business class and £2,380 in economy. Excursion fares began at £995 (source: WEXAS).

Air France have flights with several stops from Paris or you could fly from France by charter airline to Réunion and then take one of several daily flights by Air Mauritius between Réunion and Mauritius. However, not only is the fare between Réunion and Mauritius very high for the 35-minute flight, but the long, long haul from Paris to Réunion is regarded as a domestic route (Réunion is an overseas department of France) so the inflight service is less, much less, than international standard.

Air Mauritius operates non-stop or direct flights from Paris, Zurich, Geneva, Rome, Frankfurt and Munich. Condor, a German airline, also operates from Frankfurt and Munich.

Excursion fares are available from Europe but the lack of competition means they are still high. Also, the government of Mauritius has a declared policy of attracting visitors demanding quality, not a cheap price, and one way of doing that is to maintain higher air fares.

Closer gateways include Bombay, from where there is a thrice weekly service operated by Air Mauritius in conjunction with Air India (using MK's aircraft). From the Seychelles (Mahé) there are flights by BA and AF. From Madagascar (Antananarivo), MK/AF, together with Air Madagascar (MD), have three flights a week, or more via Réunion.

Singapore Airlines (SQ) has services from Singapore, as does MK, with one flight a week via Kuala Lumpur. Cathay Pacific, in November 1993, joined Air Mauritius in providing a weekly link with Hong Kong. From Australia, Air Mauritius flies once a week from Perth.

Probably the least expensive way of flying to Mauritius on direct flights from Europe is by buying a round-trip ticket from an airline ticket consolidator. A consolidator sells seats from the allocation reserved for holiday companies, offering only the seat instead of the complete holiday package, for about £700 return from London.

In London, a travel organisation called WEXAS, open to membership worldwide, can provide tickets to Mauritius (and other places) at a lot less than scheduled fares. I've used their service for full-fare tickets as well as bargain flights and heartily recommend them. WEXAS International is at 45 Brompton Road, Knightsbridge, London SW3 1DE, tel: 071 589 3315 for membership enquiries. In 1994, WEXAS quoted a member-only fare of £616 return, London-Mauritius.

For short term visitors who don't want the hassle of arranging a flight independently, a holiday package can provide the solution. Going on a package holiday need not restrict your freedom to explore the island since you are not obliged to eat, or even sleep, in the hotel although anything extra you do is, of course, at your expense and there is no refund for meals, or nights, not taken. Most of the major long haul companies offer holidays in Mauritius in hotels I rate as GRAND from around £1,250 per person for a week. Cost, according to the airline to be flown and the standard of hotel, drops to about £750 for seven nights, lower than the usual excursion fare and with B & B thrown in. A specialist in holidays in Mauritius, run by Mauritians, is Sunset Travel Holidays, 306 Clapham Road, London SW9 9AE, tel: 071 498 9922, fax: 071 978 1337.

Whichever way you fly to Mauritius, it is absolutely essential that you have a confirmed return, or onward, ticket in your possession when you arrive. Passengers without a valid ticket to leave Mauritius aren't welcome and won't be allowed in until they buy one. There is more on the immigration requirements in the Red Tape chapter (page 47).

MAJOR AIRLINES SERVING MAURITIUS

AIR FRANCE
   Rogers House, 5 John Kennedy Street, Port Louis. Reservations tel: 208 1281.

AIR INDIA
   Rogers House, 5 John Kennedy Street, Port Louis. Reservations tel: 208 6878.

AIR MAURITIUS
   Rogers House, 5 John Kennedy Street, PO Box 441, Port Louis. Tel: 208 7700/10. Reservations tel: 208 6878; fax: (230) 208 8331; telex; 4415 AIRMAU IW.

BRITISH AIRWAYS
   Duke of Edinburgh Avenue, Port Louis. Reservations tel: 208 1039; fax: (230) 212 8459.

SOUTH AFRICAN AIRWAYS
   Rogers House, 5 John Kennedy Street, Port Louis. Reservations tel: 208 1281.

SINGAPORE AIRLINES
   5 Duke of Edinburgh Street, Port Louis. Reservations tel: 208 7695.

Air Mauritius: The nation's airline
When Air Mauritius began in 1968, it was an airline without an aircraft. It has remained small ever since although it is known in international aviation circles for doing big things. In 1987 it became the first airline in the world to order higher gross weight 767/200 Extended Range jetliners from Boeing. Its two new aircraft entered service in 1988 as part of a carefully considered move into the future. This philosophy is being continued with the introduction in 1994 of Airbus A340-300 aircraft to replace the airline's ageing Boeing 747SPs. The Airbus 300 version can carry 301 passengers in three classes. Aircraft in the fleet at the end of 1993 were three B747 SP (with 12 first class, 26 business class and 249/261 economy class seats); two B767 ER (with

12 first class, 18 business class and 151 economy class seats); two ATR 42 (with 48 seats, used on the Réunion and Rodrigues routes), and two Bell jet ranger helicopters (with four seats, used for charter).

Air Mauritius, at the end of 1993, served 20 destinations: Antananarivo, Bombay, Durban, Frankfurt, Geneva, Harare, Hong Kong, Johannesburg, Kuala Lumpur, London, Moroni, Munich, Nairobi, Paris, Perth, Réunion, Rodrigues, Rome, Singapore and Zurich. Plans were in hand to open a service to Japan, it being seen as a country from where more tourists would come with better air links. Air Mauritius also acts as the ground handling agent for all other airlines at the international airport.

Flying by Air Mauritius can be fun, if the cabin crew are in a good mood. Usually they are, and you find yourself making friends even before you get to Mauritius. The menus, with drawings of Mauritian houses on the cover, are worth keeping. On some flights, caviar is served in first class and lobster in business class (I know because the chief steward gave me the menus), and drinks are free in economy class, except for champagne.

You are allowed 23kgs (50.6lbs) baggage in economy, instead of the usual 20kgs, but only 15kgs on flights to/from Rodrigues. A minor quibble: the Air Mauritius timetable booklet is somewhat eccentric in layout and it takes ages, although it is supposed to be a quick reference schedule, to find a specific flight.

The symbol of Air Mauritius is the straw-tailed tropic bird, locally known as the *paille en queue*, and this logo appears on all its aircraft. An advertisement for the airline disconcertingly states that the bird 'has been known to nosedive at you if you wave a handkerchief at it'. However, according to the airline, 'the symbol of elegance of this bird in flight made it a natural choice for the symbol of our national carrier'. Its slogan is 'non-stop caring'.

The majority of the shares in Air Mauritius is owned by the Government of Mauritius with shares also held by Air France, British Airways and Rogers & Co of Port Louis.

Air Mauritius Offices and Agents
Telephone numbers where Air Mauritius has an office, or is represented by a General Sales Agent*:

Antananarivo 222 22 or 288 65D *
Athens 3240235 *
Bahrain (973) 273001 *
Bangkok (662) 23761 45/46/47 *
Beirut (961) 343440 *
Berlin 882 75 29
Bombay 202 8474
Brussels 218 57 05
Cape Town 021 216 294

Colombo (941) 430525 *
Dubai 21 4455 *
Durban (031) 3046681
Frankfurt (069) 285256
Geneva (022) 732 05 60
Harare (4) 735738
Hong Kong (852) 5231114
Istanbul 2324100 *
Jakarta 36 7852 *

Jeddah 665 9034 *
Johannesburg 011 331 1918
Karachi 522621 *
Katmandu 41 7710 *
Kuala Lumpur 603 2429161 *
London 071 434 4375
Los Angeles 800/854 4189
Madrid (1) 559 3581
Malta 334051 *
Manila (2) 81 78680 *
Mauritius 208 6878
Melbourne (3) 654 1788 *
Milan (02) 80 4661
Moroni (269) 730686 *
Munich (089) 290 03930
Nairobi 22 9166
New Jersey 800/537 1182

Ontario 416 495 0188
Oslo (22) 835703
Paris 44 51 15 55
Perth 09481 0888 *
Réunion 202 500
Rodrigues 831 1558
Rome (06) 474 2051
Seoul (852) 7538271 *
Seychelles 22414 *
Singapore 222 3033
Stockholm 468 723 0695
Sydney (2) 221 7300
Tapei 02 5144600 *
Tel Aviv (3) 517 2163 *
Tokyo (3) 3564 5103 *
Vienna 7130444
Zurich (01) 8108411

The head office of Air Mauritius is at Rogers House, 5 President John Kennedy Street, (PO Box 441) Port Louis, Mauritius, tel: (230) 208 7700/10, 208 7836/45, 208 7900/03; fax: (230) 208 8331; telex: 4415 AIRMAU IW. The address at the airport is Air Mauritius, SSR International Airport, Plaisance, Mauritius, tel: (230) 637 3420, 637 3436; fax: (230) 637 3266; telex: 4563 AIRMAU IW. The chairman and managing director is Sir Harry K Tirvengadum.

The UK offices of Air Mauritius are at 49 Conduit Street, London W1R 9FB, tel: 071 434 4375/79; fax: 071 439 4101; telex: 24469 AIRMK, and at London Heathrow, Room 227, East Wing, Terminal 3, Hounslow, Middlesex, tel: 081 897 3545, 081 745 6510.

BY SEA

The chances of getting there by sea are slim and depend on special arrangements since there are no regular passenger sailings to Mauritius from anywhere. Cruise liners such as the QE2 occasionally call, either on round the world voyages or on cruises from South Africa. The island's location rules it out as a call for wintering yachts from Europe. Cargo ships come frequently but since few of them carry passengers you would need to sign on as a crew member to join them.

WHEN TO GO

Mauritius is the place to visit at any time of the year for someone from northern climes who craves tropical beauty and warmth. The one month which might not be idyllic is February which, although it is the hottest of the year, is also when a cyclone could occur. They don't happen every year but the cyclonic rains, which can last five days non-stop, are an annual event. Humidity is high then and it can be a depressing, unsettling time. See page 57 for more information on seasons/weather.

The peak tourist season, when holiday packages cost more, is December to early January. December is the time when local fruits are in abundance; it's summer and the temperature on the coast is about 30°C. Another peak time is mid-June to mid-September – the dry season – although for Mauritians it is cold then, the temperature at sea level being about 24°C.

Holiday prices drop between April (after Easter) and June, yet this is one of the pleasantest times of year. Package prices are lower again from September to November, another splendid time to be in Mauritius.

If climate is not the governing factor, choose when to visit according to your interests. For instance, the horse racing season is May to October and the best deep sea fishing is September to March. Flights should be less crowded outside school holiday periods.

WHAT TO TAKE

The glib answer is lots of travellers cheques. Apart from difficult personal items like prescription medicines or designer accessories, you'll be able to get everything you need. Shops seem to stock a greater variety of goods than comparative shops in Europe.

For clothes, casual elegance is a good watchword. On the coast at any time of the year, you will need lightweight, preferably cotton clothing. In the highlands something warmer will be necessary in the evenings. Hotel boutiques and shops in Port Louis and Curepipe have an excellent range of clothing appropriate for the climate.

Since imported liquor is expensive, you may want to take in your full duty-free spirit allowance. Locally made cigarettes are cheap but if you are hooked on a special brand, take it with you. Local daily newspapers in English are non-existent but international news magazines and some daily newspapers from England are obtainable, about a week old.

Maps

There are several small maps available as part of the tourist office literature and some picturesque French maps of Mauritius can be bought at hotels and bookshops. The most detailed map is the one published in English by the UK Government's Directorate of Overseas Surveys for the Mauritius Government in 1983. As well as all the major and minor roads, this shows the new motorways linking the towns of the Central Plateau with Port Louis and the newly built one that cuts through Port Louis, in front of the post office, on its way to the north, where it ends in a canefield at Mapou.

This map is to a scale of 1:100,000 (1cm to 1km) and shows all towns and villages, rivers, mountains, plantations and monuments. A detailed map of Rodrigues is also included. It is available from the Chief Surveyor's Office in the Ministry of Housing, Lands and Town & Country Planning building, Edith Cavell Street, Port Louis (tel: 2082831), or from Edward Stanford Ltd, 12/14 Long Acre, London WC2E 9LP, England. There are more detailed maps (13 in all) of different parts of Mauritius, drawn on a scale of 1:25,000, available from the same suppliers. These were compiled in 1981 from air photography in 1975 and field surveys in 1979.

More practical for the general tourist is the excellent map published by the UK firm, Macmillan: *Mauritius Traveller's Map*, which includes a Port Louis town plan and a map of Rodrigues. Not only are places of interest and hotels marked, but the restaurants and bars are shown, too. It is available through travel bookshops in the UK.

HOW MUCH MONEY TO TAKE

The thrifty, independent traveller staying in cheap, basic accommodation and eating in local eateries, travelling by bus, and enjoying free outdoor pursuits instead of spending freely in bars and casinos, could live reasonably on £20 per day. I tend to underestimate my own probable expenses because I overlook that urge to be extravagant after a period of scrimping. Since there is bound to be a time during your stay when you want to do or buy something you haven't anticipated, allow extra. See page 133, Inexpensive Mauritius, for hints on keeping costs low.

There is no published guideline on the minimum amount of spending money a visitor must possess before being allowed into Mauritius. However, if you don't have credit cards which allow you to draw cash in Mauritius, then you should have evidence of around £50 a day for entry clearance.

Statistics from the MGTO suggest that in 1992, the receipt per tourist was Rs13,857 for an average stay of 12 nights, which indicates a hypothetical daily spend per tourist of Rs1,154 which was the equivalent of about £50. If you are on a packaged holiday at an upmarket beach resort, and even if it is pre-paid, you will have the cost of extra meals (even lunch can cost £20 in some places), drinks, tea, tips and tours to worry about, so you will need more than the independent traveller.

If you're staying in prepaid self-catering accommodation you should find the cost of household items and food averaging out at less than at home.

The business visitor could find expenses high due to the cost of transport. There are excellent medium-priced business hotels, but none of them are in Port Louis which is the main business centre. Taxis, rental vehicles and chauffeur driven cars can cost more per day than hotel accommodation.

Taxis are not metered and the drivers seem impervious to sensible bargaining. They know their value, especially as resort hotels are isolated and a taxi is usually the only way to reach or leave them. So allow extra cash for unexpected taxi journeys, particularly since the excellent island-wide bus service stops running early in the evening.

Extras

With few expectations of tips outside the hotel resort areas, and the 10% service charge on meals not always applied, extras can be kept under control. There will be a 10% government tax added to your hotel bill and there is an in-built tax of 10% on food, but not on drinks. Don't forget the Rs100 departure tax payable at the airport (although, since it has been that rate for years, it is probably higher now).

WHAT INOCULATIONS

The only proof of vaccination required is against **yellow fever** if you are arriving within 10 days of leaving infected or endemic areas. It's good for 10 years. Infected areas change from time to time. Endemic areas include Kenya and Tanzania so you will need a yellow fever jab if you plan to visit or actually originate your journey there. However, passengers in transit through Nairobi or Dar Es Salaam who do not leave the airport don't need proof of vaccination.

A risk of **malaria** in the **vivax** form exists throughout the year in several rural areas, although not in Rodrigues. Prophylaxis is strongly recommended and a specialist in overseas health perils in your home country will suggest the appropriate tablets.

To combat the annoyance of mosquitoes during the night, I recommend mosquito coils in preference to electric gadgetry, creams or heavy nets suspended from the ceiling. Coils can be bought in Mauritius. They are made of some form of pyrethrum compacted so it burns for six to eight hours. They give off a smoke which mosquitoes hate. So do some humans but it is harmless to us and deadly to them.

The traveller to any tropical country will benefit from a cocktail of inoculations. The International Certificate of Inoculation has space for these. The first time traveller (and even a veteran who needs a top-up) should see about having vaccinations against **cholera** (six month effectiveness), **tetanus** (5 year effectiveness), **polio** and **typhoid**.

Gamma Globulin as a means of protection against **hepatitis** is only limited in value.

There is a Vaccination Centre and Malaria Surveillance Unit at Victoria Square, Port Louis, tel: 212 4464, and a vaccination centre at Air Mauritius, Rogers House, tel: 208 7700.

Although the water in Mauritius is safe to drink in most places (but be careful after a cyclone), water, especially ice, can be the cause of minor upsets. A sensible precaution is to drink only bottled water (obtainable everywhere very cheaply) and to do without ice in your drinks. Bottled soft drinks, mixers and soda water are usually served cold.

WHERE TO GET INFORMATION IN ADVANCE

The head office of the MGTO will answer specific questions. The full address is:

Mauritius Government Tourist Office
Emmanuel Anquetil Building
Sir S Ramgoolam Street
Port Louis, Mauritius
Tel: (230) 201 1703; fax: (230) 212 5142; telex: 4249 EXTERN IW

Information and Public Relations Offices in other countries:

AUSTRALIA
Mauritius Tourist Information Bureau
313 Abernathy Road
Belmont 6104, Perth
Tel: (9) 479 4283, fax: (9) 479 4322

FRANCE
Bureau d'Information de l'Ile Maurice
41 rue Ybry
92200 Neuilly Cedex
Tel: (1) 46 40 37 47, fax: (1) 46 40 11 23

GERMANY
Mauritius Informationsbüro
Hohenwaldstrasse 10
61449 Steinbach (Taunus)
Tel: (6171) 980354, fax: (6171) 980652

HONG KONG
Mauritius Tourist Information Bureau
Suite C, 23/F, Eton Building
288 Des Voeux Road
Central
Tel: 8511036, fax: 8052416

INDIA
Mauritius Tourist Information Bureau
c/o Trikaya Grey
28 Rampart Row
Kala Goda Fort
Bombay 400 023
Tel: (22) 285 6746, fax: (22) 287 2270

JAPAN
Mauritius Tourist Information Bureau
Ginza Stork Building 5F
1-22-10 Ginza
Chuo-Ku
Tokyo 104
Tel: (3) 5250 0175, fax: (3) 5250 0176

ITALY
Ufficio del Turismo delle Isole Mauritius
Foro Buonaparte 46
20121 Milan
Tel: (2) 86 59 84/86 70 26, fax: (2) 86 46 05 92

SWITZERLAND
Mauritius Tourist Information Service
Kirchenweg 5
CH-8032 Zurich
Tel: (1) 383 87 88, fax: (1) 383 51 24

UNITED KINGDOM
Mauritius Government Tourist Office
30-33 Elvaston Place
London SW7 5NW
Tel: 071 584 3666, fax: 071 225 1135

USA
Mauritius Tourist Information Service
15 Penn Plaza
415 Seventh Avenue
New York
NY 10001
Tel: (212) 239 8367, fax: (212) 695 3018

MAURITIUS HIGH COMMISSIONS AND EMBASSIES

AUSTRALIA
Mauritius High Commission
43 Hampton Circuit
Yarralumla ACT 2600
Canberra
Tel: (6) 281 1203, fax: (6) 282 3235

BELGIUM
Mauritius Embassy
68 rue des Bollandistes
Etterbeek
1040 Brussels
Tel: (2) 733 9988, fax: (2) 734 4021

EGYPT
Mauritius Embassy
72 Abdel Moneim Riad Street
Agouza 11111-Giza
Cairo
Tel: (2) 3467642, fax: (2) 3452425

FRANCE
Mauritius Embassy
68 boulevard de Courcelles
75017 Paris
Tel: (1) 42 27 30 19, fax: (1) 40 530291

INDIA
Mauritius High Commission
5 Kautilya Marg
Chanakyapuri
New Delhi 110021
Tel: (11) 30 11112, fax: (11) 30 19925

MADAGASCAR
Mauritius Embassy
Lot 6 – 21B Bis
Anbarotoka
Ambanidia
Antananarivo
Tel: (2) 23 21 57, fax: (2) 21 939

MALAYSIA
Mauritius High Commission
Suite ABC, 14th Floor
Bangunam Angkasa Raya
Jalan Ampang
Kuala Lumpur
Tel: (3) 2431992, fax: (3) 2415115

PAKISTAN
Mauritius Embassy
House No 27, Street No 26
Sector F-6/2
Islamabad
Tel; (51) 823345, fax: (51) 210076

UNITED KINGDOM
Mauritius High Commission
32-33 Elvaston Place
London SW7 5NW
Tel: 071 581 0294, fax: 071 823 8437

UNITED NATIONS (SWITZERLAND)
Mauritius Mission to the UN
Studio 34, Residence St James
3 rue Versonnex
1207 Geneva
Tel: (22) 73 62 354, fax: (22) 73 64 374

UNITED NATIONS (USA)
Mauritius Mission to the UN,
211 East 43rd Street,
New York, NY 10017
Tel: (212) 949 0190, fax: (212) 679 3829

USA
Mauritius Embassy
Suite 134 or 441 Van Ness Center
4301 Connecticut Avenue NW
Washington DC 20008
Tel: (202) 244 1491, fax: (202) 966 0983

Red Tape

ARRIVAL

Health
Before you'll be allowed off the aircraft on arrival, the passenger cabins will be sprayed and a brief inspection made by a Mauritian health official. Inside the arrivals building the first desk you come to is the Health Authority where you will be asked where you've come from. As long as it isn't a Yellow Fever area, you don't need an inoculation, except for your own peace of mind.

The health official will want your name and the address of the place where you intend to stay. This is part of the continual campaign against malaria. If you have come directly from a malaria infected country you could be visited by the health authorities at your hotel within a few days of arrival and be asked to give a blood sample for precautionary analysis.

Passport
The immigration desks are next. A full passport is required to enter Mauritius. However, holders of a Certificate of Identity issued by the Government of Mauritius or of a *Laissez Passer* issued by the United Nations will be admitted without passports.

Seamen who are travelling on duty can enter the country on a Seaman's Book issued by any country, providing the book itself is written in English or French. If a seaman is arriving by air to join his ship in Mauritius, he will need documentary proof from the ship's agent in Port Louis and this should state that the agent will meet the seaman at the airport.

Passports issued by the Governments of Ciskei, Bophuthatswana, Transkei, Venda and Taiwan are not recognised by Mauritius. Those passport holders will have to apply to the Immigration Authority for an entry permit.

On the plane before arrival you should expect to be given an International Embarkation/Disembarkation card. This should be filled in before you join the immigration queue.

My experience of the immigration officials at the airport has always been pleasant, giving a warm welcome to the country. On one visit, when the official saw 'author' in my passport, he said his favourite author was Dickens and quoted something apt to prove it. I have heard, though, of people experiencing problems when they don't comply with the formalities.

For instance, if you don't know where you're going to stay, expect questions since immigration needs an address for you. Avoid that by putting the name of an appropriate hotel on the embarkation card. The low budget traveller who wants to look around for a cheap guest house should not give the name of a luxury hotel because it won't be believed. Put down the name of an inexpensive guest house taken from this guide instead. If you intend to camp, don't tell a soul.

There are visitors who don't know where they're going to stay because their accommodation is being arranged by business contacts in Mauritius. In that case, the contact should be at the airport to provide the information. If you say you know people in Mauritius you may be asked to name them as proof that you are what you say you are.

You will be asked to show your ticket to leave Mauritius. A wealthy friend of mine who didn't have a ticket had to buy one at the airport before being allowed entry, despite his wallet full of credit cards.

Proper financial arrangements to cover your stay are absolutely necessary. The amount of money that you have in your possession is not the sole criteria; your access to funds in an emergency is important too. The reason for this (as well as why you need a ticket out of Mauritius) is because the casinos there are open to everyone. If you gamble away all your money, you could become a charge on the State.

The visitor who comes on a package holiday does not raise the same doubts that independent travellers do because the package tourist has prepaid accommodation and is under the auspices of the tour company. However, providing the independent traveller is a genuine tourist who will not take up 'gainful employment' which is forbidden, entry is granted after the short interview at the desk. But don't expect to be granted a six month permit. One month is more likely. If you want to stay longer you must apply for an extension.

There is a list of undesirable types who will not be admitted to Mauritius. Anyone who is likely to be a charge on public funds will be refused entry, as will chronic alcoholics, so don't overdo the drinks on the plane.

Visa

Generally speaking a visa to visit Mauritius is not required but if you are travelling on an exotic passport, such as one from South America or even from a close neighbour like Sri Lanka, you will probably need a visa. The rules change so, if you are in doubt, check with your nearest Mauritius representative. British passport holders and citizens of other European countries, and of the USA, Canada, Australia, New Zealand, South Africa and Scandinavia can enter visa free.

Bonafide visitors are usually granted a stay up to one month or for the duration of their visit if less. Extensions are possible.

Visa issue

Getting a visa in advance is not easy since there are only a few places in the world where this can be done, namely through the diplomatic representatives listed in the previous chapter. If there is not one near you, your contact in Mauritius, or yourself, should request an application form from the Passport & Immigration Office, Line Barracks, Port Louis (tel: (230) 208 1212; telex: 4249 EXTERN IW, no fax). This has to be filled out and submitted with two photographs. A letter of approval will be issued, free of charge, which you have to show to immigration at the airport. If you need a visa and have not got one (and if you manage to get on a flight to Mauritius), entry will be refused.

Luggage

Delivery of luggage is usually prompt unless there are several aircraft arriving at the same time. Trolleys are available and there are porters. There are two duty free shops *on arrival*; the one selling liquor is before immigration, the one with electronics is after immigration. Both are before customs.

Customs

The red and green channel system operates here but even if you opt for the green channel, you are likely to be questioned before being allowed through it.

Incoming visitors age 16 and over are allowed to import free of duty:

Cigarettes: Not exceeding 250g.
Spirits: One litre.
Wine: 2 litres of wine, ale or beer.
Perfume: 10cl of perfume and about 25cl of toilet water.
Personal Effects: Wearing apparel and used personal effects which will be taken out when leaving.

Plants

Be careful! All plants and plant material must be declared to customs and will be subject to inspection. Sometimes an announcement about this will be made on the plane before arrival. A plant import permit must be obtained in advance from the Ministry of Agriculture even for cuttings, bulbs, fresh fruit, vegetables and seeds. You can't import sugar cane or fresh fruit from Asia east of 60° longitude (that means India, Pakistan and Sri Lanka), or soil and micro organisms.

Drugs such as ganja, opium, cocaine and other illegal substances are banned. A notice at the airport warns: 'Penalty for drug trafficking is death'.

Pets

The import of dogs and cats from areas within 100kms radius of anywhere rabies occurred in the previous 12 months is prohibited; so too are invertebrate animals.

Animals, and animal material, can only be imported with a permit from the Ministry of Agriculture, obtained in advance, and a veterinary certificate from the country of origin. Animals must be declared on arrival. Imports will only be allowed if details on the certificate from the exporting country agree with those on the import permit.

Dogs and cats are subject to six months quarantine. Birds are quarantined for three weeks. The cost is met by the importer.

Changing money

There are bank desks open during all international arrivals. These desks operate more efficiently than some of the banks in Port Louis and will exchange cash or travellers cheques rapidly at the official rate. Keep all receipts in case you need to buy back foreign currency on leaving. There is a high charge of Rs35 when you cash travellers cheques, regardless of the total amount. Some banks allow you to cash five cheques before they charge more, others permit up to 12. The Mauritius Commercial Bank, which operates money changing counters where there are no hassles, cashes up to 11 cheques for Rs35, then charges Rs3 each additional cheque. To offset this cost (it's about £1.30, perhaps acceptable on £100 but it doesn't leave much change from a £10 cheque) it is better to change high domination cheques, or a lot of small denomination ones at the same time.

There is no restriction imposed on the importation of foreign currency either in cash or drafts, letters of credit or travellers cheques. Visitors may import Mauritius notes up to a maximum of Rs700 and take out Rs350.

The legal unit of currency is the rupee (Rs) which is divided into 100 cents. The largest note is for Rs1000; also new is the Rs500 note. The Rs200 note is green, the Rs100 one is red, and slightly smaller in size. There are also Rs50, Rs20 and Rs10 notes. The Rs5 note was replaced in 1988 with a Rs5 coin. There is also a Rs1 coin and coins for 5, 10, 20, 25 and 50 cents.

Getting to your hotel

There are two desks at the airport where car hire can be arranged. If someone is meeting you, look outside for them since the general public are not allowed into the arrivals lobby and have to congregate with the taxi drivers, beyond the doors. Hotel representatives wait in the lobby.

If you need a taxi it helps to know the current fare to your destination. There is a tourist information counter, run by the MGTO, at the airport, where you could ask for advice about the fares. If you don't like the rate, some taxi drivers might agree to drive you in exchange for cigarettes or liquor from your duty free purchases. It happened to me once. At night you could well be charged double and be unable to find an airport taxi to take you for less since the drivers don't usually undercut each other. Always agree the price with the driver before getting in. There are public bus services to Mahebourg and Curepipe, from where buses serve other parts of the island.

Tipping
Your porter should be tipped according to what he does for you. Since my bag is usually too heavy for me to carry after a long flight, I feel one US dollar is fair payment; Rs10 should be sufficient though. Taxi drivers don't expect tips. In your hotel, see if a service charge is going to be added to your bill before dishing out tips since they may not be necessary. In restaurants where there is no service charge added, you could leave 5% to 10% of the bill according to your satisfaction with the service. In eateries graded in this guide as *basic* tipping is not expected.

STAYING ON

Extending visit visa
Each application to stay longer than the period written by the immigration officer in a visitor's passport is treated according to the individual visitor's circumstances, not by standard published guidelines.

The Immigration Office is in the Police Headquarters complex at Line Barracks, originally built by the French in 1736 to accommodate 6,000 soldiers. Do not be daunted by the foreboding appearance of the fortress wall surrounding the complex which lies on the western edge of Port Louis. The Police Station entrance is in Kitchener Street, behind the Victoria Square Bus Station, but don't go through there in case you get involved in helicopters landing and training activities in the barrack square.

The entrance for the Passport Office is the East Gate in Jemmapes Street, off the main shopping thoroughfare of Chaussée Street, which becomes Barracks Street as it leads up to the gate. Go straight through (there is no checkpoint) and you'll find yourself in a huge quadrangle surrounded by the solid stone walls of the two-storey barrack rooms. The Passport and Visa Offices are on the right and there are benches in the shade of the cloisters where passport applicants await their turn.

The Visa Office (open 10.00 to 12.00, Monday to Friday) is next door to the Passport Office and your quest for an extension to your visitor's visa begins downstairs. Interviews are conducted upstairs.

You will need to take with you a letter addressed to the Officer In Charge, Passport and Immigration Office, Line Barracks, Port Louis, in which you explain your reason for wanting to stay longer, and until what date you want to stay. You should state also that you have a ticket out of Mauritius and give details of your confirmed reservation to leave. Include details of where you are staying and of the amount of funds you have available to cover your costs, including lodging and personal expenses. Be prepared to furnish proof of everything you say in the letter.

If your case is genuine and you satisfy the examining officer that you do not intend to work and will not become a charge on public funds, an extension can be granted for up to six months for one visit. There is no fee.

Work permit

Because Mauritius is developing with the aid of considerable private foreign investment, the authorities accept the need of those foreign investors to employ foreign personnel (usually as directors or financial controllers) to represent their interests. Expatriates with technical or professional ability are also likely to be granted work permits where qualified nationals are not available. So if you want to stay and work in Mauritius, it *is* possible, as long as you can find employment with a foreign company at director level or have a skill that is in short supply.

Your potential employer will apply for the work permit and pay the fee (which rises for each year of employment) payable in respect of employment of expatriates. It is likely to take several weeks before it comes through. If you plan on being self-employed, a permit is still required, as is a local associate.

Residence permit

Application for a residence permit has to be made to the Prime Minister's Office. Each application is investigated thoroughly and if it is from a foreigner wishing to invest in Mauritius, it is considered in conjunction with the proposed investment project.

An individual not involved in an investment project who wants to reside in Mauritius has to satisfy the authorities that maintenance will be provided wholly from funds outside Mauritius. A deposit in some form for maintenance support or repatriation may be required. A foreigner who is the spouse of a citizen can achieve the status of resident after a protracted process.

Retirement

Retired foreigners who want to buy a house and spend their days in retirement in Mauritius have to apply for permission to the Prime

Minister's Office, Government House, Port Louis. This practice, I am officially informed, is not encouraged by the government.

Attitude of officials

Generally positive. The police, in a uniform of dark blue trousers and lighter blue shirts, are not menacing. The legacy of British colonial training lingers on and they seem polite and helpful, if unobtrusive, to visitors and law-abiding citizens. Bureaucrats, too, once convinced of a visitor's genuine need for help, are forthcoming as people rather than as regulation-bound civil servants.

DEPARTURE

Airport procedure

The terminal building at Mauritius has a knighthood. It is called Sir Seewoosagur Ramgoolam Air Terminal and is located 45km from Port Louis at Plaisance, in the southeast corner of the island (see chapter on Grand Port). The terminal was opened in 1987, replacing one that had become rather like Curepipe market with its loiterers and noisy confusion.

There is a block of snack bars in the car park offering local delicacies and pleasant banter if you are waiting for friends to arrive. Only departing passengers, who go through a security check at the entrance, are allowed into the terminal.

Bank counters are situated in the lobby before check-in for those who want to change money. Trolleys and porters are available to assist with passengers' luggage and will carry this to the check-in desks. The ground handling for all airlines is done by Air Mauritius with an airline representative on call if needed. There are separate check-in desks for first, business and economy class passengers.

In theory only one carry-on bag per passenger is permitted in the cabin and the fragile wooden model ships, which are made in Mauritius and are popular souvenirs, are not allowed. They should be securely packed and checked in with the hold luggage.

It is advisable to reconfirm your flight arrangements soon after arrival in Mauritius, even if the airline does not ask you to do so. You'll be told then of the check-in time. Minimum check-in time is at least 90 minutes for British Airways, longer for some airlines. It is smart to check in as early as possible as queues build up for major flights, not just as check-in but also at the immigration desks, for hand luggage security checking (after immigration) and for seat selection (done in the departure lounge, not at check-in). Check in too late and you won't have time for duty free shopping.

There is a private departure lounge for government guests and another for first class passengers or those invited by the airline's man-

agement to use it. Members of the British Airways Executive Club
can also use the private lounge facilities.

Departure tax
An airport service charge is levied on most departing passengers. In
1993 it was Rs100, payable in cash at the check-in desk. Those in
transit who continue their journey by the first connecting flight within
48 hours are exempt. So, too, are certain government and diplomatic
officials, United Nations personnel and their families, military forces
and their families stationed in Mauritius, and children under two.
There is no requirement for an exit visa either for tourists, expat
workers or nationals.

Duty free shops
The duty free shops at the airport offer a remarkable range of goods
at prices which really are duty free and have none of the hidden taxes
on items bought at so-called duty free shops in Port Louis (see next
chapter on Shopping). If you have bought duty free diamonds or jewellery, don't forget to pick up your purchases after you pass through
immigration.

On the left, after the security check, is the main duty free area with
a shop selling sports goods (from socks to full sets of golf clubs).
There is also a bookshop with books on Mauritius (including this
one), at the other side of the entrance to the first class and CIP
Lounge. Opposite is the counter for perfumes (claimed to be the
lowest priced in the region), a counter for electronics, and an island
counter for watches and other goodies. At the other end of the departure lounge is the self-service cigarette, liquor and savoury delicacy
shop.

Departure lounge
There is a stand-up bar and also a sit-down restaurant in the departure lounge. There are three main departure gates with corridor access
to aircraft on the upper level. For flights to Rodrigues or Réunion
passengers go downstairs and walk across the tarmac to the aircraft.

LOCAL TRAVEL AGENTS RECOGNISED BY IATA
Air International Travel & Tours
4 Ter St Georges Street, Port Louis
Tel: 208 3762; telex: 5258 IW

Al-Labbaik Travel Agency
20 Sir Virgil Nez Street, Port Louis
Tel: 212 6454; fax: 212 6454

Atom Travel Agency
22 Royal Street, Port Louis
Tel: 208 0164; telex: 4879 ATOMIW

Atlas Travel Service
Cnr Sir S Ramgoolam & Eugene Laurent Streets, Port Louis
Tel: 208 1497; fax: 208 7717

Budget Travel
35 Sir William Newton Street, Port Louis
Tel: 208 1277; fax: 240 1479

Bonny Air Travel
Edith Cavell Street, Port Louis
Tel: 212 5688; fax: 208 5727

Century Travel
Lord Kitchener Street, Port Louis
Tel: 208 6707; fax: 208 6707

Concorde Travel & Tours
La Chaussée, Port Louis
Tel: 208 5041; fax: 212 2585

Coop Travel & Tours
Dumat Street, Port Louis
Tel: 212 2922; telex: 4348 ATSOOSA IW

Chinese Travel Agency
6 Jummah Mosque Street, Port Louis
Tel: 240 0196; telex: 5253 CATOUR IW

Grand Bay Travel & Tours Ltd
Royal Road, Grand Bay
Tel: 263 8771; fax: 263 8274

Harel Mallac Travel
Edith Cavell Street, Port Louis
Tel: 208 8580; fax: 208 1674

IKS Travel
Cnr La Paix & Farquhar Streets, Port Louis
Tel: 242 4032; fax: 240 4435

Mauritius Air Travel & Tours
Cnr Sir S Ramgoolam & Sir W Newton Streets, Port Louis
Tel: 242 5026; fax: 208 2417

Mauritius Travel & Tourist Bureau
Royal Street, Port Louis
Tel: 208 2041; fax: 208 0390

Mauritours
10 Sir W Newton Street, Port Louis
Tel: 208 5241

Oceania Travel
44 Jummah Mosque Street, Port Louis
Tel: 208 1230; fax: 208 8868

Rogers Travel Ltd
Rogers House, 5 Kennedy Street, Port Louis
Tel: 208 6801; fax: 212 0218

Silver Wings Travel Ltd
21 Louis Pasteur Street, Port Louis
Tel: 242 6405; fax: 208 8133

Skyline Travel & Tours Ltd
3 Eugene Laurent Street, Port Louis
Tel: 208 5038; telex: 4453 SKYLINE IW

Stella Travel Agents Ltd
Sharon Building, 3rd Floor, Sir W Newton Street, Port Louis
Tel: 212 0258; telex: 4325 KAILASH IW

Sun Travel & Tours Ltd
2 St Georges Street, Port Louis
Tel: 212 1639; telex: 4487 IKS IW

Transworld Travel Ltd
Place Foch, Port Louis
Tel: 212 4101

Tropic Tours Ltd
Fan Sing Building, Edith Cavell Street, Port Louis
Tel: 208 8578; fax: 208 8579

White Sand Travel
La Chaussée, Port Louis
Tel: 212 6092; fax: 208 8524

Facts of Life

GENERAL

Seasons/weather
Basically, there are two seasons: *Summer* when it is hot, from November to April, and *Winter* when it is warm, from May to October. The sugar cane cutting season is June to November. The rainy season is roughly January to May although rain is spasmodic, not a constant downpour for the entire five months. On the west coast the rainfall is about one metre or less a year. The central plateau and windward slopes can have up to five metres in a year.

Temperatures during summer range from 24°C at dawn to 30°C at noon on the coast, and during winter are about 18°C at dawn to 24°C at noon. On the central plateau it is normally about five degrees cooler. Its proximity to the Tropic of Capricorn assures Mauritius of a subtropical climate that is typically warm and humid. Cyclones can occur in January, February and March.

A cyclone is a tropical storm that often has a devastating effect on insecure buildings and vegetation. They form in the southwest Indian Ocean, north of Mauritius, embracing the island as they move southwards. As well as high winds, a cyclone brings great dark, brooding clouds and torrential rain. The island thrives on this rain but since the cyclonic rains occur on an average of five days a year, they are only a minor inconvenience to the sun-worshipper. A severe cyclone, when everyone has to batten themselves indoors, is a rare occurrence, although there was one in 1994.

The trade winds blow in winter, relieving the humidity of the coast, and sea breezes keep down the humidity during the hottest months of January, February and March. Port Louis can be hot and sticky then and the humidity is higher on the central plateau. The south coast is the breeziest.

For the tourist staying in a coastal resort, any time of the year is suitable for a vacation. For the business visitor who has to keep to the towns, the dry and cooler months of April to November would be more tolerable.

Time
Mauritius time is Greenwich Mean Time (GMT) plus four hours.

There is a sudden dawning and a brief tropical twilight. In the

winter months, daylight extends from 0600 to 1800 hours, and in
summer from 0500 to 1900 hours.

Electricity

Electricity is supplied by the Central Electricity Board (CEB) whose
head office is in Royal Road, Curepipe (tel: 675 5010). Power comes
mainly from hydroelectric plants with reservoirs located at Mare aux
Vacoas, Mare Longue, La Ferme, Eau Bleue and Tamarin Falls.
There is a wind-generated plant at Grand Bassin.

During the sugar cane harvest, sugar factories produce their own
electric supply from *bagasse* and the surplus of electricity is sold to
the CEB. Other methods used by the CEB for producing electricity
are through oil (at St Louis and Fort Victoria power stations) and
charcoal (FUEL power station).

The distribution voltage is 230V single phase and 400V three phase.
Incoming high voltage is 6,600V or 22,000V or 66,000V with 50HZ
frequency. Tariffs vary according to consumer requirements with
special industrial and EPZ rates.

A variety of electrical sockets are to be discovered in buildings but
plugs are available for all types in the shops if you don't have an
adapter. The more modern buildings are equipped to take the international standard square 3-pin plug. There are occasional power fail-
ures so it is prudent to carry a pocket torch for emergencies.

Water

Water distribution, subsidised by government, is by the Central Water
Authority (CWA) with head office in St Paul, Phoenix (tel: 686 50712).

Can you drink it? Sometimes. It is not safe to drink in certain
areas, especially when there are filter and treatment problems such as
in Port Louis after prolonged rains.

Media

Newspapers in Mauritius enjoy a reputation for lively debate and a
freedom of expression, with the independent press curbed only by
self-censorship. The first newspaper was published in 1773 and there
have been more than 600 titles since then, including *Le Cernéen*, started in 1832 as the first newspaper which did not have to be submitted
to the government for approval.

The most popular daily papers are *Le Mauricien* and *L'Express*,
which are published in French, although *L'Express* occasionally carries
articles, news reports and advertisements in English. There is no English daily newspaper but there are two Chinese dailies. There are also
weekly and monthly publications propagating a particular political
viewpoint. Newspapers are sold at kiosks and street corners and
attract an avid readership with sales put at over 70,000 copies daily.
The address of *Le Mauricien* is 8 St George Street, Port Louis, tel: 208

7808; *L'Express* is at 3, Brown Sequard Street, Port Louis, tel: 212 1826.

There is one government controlled radio station which broadcasts in English, French, Creole and Hindi and there are estimated to be close to a quarter of a million radio sets in the country. The BBC has a Mauritian as its local correspondent and the BBC World Service can be received clearly.

The Mauritius Broadcasting Corporation's television service is popular. It was introduced in 1965 and splits its daily nine hours of programmes into English, French and Hindi, with Creole news summaries and occasional Chinese movies with subtitles. (Mauritius Broadcasting Corporation, Louis Pasteur Street, Forest Side, tel: 675 5001.) The service was extended in 1987 to Rodrigues. There is a College of the Air on radio and TV. Television viewers also receive programmes from Réunion's TV station.

Churches
For Christians there are both Roman Catholic and Anglican cathedrals in Port Louis with Presbyterian and Evangelical churches close by and churches of all denominations throughout the island. Hotels display details of religious services held near them on their notice boards.

Begging
In recent years there has been an increase in the number of older people begging, and many have developed a network of people, such as restaurant staff, to help them. There is also occasional part-time begging, especially around the main commercial areas and markets. Some of the younger beggars are from Diego Garcia and have resisted integration into the community. In Port Louis, I found that when I once needed change for a Rs200 note, the only person who had it was a beggar.

Uniforms
The presence of uniformed personnel on the streets of Mauritius is rare enough to be remarkable. The most frequently seen are the **police** who wear light blue shirts and dark blue trousers, with black flat caps. **Firemen** wear a brown uniform with red belts.

There is no proper army. A para-military unit called the **Special Mobile Force** (SMF) numbers less than a thousand and has its HQ at Vacoas. It has some tanks, jeeps and other military vehicles. The top soldiers have been trained in Europe and India. French military advisers offer supervision and further training and there is also a lingering British connection. SMF regulars wear khaki, soldier style uniforms, quite distinct from that of the normal police or riot unit. They have combat and parade uniforms.

There is no airforce but a small navy unit does exist. There is also

a coastguard service. The absence of security guards around government buildings and foreign embassies is evidence of the island's
peaceful way of life.

Social Organisations

The **Rotary Club** of Port Louis meets every Wednesday, 12.00–15.00,
at the Flore Mauricienne restaurant, while the Citadel branch of the
club meets at the same place at 07.30 on Tuesdays. In Curepipe, the
club meets every Thursday at 18.30 at the Continental Hotel. The
Rotary Club of Grand Bay meets on Tuesdays from 18.30 at Le
Mauricia Hotel. In Quatre Bornes, the Rotary Club meets at the
Gold Crest Hotel on Wednesdays at 18.30 and the Rotary Club of
Beau Bassin Rose Hill meets on Wednesdays at 18.30 at the Maison
de la Culture et des Loisirs, Sir Harilal Vaghjee Arcades. There are
also Rotary Clubs in Mahebourg, Black River, Vacoas and Rodrigues
(where meetings are on Tuesdays at 17.00 at Les Filaos, English Bay).

There are **Lions Clubs** in Port Louis, Curepipe and Quatre Bornes.
The Port Louis chapter meets on the second Monday of each month
at 16.30 at 10 Dr Ferriere Street, Port Louis. The address of the
Mauritius Round Table is PO Box 181, Port Louis. There is also a
branch of the **SKAL Club** association of tourism professionals.

Foreign Countries and Organisations Represented in Mauritius

EMBASSIES/HIGH COMMISSIONS

AUSTRALIA   Rogers House, Port Louis. Tel: 208 1700; fax: 208 8878
CHINA   Royal Road, Belle Rose, Quatre Bornes. Tel: 454 9111; fax: 464
6012
EGYPT   8 King George Avenue, Floreal. Tel: 696 5012; fax: 686 5775
FRANCE   14 St George Street, Port Louis. Tel: 208 3755; fax: 208 8145
INDIA   Bank of Baroda Building, Sir William Newton Street, Port Louis.
Tel: 208 3775; fax: 208 6859
MADAGASCAR   Queen Mary Avenue, Floreal. Tel: 686 5015
PAKISTAN   Anglo Mauritius House, Intendance Street, Port Louis. Tel:
212 6547
RUSSIA   Queen Mary Avenue, Floreal. Tel: 696 1545
UK   King George V Avenue, Floreal. Tel: 686 5795; fax: 686 5792
USA   Rogers House, Port Louis. Tel: 208 2347; fax: 208 9534

CONSULATES

AUSTRIA   Rogers House, Port Louis. Tel: 208 6801
BELGIUM   Blyth Brothers, New Quay Street, Port Louis. Tel: 208 1241
BRAZIL   Harel Mallac Building, Edith Cavell Street, Port Louis. Tel: 208
5434; fax: 208 1674
CANADA   Blanche Birger Co Ltd, 18 Jules Koenig Street, Port Louis. Tel:
208 0821

DENMARK   4 Edith Cavell Street, Port Louis. Tel: 208 5051
GERMANY   32 bis, St George Street, Port Louis. Tel: 240 7425; fax: 208 5330
FINLAND   Rogers House, Port Louis. Tel: 208 6801
JAPAN   Ireland Blyth Ltd, Dr Ferriers Street, Port Louis. Tel: 208 2811
NETHERLANDS
   New Quay, Port Louis. Tel: 208 1241
NEW ZEALAND   Anchor Building, Les Pailles. Tel: 212 4920; fax: 208 4654
NORWAY   Rogers House, Port Louis. Tel: 208 6801
PORTUGAL   Harel Mallac Building, Edith Cavell Street, Port Louis. Tel: 208 4802; fax: 208 1674
SPAIN   10 Dr Ferriere Street, Port Louis. Tel: 208 2811; fax: 208 1014
SWEDEN   Rogers House, Port Louis. Tel: 208 6801
SWITZERLAND   2 Jules Koenig Street, Port Louis. Tel: 208 8763

ORGANISATIONS
COMMONWEALTH DEVELOPMENT CORPORATION Chancery House, Lislet Geoffroy Street, Port Louis. Tel: 208 4885
EUROPEAN COMMUNITY   61-63 Floreal Road, Vacoas. Tel: 686 5061; fax: 686 6318
UNITED NATIONS   Anglo-Mauritius House, Port Louis. Tel: 212 3726; fax: 208 4871
WORLD HEALTH ORGANISATION   c/o Ministry of Health, Port Louis. Tel: 201 1899

Public holidays
Public holidays for religious and state occasions threatened to overwhelm working life in Mauritius, multiplying until there were 28 official days off work a year, in addition to weekends. Now the number of statutory public holidays has been reduced to 13. These are as follows:

New Year's Day	January 1
New Year	January 2
Chinese Spring Festival	Variable (January/February)
Thaipoosam Cavadee	Variable (January/February)
Maha Shivaratree	Variable (February/March)
Republic Day	March 12
Ougadi (Telegu New Year)	Variable (March/April)
Labour Day	May 1
Id El Fitr	Variable (May/June)
Ganesh Chaturthi	Variable (August/September)
Divali	Variable (October/November)
All Saints Day	November 1
Christmas Day	December 25

Employees are also permitted to have two additional days leave a year to celebrate religious festivals which are no longer official public holidays. Leave is granted at the employee's request even if the employee doesn't belong to the religion celebrating the festival. Some of these festivals are so popular with everyone, regardless of their religion, that they become like public holidays, with everywhere closed in certain areas.

Since these holidays depend on different religious calendars, the days on which they are held vary each year and will not always be in the months shown here.

Sankranti	January
Holi	March
Mehraj Shariff (Muslim)	March
Varusha Pirappu (Tamil New Year)	April
Shabbe Baraat (Muslim)	April
Good Friday	March/April
Easter Monday	March/April
Seemadree Appana Parsa (Telegu)	May
Sittarai Cavadee (Tamil)	May
Corpus Christi	May/June
Id El Adha (Muslim)	August
Raksha Bandhan (Hindu)	August
Assumption Day	August
Father Laval's Death Anniversary	September
Mid Autumn Festival (Chinese)	October
Yaum Un Nabi	November
Ganga Asnan	November
Boxing Day	December

The weekend in Mauritius is Saturday afternoon and all day Sunday.

FESTIVALS

Sankranti
The first of the year's religious festivals, it is celebrated in the beginning of the Tamil month Thai, and is also known as Thai Pongal. It is an occasion of thanksgiving for the harvest which is represented by the ceremonial boiling of rice. It is customary to wear new clothes at this time.

Chinese Spring Festival
This is New Year's Day and spring-cleaning combined. The festival begins on the eve of the Chinese New Year with an explosion of fire crackers to chase away evil spirits. New Year's Day is in January or February and does not fall on the same day every year due to the irregularity of the lunar month.

During the week before New Year's Day there is a thorough spring-cleaning of the home. Traditionalists make visits to pagodas on New Year's Eve with offerings and prayers of thanksgiving. The Day itself is a holiday for the Chinese community who celebrate by going to the beach. Neither scissors nor knives are used on the Day and the colour red, symbolic of happiness, is favoured. Food is displayed in an honoured place in the home in the hope of abundance in the coming year. Cakes made of rice flour and honey, called wax cakes because of their texture, are shared with relatives and friends.

Thaipoosam Cavadee
This Tamil ritual is named after the wooden yoke – the *cavadee* – decorated with flowers and palm leaves and with a pot of milk suspended from each end, which a devotee fulfilling a vow carries across his shoulders in procession to his temple. There it is placed before the deity when, despite the long, hot ordeal, the milk should not be curdled.

The *cavadee* procession, while colourful and spectacular, is awe-inspiring because of the penance undergone by the participants who walk with their bodies pierced with needles, hooks hanging from their flesh and skewers threaded through their tongues and cheeks.

Maha Shivaratree
The Great Night of Shiva is a solemn occasion for Hindus which begins with a night-long vigil in worship of the God Shiva. The following day, devotees dressed in pure white carry the Kanwar, a wooden arch decorated with flowers, paper and tiny mirrors, in procession to Grand Bassin. This lake is in the Savanne district, about five kilometres by motorable road from the Mare aux Vacoas reservoir.

The lake is holy to Hindus who carry water from it home to their own temples. *Poojas* (worship with food) are celebrated that night in the temples dotting the banks of the lake, the air heavy with the sweet smell of burning incense sticks and reverberating with prayers broadcast from loudspeakers. This is reputed to be the largest Hindu festival celebrated outside India and is reminiscent of the great rituals on the banks of the holy Ganges. Worshippers believe the lights they launch on the lake on banana leaves and their offerings of flowers will float somehow to the Ganges.

Holi
A happy time for Hindus when greetings are exchanged and revelry erupts with the squirting of coloured water and the spraying of coloured powder on one another, and on everyone else the revellers come across. A noisy and cheerful festival.

Mehraj Shariff
Muslim celebration.

Ougadi
Telegu New Year.

Varusha Pirappu
Tamil New Year.

Shabbe Baraat
Muslim celebration.

Seemadree Appana Parsa
Telegu religious celebration.

Sittarai Cavadee
Tamil religious celebration (April/May).

Id El Fitr
The annual month of fasting (Ramadan) by Muslims, during which
they neither eat nor drink between sunrise and sunset, comes to an
end with this festival.

Ganesh Chaturthi
Celebrated on the fourth day of the lunar month of August/Septem-
ber by Hindus of Marathi faith as the birthday of Ganesh, the god of
wisdom and remover of all obstacles. In Baie du Cap processions are
held with devotees escorting pink, elephant-nosed effigies to the sea
and dusting onlookers with scarlet powder.

Corpus Christi
Devout Roman Catholics join in a procession through the streets of
Port Louis in May or June on the occasion of Corpus Christi.

Id El Adha
Sheep and goats are sacrificed in ceremonial slaughter for this Muslim
festival and the meat is shared by family and friends. The day commemorates the sacrifice by Abraham of his son and the events sym-
bolise the Muslim ideal of sacrifice and dedication.

Raksha Bandhan
Hindu celebration.

Father Laval
Throughout September, but especially on September 9 which is the
anniversary of the death in 1864 of Father Jacques Desire Laval

(known locally as Père Laval), pilgrims gather at the priest's grave in Ste Croix. Father Laval was born in France in 1803 and brought up in a strict religious atmosphere, qualifying as a medical doctor before becoming a priest. In 1841 he arrived in Mauritius as a missionary and converted thousands of recently freed slaves to Catholicism, becoming known as the Apostle of the Blacks. He is regarded as the 'national saint' of Mauritius, recognised by the Vatican and venerated by followers of all faiths who attribute miraculous healing powers to his name.

Mid Autumn Festival
Chinese feast.

Divali
Clay oil lamps and paper lanterns with candles in them are placed in front of every Hindu and Tamil home on this Festival of Lights. Hills and valleys sparkle in the night as lights burn to celebrate the victory of Rama over Ravana, and Krishna's destruction of the demon Narakasuran; the victory of good over evil.

All Saints Day
The day on which cemetery cleaning takes place and flowers are placed by Roman Catholics on the graves of the dead.

Yaum Un Nabi
The birth and death anniversaries of the Prophet Mohammed are commemorated on the Prophet's Day, following twelve days during which the faithful gather in mosques throughout the island, devoting themselves to religious study.

Ganga Asnan
For Hindus this is the time of ceremonial bathing in the sea for purification, since they believe the holy water of the Ganges will be able to purify them through it. At the beaches of Albion, Belle Mare, Baie du Tombeau, Blue Bay, Flic-en-Flac, Mont Choisy, Pereybère, Pte aux Roches, Pte aux Sables and Tamarin, special lifeguard units are set up from 09.00 to 17.00 hours to ensure the safety of bathers.

Muharram
An important Muslim festival known in Mauritius as Yamsey, featuring figures and towers called *ghoons*, carried in procession through the streets in commemoration of the death of the grandson of the Prophet.

Chinese festivals
The Chinese dragon, a six metre long monster, has been known to make appearances, dancing and twisting in a pageant symbolising

peace and prosperity. In March, ritual cleaning of the statues in Buddhist temples takes place.

Firewalking
At the Tamil temple in Terre Rouge and at other temples in predominantly Tamil areas, can be witnessed *Teemeedee*, or firewalking, between October and March. Worshippers walk over beds of red hot embers which represent the outstretched sari of Draupadee. They prepare for the ordeal by fasting, a ritual bath and a blessing before walking unscathed on the glowing embers to the accompaniment of chants from supporters.

Details of where to see firewalking, and the dates each year of the Religious Festivals and Public Holidays, are given in a leaflet about 'Coming Events' available bi-monthly from the Tourist Office.

HOW TO GET AROUND

Tour operators and their programmes
The easiest way to get around and see the sights of Mauritius is by taking one of the conducted tours run by a tour operating company. They provide an instant introduction to the island, enabling visitors to discover places they can return to later to explore independently. Inbound tour operators meet arrivals at the airport on behalf of the hotels. They provide leaflets about their services to incoming guests and many have desks at the major hotels.

The most innovative is **MauriTours Ltd** who have standard tours from every hotel on most days of the week, as well as special tours such as big game fishing, tea or spice plantation visits, walking in the Macchabée forest, and bird watching.

MauriTours issue an occasional newsletter about Mauritius which reflects the company's concern that the booming economy might represent a threat to the environment. Their interest in natural Mauritius is shown by the special tours they organise for birdwatchers to the Cryptomeria forest on the southern border of the Central Plateau to watch the pink pigeon, to the Macchabée forest, habitat of the Mauritian merle, the cuckoo shrike and the echo parakeet, and to Black River Gorges to look for the Mauritius kestrel.

These expeditions, led by professional biologists, could not be undertaken easily by an individual. Neither could the trip to Round Island and Serpent Island which is also organised by MauriTours, since a special permit is needed. This trip is by boat (2½ hours) or by helicopter to islands famous for their colonies of nesting sea birds, with 30,000 on Serpent Island alone. Private estates can be visited on the 'Bel Air and Andrea' tour which includes a tea break in a private

villa overlooking the blustery south coast and a lunch of local delicacies in a sugar estate bungalow.

MauriTours guides are trained thoroughly and given regular
refresher courses throughout the year. They have two Japanese guides
for their Japanese clients. The company maintains a fleet of
European-standard tour coaches and nearly 50 minibuses. All vehicles
are linked by radio telephone with HQ and the airport desk. They
also run a VIP limousine service to provide guests who represent it
with a special, personal welcome at the airport and an exclusive,
deluxe transfer to and from the hotel. They run a 24-hour service
with a duty manager of executive level available around the clock at
MauriTours' HQ.

Clients of **White Sand Tours** are given a letter on arrival at the
airport describing the excursions the company offers as well as
giving tourist advice. White Sands operates its own vehicles and also
has hospitality desks at over a dozen major hotels. As well as standard tours – all of which allow plenty of time for shopping – the
company can arrange deep sea fishing, deer hunting, helicopter
'flips', horse riding, and a box of anthurium flowers as a souvenir
on departure.

The Mauritius Travel and Tourist Bureau Ltd, known as MTTB, is
a Mauritian company established in 1953. They concentrate on a
complete service for the visitor, with three Port Louis offices and ones
in Curepipe and Rose Hill, as well as desks at major hotels. One
hotel, the Verandah Bungalow Village in Grand Bay, is owned by
MTTB. The company is the representative in Mauritius for American
Express. It is particularly strong on deep sea fishing events.

The Mauritius Touring Company known as **Hertz Mauritourco** is
the Hertz licensee in the island. They have a range of tours to appeal
to the holiday visitor with the attraction of exceptionally knowledgeable guides. With an individual approach, these guides tailor tours to
suit the participants since they know by experience that what intrigues
a French visitor, for instance, would be of no interest to a South
African.

Another company offering tours is **Ebrahim Travel & Tours**, based
in Grand Bay. Their prices, which do *not* include entrance fees, meals,
etc, are highly competitive, and would suit the independent traveller
staying in Grand Bay. They also arrange sailing around the northern
islands, scuba diving, deep sea fishing, glass bottom boat rides and
hire of bicycles, moppets (sic), motorbikes, cars and bungalows.

The cost of conducted tours is not cheap and standard excursions
such as visits to Port Louis or the Botanical Gardens can be done
independently using buses. However, an organised excursion is worth
the expense for its saving in hassles and the accuracy of information
obtained. Many places and experiences can actually only be enjoyed
on an organised tour.

Daily Tours

(*Note*: Maurtourco also operate similar tours which can be arranged for small groups on any day. Tour days are subject to change.)

Monday
Garden of President's residence, Eureka Creole Mansion, Casela Bird Park (Mauritours, MTTB)
Emerald Cruise to Coin de Mire and Ilot Gabriel (Mauritours)
Pamplemousses Garden and Port Louis (White Sands)
Plantation Tour (MTTB)

Tuesday
Port Louis and Pamplemousses Garden (Mauritours)
Curepipe, Black River Gorge, Chamarel (White Sand, MTTB)

Wednesday
Bel Air and Andrea and Vanille Crocodile Farm and Anthurium Nursery (Mauritours)
Le Val Nature Park, Mahebourg and Domaine du Chasseur (Mauritours)
Shopping in Grand Bay (White Sands)
Domaine les Pailles (White Sands)
Ile aux Cerfs (MTTB)
Catamaran cruise, east coast, to Ile aux Cerfs (MTTB)
Isla Mauritia (built 1892) cruise from Grand Bay (MTTB)

Thursday
Ile aux Cerfs (Mauritours)
Curepipe, Grand Bassin, Black River Gorge, Chamarel (Mauritours)
Turquois cruise from Pointe d'Esny to Ile aux Cerfs (Mauritours)
Isla Mauritia cruise from Grand Bay (Mauritours)
Cruise to Port Louis (Mauritours)
Port Louis, cruise to Grand Bay, Pamplemousses Gardens (White Sands)
Port Louis, Grand Bay, Pamplemousses Gardens (White Sands)
Port Louis, Pamplemousses, Grand Bay (MTTB)

Friday
Ile aux Cerfs (Mauritours)
Curepipe, Grand Bassin, Black River Gorge, Chamarel (Mauritours)
Ile aux Cerfs (White Sands)
Catamaran cruise and Domaine du Chasseur (White Sands)
Isla Mauritia cruise from Grand Bay (MTTB)

Saturday
Domaine les Pailles (Mauritours)
Shopping in Quatre Bornes and Rose Hill (Mauritours)
Isla Mauritia cruise from Grand Bay (Mauritours, White Sands)
Sinuhe cruise from Grand Bay (Mauritours)

Shopping in Curepipe (White Sands)
Mahebourg and Domaine du Chasseur (MTTB)

(Personal recommendation: If you only take one organised tour
during your stay in Mauritius, the Bel Air and Andrea one operated
by Mauritours is more interesting than most, and is something you
could not do independently.)

Tour operators: Travel agents specialising in local tours and sightseeing

CONCORDE TRAVEL & TOURS
Chaussée Street
Port Louis
Tel: 208 5041
Fax: 212 2585
Telex: 4305 CONCORD IW

EBRAHIM TRAVEL & TOURS
Ebrahim Flats
Grand Bay
Tel: 263 7831

HERTZ MAURITOURCO
Froberville Lane
Curepipe
Tel: 675 1453
Fax: 675 6425
Telex: 4435 HERMCO IW

MAURITOURS
S Venkatasananda Street
Rose Hill
Tel: 454 1666
Fax: 454 1682
Telex: 4349 MORITUR IW

MAURITIUS TRAVEL &
TOURIST BUREAU (MTTB)
Royal Street
Port Louis
Tel: 208 2041
Fax: 208 8607
Telex: 4613 MTTB IW

WHITE SAND TOURS
M1 Motorway
Port Louis
Tel: 208 5424
Fax: 208 8524
Telex: 4217 IBLTO IW

Driving

The main self-drive car hire companies of Hertz, Avis and Europcar
operate in Mauritius. The visitor need not feel nervous about road-
manship since the standard of driving is good and, outside the towns,
there are stretches of open road without traffic, which make driving
pleasant. There are over 1,600kms of tarred road throughout the
island. The motorways and the road between Port Louis and
Curepipe are the best; little used country roads are not in such good
condition. Driving is on the left.

Negotiating Port Louis by car requires patience as traffic builds up
to horrendous proportions during the day, complicated by the trucks
and handcarts which stop to unload goods from the port at warehouses in the city centre, and by the vans that come at the same time
to collect the goods for distribution to the country districts. Most of
the streets are one-way, which adds to the confusion for the uninitiated. Parking in Port Louis, 09.00–16.30, is only permitted with a

parking ticket which must be purchased in advance from a filling station and displayed inside the windscreen, with time of parking entered
on it by the driver. Police check on its validity (and your honesty).

Car hire in Mauritius is expensive. Cars can be rented from independent companies, especially those in the Grand Bay area, for a few
rupees a day less. Cars can be delivered and recovered anywhere on
the island and there are car hire desks at the airport. Some companies
keep cars available at the major hotels.

The minimum age for hiring a self-drive car depends on the company. Europcar and Avis stipulate 23 years while Hertz are happy
with drivers of 21 years minimum. All require that the driver has
been in possession of a valid driver's licence for at least one year.
Since an international driving licence is only valid for one year it is
advisable to carry either your own home country licence as well, or
an old International Licence as proof of more than a year's driving
experience.

If you don't want to drive yourself, the car hire companies will
provide a driver. Not only does this save you having to cope with
local driving conditions but there is also the bonus of having a private guide too. The cost of an experienced driver starts at Rs150 per
day (09.00 to 18.00), in addition to the car hire cost, with overtime
and Sundays extra.

If you intend to import your own vehicle to drive in Mauritius,
duty will be payable on its whole value. Details are available from the
Controller of Customs, Customs and Excise Department, IKF Building, Trou Fanfaron, Port Louis (tel: 240 9072). There are several
vehicle spare parts shops and a wide range of cars are driven, with
Japanese makes predominant. Both petrol and diesel are readily
available at filling stations throughout the country, but it is worth
keeping your tank full, especially for distance driving at night. Seat-
belts must be worn.

Some car hire companies

AVIS
M1 Motorway, Port Louis
Tel: 208 1624

BEACH CAR LTD
Royal Road, Grand Bay
Tel: 263 8759

BUDGET RENT-A-CAR
Link Road, Roche Bois
Tel: 242 0341

EUROPCAR
Motorway 2, Pailles
Tel: 208 9258
Fax: 208 4705

HERTZ MAURITOURCO
Froberville Lane, Curepipe
Tel: 675 1453
Fax: 675 6425

MASK TOURING CO LTD
(Ground Floor of the Gold Crest
Hotel Building)
St Jean Road, Quatre Bornes
Tel: 454 6975

Motorbike hire

Motorbikes are available for hire but you will have to hunt for them. The best area to look is Grand Bay where one company, Grand Bay Travel and Tours (Royal Road, Grand Bay, tel: 263 8771), acts as agents for individual motorbike owners and can arrange rental from Rs125 a day. There are other places in Grand Bay but availability elsewhere on the island depends on private arrangements. Crash helmets are compulsory when driving or riding a motorbike.

Bicycle hire

Bicycles can be hired from the major hotels by the hour, half day and day. Some hotels organise half-day bicycle tours for youngsters. Bicycle riding is regarded as a diversion rather than a means of getting around the island.

Taxi hire

A visitor who had been in Mauritius for a week walked into the tourist office in Port Louis and looked around the room for a few minutes.

'I must congratulate you', he said to the girls at the information counter. 'Yours is the first tourist office I have visited which has a portrait of a taxi driver on its walls.'

The girls were puzzled until the tourist pointed mockingly to the stuffed head of a shark hanging above the counter.

Taxi drivers in Mauritius have won a reputation for being rapacious because their charges are neither standardised nor regulated effectively, and they don't have meters. Licensed taxis at the airport operate at a uniform rate and you could get an idea of the current charges to your destination from the tourist counter.

Taxis are available on call from all the major hotels and the concierge will have a list of their prices, which will be higher than independent taxis which don't have a hotel concession. Although the official guideline for fares, dating back to 1989, was Rs5 per return km (not mile), don't expect to find a taxi at that price. Most taxi drivers seem agreeable to sensible bargaining (if they do not have to stick to a price fixed by a hotel) and the drivers are generally pleasant and helpful. (One I encountered outside a luxury hotel was keen to offer 'pleasures and access not available in the hotel'.)

Since a taxi charges for the return trip it is worth asking the driver to wait so you can make the return trip with him instead of in another taxi. In theory that's fine, but in practice you'll find the fare increases to cover the return trip. If you are fortunate in finding a taxi driver whose charges are reasonable, encourage him to keep his rates low by giving him all your business.

There are taxi stands throughout Port Louis. A Mercedes picked up at the Central Place d'Armes stand will cost more than a Morris Minor hired at the Immigration Square car park.

Taxis are recognisable by their white registration plates and black figures, whereas private cars have black number plates with white figures. Yellow plates with black figures means a hire car on contract. There are a number of private cars operating as illegal taxis (*taxi marron*). In towns, taxis tend to be available only at conventional times: 06.00 to 20.00 hours. Getting a taxi outside those hours is difficult and only a few offer night service. There are 40 taxi stands and services listed in the island-wide telephone book. Taxis are usually to be found close to the bus stations in the main towns and do not ply the streets looking for passengers.

The exceptions are the **taxi trains**, taxis that tout for custom among passengers queuing for buses, or those that follow regular routes picking up passengers on the way and charging little more than the bus fare for a seat in a shared car. These taxis are usually old bone shakers but they do offer a cheap alternative and will operate late into the night on popular routes. Another way of saving on taxi fares is to travel with a knowledgeable Mauritian. A journey that I made one night by myself cost on the next night a tenth of what I paid, because my Mauritian companion did the negotiating. So taxi drivers aren't all sharks, and at least they don't expect tips.

Helicopter hire

The Air Mauritius Bell Jet Ranger helicopter, with seats for four passengers, is available for hire with pilot for sightseeing and for transfers from/to the airport. In 1993, the cost of transfer from the airport to hotels in the north of the island was Rs7,180, and to elsewhere in Mauritius Rs5,620; the rate for one hour was Rs9,980. Tel: Air Mauritius 637 3420. There are also scheduled sightseeing trips available through the major hotels or tour operators.

Bus

Mauritius is blessed with an excellent bus service, a boon to the independent traveller. It is run on a cooperative basis by different operators: the National Transport Corporation (NTC), tel: 426 2938; Rose Hill Transport (RHT), tel: 464 1221; United Bus Service (UBS), tel: 212 2028; Triolet Bus Service (TBS), tel: 261 6516; Mauritius Bus Transport (MTB), tel: 245 2539, and individual operators. Since so many people live outside the towns where they work, they depend on the bus service for transportation and their patronage keeps it flourishing.

Compared with the bus service of Africa and Asia it is a disciplined, well-run operation. Tickets are issued from a machine roll by conductors, and there are comfortable seats in the coach-type vehicles which generally carry about 46 seated passengers and 18 standing.

Overloading is not typical. Queuing at bus stops is orderly with the
queue forming to the right of the stop. At the Port Louis terminal in
Victoria Square, passengers line up in single file between railings. In
Rose Hill there is a new bus station with individual shelters like gaze-
bos attractively painted in white and green.

Express buses are not non-stop but take a shorter route between
points, although charging the same fare as the slower buses. The fares
are low, with a trip across the island from Port Louis to Mahebourg
(which involves a change) costing around Rs16. It is important when
getting on a bus to ask the conductor where it is going since the town
on the front is not necessarily its destination. There are no buses that
do a round trip tour of the island. To go across the island from
Mahebourg via the airport to Port Louis, it is usually best to take a
bus to Curepipe and change there, as the scheduled service (route
198) can be irregular.

Since the usual flow of passenger traffic is to Port Louis in the
morning and out of Port Louis in the evening, making a connection
in country districts sometimes takes ages. Another problem is that the
rural services finish operating at 17.30, and even the buses linking the
major towns stop running about 20.00, although there is a service up
to 23.00 between Port Louis and Curepipe.

During the day, the outward and return services operate as the bus
fills up rather than to a strict timetable. The principal services are
listed here with the main bus stations in Port Louis being at Victoria
Square, southwest of the Place d'Armes, and Immigration Square to
the northeast.

Bus itineraries

This list is not complete, as new services are introduced, or disappear,
from time to time. Departures are listed according to point of origin,
not the departure point of the return journey.

From Port Louis (Victoria Square)

1	via Coromandel, Beau Bassin to Place Margéot, Rose Hill
1A	via Coromandel, Buckingham, Hugnin Street to Rose Hill
1B	via Balfour Garden, Vandermeersch Street to Place Margéot, Rose Hill
2 & 2A	via Beau Bassin, Place Margéot, Rose Hill, Phoenix to Curepipe, with extension to Forest Side
3	via Beau Bassin, Rose Hill, Quatre Bornes to Vacoas
3A	via Rose Hill to Phoenix
93	via Quartier Militaire to Camp Thorel
102	via Rose Hill, St Paul, Floreal to Curepipe
103	via Moka, St Pierre to Nouvelle Découverte
162	to Forest Side (express)
163	to Vacoas (express)
170	via Quatre Bornes, Vacoas, St Paul to Curepipe

From Port Louis (Immigration Square)
19   via Terre Rouge, Montagne Longue to Crève Coeur
20   via Triolet, Mon Choisy, Grand Bay, Cap Malheureux to St François
20A   via Triolet to Grande Pointe aux Piments
20C   via Triolet, Trou aux Biches, Grand Bay, Pereybere to St Antoine
21   via SSRN Hospital, Pamplemousses, to Goodlands
22   via Pamplemousses, Goodlands, St Antoine to Grand Gaube
33   via Jeetoo Hospital to Pailles
36   to St Croix Church
41   to Vallée des Prêtres with extension to Caroline
42   via Roche Bois to Le Goulet
43   via Pamplemousses road to Cité Martial
48   to St Croix Church
48A   via Cité La Cure to St Croix
49   to Plaine Verte
51   via Grand Rivière Northwest to Pointe aux Sables
52   via Petite Rivière Bambous to Médine
69   via Rose Hill to Beau Songes
70   via Cocoterie Street to St Croix Church
71   via Cottage to Poudre d'Or
77   via Baie du Tombeau to Terre Rouge
82   via Triolet, Trou aux Biches, Cap Malheureux to St François
86   via SSRN Hospital to Rivière du Rempart
112   via Bon Accueil, Lalmatie, Constance to Centre de Flacq
126   via Ile d'Ambre to Rivière du Rempart
171   via SSRN Hospital to Grande Pointe aux Piments
190   to Victoria Square and back

From Plaine Verte
33A   via SSR Street to Plaine Lauzun

From Grois Bois
92   to Jan Palach Square, Curepipe

From: Cité La Cure
148   via St Croix Church to Plaine Lauzun

From Pailles
150   via La Butte to Vallée Pitot
165   via Cassis to Immigration Square

From Plaine Lauzun
152   via Plaine Verte to Baie du Tombeau

From Vallée des Prêtres
160   via SSR Street to Plaine Lauzun

From Triolet
75   to Pamplemousses

From Goodlands
26   via Poste la Fayette to Centre de Flacq

From Rivière du Rempart
27A   to Roches Noires
27B   to Plaine des Roches

From Piton
29   via Fond du Sac, Scottise to Grand Bay

From SSRN Hospital, Pamplemousses
75A   to Pamplemousses Centre
175   to Crève Coeur

From Place Margéot, Rose Hill
130   via St Pierre to La Laura Malinga
13   via Montagne Ory to St Pierre
13A &
13B   via St Pierre to Nouvelle Découverte
15   via Quartier Militaire, Providence to Centre de Flacq

From St Antoine
95   via Grand Gaube, Cap Malheureux, Mon Choisy, Triolet to Pamplemousses

From Rue Edward VII, Rose Hill
45   via Mont Roches to Albion

From Quatre Bornes
4A   via Floreal to Jan Palach Square, Curepipe
5   via Bambous to Baie du Cap, La Gaulette
57   via Bambous, Flic en Flac to Wolmar

From Jan Palach Square, Curepipe
6 & 6A   via Rivière des Anguilles to Chemin Grenier, Chamouny
9 & 9A   via Rose Belle, Airport to Mahebourg
17   via Quartier Militaire to Centre de Flacq
61A   via Rivière des Anguilles to Camp Diable
62   via Rose Belle to Rivière du Poste
191   via La Vigie to Immigration Square, Port Louis
133   via Nouvelle France, Baie du Cap to Choisy
142   via Beau Bois to Souillac
168   via Bois Chéri to Grand Bassin
179A   via Floreal to Wolmar

From Centre de Flacq
18   via Grand Sable to Mahebourg
54   via Quartre Cocos to Palmar
55   via Boulet Rouge to Trou d'Eau Douce
101A   via Lalmatie to SSRN Hospital, Pamplemousses

From Baie du Cap
5A   via Chamarel to St Anne

From Souillac
8   via Rivière des Galets to Baie du Cap

From Mahebourg
10   via L'Escalier to Souillac
11   to La Val
46   to Blue Bay
177   to Bois des Amourettes
186   to Savinia
198   to Port Louis

Hitchhiking

Hitchhiking is seldom practiced by Mauritians. With the bus service reaching the depths of nearly every village, Mauritians are knowledgeable about how to get around their island easily and inexpensively. Foreigners do hitchhike though and cars will stop. Hitchhiking is not disapproved of by the police but it is difficult to assess what Mauritians themselves think of it.

AROUND TOWN

Shopping

Shops in Port Louis open on weekdays at 09.00 and close at 17.00, with Saturday as a half day. Some open on Sunday mornings, too. Corner grocery/liquor stores on the outskirts of Port Louis open earlier and stay open later like the village shops, and are also open on Sunday mornings. The Port Louis market is open every day including Sundays, although trading is not so hectic then. Port Louis shops sell everything from the latest video recorders and digital watches (sometimes also available from streetside pedlars) to coconut husks for polishing wooden floors.

Shopping in the interior towns of Curepipe and Quatre Bornes is more conventional, without the colour and bustle of street life in Port Louis. Shops in Curepipe stay open all day Saturday but close on Thursday afternoons, as do those in the other plateau towns. They generally close later (at 18.00 hours) than the shops in Port Louis and their prices may not be as low as in the city. There are supermarkets in Curepipe and Quatre Bornes. Every town has a market, although not every day, in a bazaar-like setting. Those at Curepipe and Rose Hill are interesting and lively. Shops in villages are open at irregular hours and until late to meet customer demand.

Discounts on marked prices may be available if you have the effrontery to ask, although it's usually Mauritians who are successful.

Bargaining on unmarked prices is acceptable if you have time, but do not expect to lower the price significantly since it's more a game than an essential part of the deal. Never agree to purchase anything until you know its price.

The usual souvenirs of a tropical island (basket work, wood carvings, tortoise and seashell creations) are available, sometimes imported from the Philippines, so check those shiny/varnished shells are genuine. Shops have enough junk such as T-shirts emblazoned with "No Problem" and atrocious ashtrays and paperweights to satisfy the worst possible taste. However, quality souvenirs, such as the models of old sailing ships made in workshops around Curepipe, can be found at the better hotel gift shops and in the cabin boutiques in the grounds of Eureka House.

Duty free diamonds can be obtained at the cutting works in Floreal, and other duty free goods are available at shops in Port Louis. But take care. Some shops that claim to sell duty free goods, especially watches, don't, since their prices include an import levy of 17% and a sales tax of 5%. Genuine duty free items can be bought at the Port Louis offshoot of the airport's **Mauritius Shopping Paradise** and at the Port Louis jewellers, **Poncini**. Buyers will need to show a foreign passport and an air ticket, and must pay in foreign currency or credit card on purchase; goods are delivered to buyers at the airport on their departure.

There are only a few quality jewellers on the island and one that is known to the discerning is **Ravior** in Quatre Bornes. The Duke of York visited there in October 1987 and signed the clan book of the owner, himself a descendant of Gujarathi royalty. Whether he bought one of the superb range of stones on display there is 'a professional secret'.

Dressmakers and tailors really can make clothes in 24 hours but better work takes longer. The short-term visitor who wants a dress copied should commission the work on arrival to make sure it is ready in time for her departure. Some towns have florists and the wax-like pink anthuriums grown in Mauritius make a delightful present. They are sold packed in carboard boxes for travelling and will keep for up to six weeks when you get them home.

The prices of everyday household items are difficult to compare in general terms since some items are more expensive (instant coffee for instance is double the UK price) while others (such as Kleenex tissue, sardines and evaporated milk, all imported) are cheaper than in England. Imported wines and spirits and cigarettes are more expensive, an encouragement to buy the locally produced alternative. As ever, it pays to explore when you are shopping, both for bargains and novel souvenirs which can often be found in village hardware stores that sell everything from authentic garlic crushers carved out of wood to pink plastic models of a despondent dodo.

Bookshops
For its population and high literacy rate, Mauritius is poorly served for bookshops. While there are a score of *Libraries* on the island, most of these combine stationery supplies with a stock of books for students and a few general volumes in French and some in English. Although there is no duty levied on the import of books into Mauritius, prices are high.

The best shops for books are in Curepipe and Port Louis. In Bourbon Street in Port Louis there is a fascinating bookshop that specialises in selling and exchanging secondhand paperbacks. There's not much space to browse but there are lots of novels in English as well as new books on Mauritius.

Beauty care
The major hotels have beauty and hair salons and, since these are not restricted to hotel guests, anyone in need of international standard hair and beauty care can use them. Hairdressers do not expect a tip. Herbal remedies are very popular among Mauritians for beauty care and there are herbal beauty salons. These offer herbal facials and local solutions to skin and hair problems as well as massage, pedicure, haircut and hair styling. There is also a herbalist in Flacq who is recommended by visitors.

In the market in Port Louis there are some much-photographed stalls displaying heaps of herbs with signs saying, in French, what complaints they can cure if drunk as a *tisane* (tea). The father and son team of **KG Naiken** have well over half a century of experience and have won medals for their herbal remedies. Tell Mr Naiken your complaint and he will supply a mix of herbs to cure it. For a hangover he gave me three different kinds of leaf, to be boiled in three glasses of water until reduced to two, and then drunk.

Laundry
While hotels will look after the laundry of guests, so, too, will the inexpensive guesthouses, usually by private arrangement with the room maid. The climate ensures that clothes dry quickly. **The Dry Cleaning and Steam Laundry Company** at Cassis near Port Louis has depots in Port Louis (six), Curepipe, Rose Hill, Grand Bay, Mahebourg, Flacq, Rivière des Anguilles, Souillac, Quatre Bornes, L'Escalier and Black River; tel: 212 2048.

Business hours
Government offices are open 09.00 to 16.00, Monday to Friday. Because of the optional religious holiday scheme, they may be understaffed, although open, on special leave of absence holidays. Commercial offices keep the same hours but will be also open on Saturday 09.00 to 12.00.

Punctuality is expected for appointments and dress should be smart with a tie and jacket for men creating a favourable impression, although safari suits are also acceptable. A woman should dress conservatively. While men wear western dress in offices (usually tie and shirt, no jacket), many women favour saris.

Public toilets

'Where's the loo?' is a question of concern to tourists. An experienced tour guide told me that a good toilet is the main criterion for recommending an establishment, whether it's a restaurant or souvenir shop, to her clients. There are public toilets in Port Louis, Curepipe and other towns located near bus stations. While they pong a bit, they are generally well maintained.

In an emergency, a visitor need not feel embarrassed about asking to use the facility of a high standard restaurant, town hotel or tourist shop without actually buying anything. Office buildings, too, have well kept conveniences which a visitor could seek permission to use. Sometimes they are locked rather than occupied so just ask at the bar/reception for the key.

Photography

Processing of colour print film in 24 hours is available at several outlets in Port Louis and Curepipe. The cost of processing and of film may be higher than in your home country. Prints are the 12.5 × 9cm size, not the larger postcard size which is standard in Europe.

Mauritians are quite happy to have photos taken of themselves but you should ask their consent first; no fee will be demanded. Permits are not required for photography but, officially, you are not allowed to take photographs of the harbour and the airport.

Banking

Banks are open from 09.30 to 14.30 hours on Mondays to Fridays and from 09.30 to 11.30 on Saturdays. They are closed on Sundays and public holidays. The Mauritius Commercial Bank (MCB) has special foreign exchange counters. In Grand Bay, the counter is open on weekdays and Saturdays and public holidays 08.00–18.00; Sundays 09.00–14.00. The counter in Port Louis opens on weekdays 08.30–15.30; Saturdays 08.30–12.00. In Rose Hill and Curepipe, the counters are open on weekdays and Saturdays 09.00–17.00. At the airport, bank counters are open for the arrival and departure of all international flights. Tourists can also change travellers cheques and cash at principal hotels.

The Bank of Mauritius (the Central Bank) was established in 1967 to oversee the proper functioning of the banking system, implement the financial and monetary policies of the Government, and also administer exchange control. In 1976 the bank tied the rupee to the

Special Drawing Rights (SDR) of the International Monetary Fund (IMF) instead of to sterling. In 1983 this was changed again and the rupee was linked to a basket of currencies relevant to foreign trade. The exchange rate fluctuates daily, determined by the Central Bank, and is the same in all commercial banks.

The method of exchange is not the same, however. Some banks require a lot of form filling to exchange travellers cheques and then tell you to join a queue at another counter to collect the rupees. The Mauritius Commercial Bank (MCB) is one of the quickest, since you join only one queue to a teller who simply notes your passport number together with the amount being exchanged and the day's rate and issues a computerised receipt to record the transaction, along with the cash. A service fee of Rs35 is charged whatever the amount, or number of cheques, changed.

Credit card holders can get cash locally from MCB (Mastercard) and Barclays (Visa) among other banks. Personal cheques can be cashed by American Express card holders; check first with the American Express representative: Mauritius Travel and Tourist Bureau (Royal Street, Port Louis, tel: 208 2041).

COMMUNICATIONS

Mail

In 1815 it took 17 weeks for news of Napoleon's defeat to reach Port Louis. Now mail from, and to, Europe takes less than a week and approximately 10 days from/to the USA. Airmail rates are reasonable, from Rs4 per 5gms according to destination, and post offices sell aerograms with a Rs3 stamp already printed on them. Inland letters cost 40 cents for the first 40 grammes, while mail to Rodrigues goes by air at a cost of 40 cents for five grammes. A useful service is Express Delivery which can result in a letter mailed before 09.00 being delivered to an address within a radius of three miles a few hours later the same day. Two forms have to be filled in for this service.

The main post office is a squat Victorian granite block building in Quay Street, now isolated from the rest of Port Louis by the new motorway which runs along the waterfront to link the south and central districts of the island with the north. The PO's dowdy exterior matches its dull interior but the clerks behind the panes of glass which separate them from the public are bright and helpful. There is another post office in the plaza of the Emmanuel Anquetil Building at the corner of Sir S Ramgoolam Street and Pope Hennessy Street, opposite the town hall. Altogether there are nearly 70 post offices throughout the island and in Rodrigues.

The post office opens at 08.00 every day except Sundays and public

holidays. There is a break for lunch from 11.15 to noon after which
they open again (except on Saturdays) until 16.00. Business after
15.15 on weekdays, and from 11.15 to 11.45 on Saturdays is confined
to the sale of postage stamps only.

Visitors who need a temporary mailing address for their incoming
mail should seek the approval of the Postmaster General, General
Post Office, Headquarters, Quay Street, Port Louis, tel: 208 2851, in
order to have their mail addressed c/o Post Restante. Holders of
American Express cards can have their mail sent to them c/o MTTB,
Royal Street, Port Louis, tel: 208 2041.

Telephone

The telephone system is run by Mauritius Telecom, whose corporate
office is at 2nd Floor, PCL Building, Sir William Newton Street, Port
Louis, tel: 208 7000; fax: 208 1070. There are customer service centres
(where faxes and telexes can be sent, and which have pay phones) at
Port Louis, Plaine Vert, Terre Rouge, Rose Hill and Forest Side.

All telephone numbers have an area code of three digits and the
local number of four digits; the entire number has to be dialled for a
call. The exchange number and directory enquiries is 90. Local calls
cost Rs1 for every eight minutes or part; national calls cost Rs1 for
every three minutes or part (06.00–18.00) or the same as local calls
(18.00–06.00). In Rodrigues all calls within the island are charged as
local calls.

It costs Rs1,000 to have a telephone installed, with a deposit of
Rs1,000 required from a Mauritian or Rs5,000 from a foreigner. The
monthly charge is Rs100 for a business, and Rs60 for a residence.

The charge for inter-island calls by IDD is Rs5 per minute, or Rs15
for operator-connected calls with reduced rates Saturday 12.00–
Sunday 24.00. IDD phones are nationwide; just dial 00 as the international code followed by the country code, area code and local
number. International directory enquiries (a free call) is 10090; international enquiries is 10092. For operator assistance, dial 10091.
Certain credit card calls and pay card calls are available.

IDD calls are charged per minute. In 1994, an IDD call to the UK
from Mauritius cost Rs30 for every minute; to the USA Rs35; to
Germany Rs40; to Italy Rs35; to France Rs30; to South Africa Rs30;
to India Rs30. Hotels, of course, add their own mark up to the basic
cost. Pay phones are available throughout the island.

Emtel Ltd (1 Boundary Road, Rose Hill, tel: 454 5400; fax: 454
1010) provide a cellular mobile telephone service and telephones can
be rented on a temporary basis at Rs400 per day, deposit Rs8,000, call
charges Rs5 per minute; all major credit cards accepted. No special
access code is required to call a mobile phone number. There is also a
Phonelink paging service available from Phonelink, 29 Sun Trust
Building, Edith Cavell Street, Port Louis, tel: 212 8899; fax: 212 0355.

A telephone, fax and telex directory is published every year. There are also a dozen (pink) pages detailing the numbers of government offices. The yellow pages section consists of only 22 pages in the 1993 directory, although the main section of 520 white pages features advertisements for commercial establishments. The directory is in English. The alphabetical listings are confusing since, for example, La Pirogue Hotel is listed under 'L' and not 'P'. Similarly, The Islamic Circle is under 'T' not 'I'. The IDD code to call Mauritius is 230.

Telegrams
Telegrams can be handed in to any post office.

Telex
Telex services extend throughout the country. The Mauritius answer-back suffix is IW. There are public telex machines at the Mauritius Telecom offices, where telexes can be sent at the normal rate, plus Rs10 when an operator sends it. The telex code for Mauritius is 0966.

Facsimile service
Faxing is the fashion in Mauritius both for internal as well as international messages, especially as airmail takes so long. Hundreds of subscribers are listed in the telephone directory. Faxes can be sent through the Mauritius Telecom service centres.

Mauritius for Pleasure

Beaches

Thanks to the coral reefs that encircle Mauritius, its coastline glistens with beaches of powdery white sands, lapped gently by the translucent waters of a lagoon. The best beaches have hotels close to them but these are not exclusive tourist enclaves and most have public access. There are also public beaches and it is still possible, away from the hotels and coastal roads, to find secluded stretches of sand.

The areas beach seekers should avoid are those where the breaks in the coral reef lead to rough seas and a rocky foreshore, especially in the south between Gris Gris, near Souillac, and eastwards towards Pont Naturel, before reaching the Shandrani beach area. On the west coast, Tamarin and some areas north of Flic en Flac are also unprotected by reefs but the huge waves that used to roll in through the narrow channel to Tamarin Bay, delighting surfers, are rare now.

Also rare on Mauritian beaches are the lush groves of coconut palms normally associated with tropical island paradises. Instead, the long stretches of sand are fringed with pine-like casuarina trees, their jointed branches resembling gigantic horse-tails. These trees add a formal touch to the landscape since, in many places, they have been planted in close formation to act as windbreaks. They are known locally as *filaos*.

Not all beaches in Mauritius are walled with hotels and many have only a public 'kiosk' or picnic pavilion as their closest building. Few hotels are actually grouped together, monopolising a whole beach, although they do try to control what happens on their share of the foreshore for the comfort of their guests. Hotel beaches are kept clean, beach hawkers are licensed and not a nuisance, and there is unobtrusive patrolling by security staff in front of the larger hotels. Topless sunbathing is the way of beach life in Mauritius.

Swimming or paddling off some of the beaches is hazardous, not because of underwater currents but due to the sharp-spined sea urchins (*Echinoidea*) that lurk to prick the unwary with their poison-tipped barbs. It's a good idea to wear sandals when walking in the shallows. Hotels will advise where the urchins are dangerous.

The most popular beaches are on the northern coastline, from Tombeau Bay up to Grand Bay and beyond. **Trou aux Biches** is a long stretch, much of it surrounded by the hotel complex of the same name. **Choisy**, further up the coast, is a favourite spot with locals as well as tourists. The beach at **Pointe aux Cannoniers** is encircled by the Club Mediterranée camp. **Grand Bay** has smaller beaches and a kind of after-beach life akin to Mediterranean resorts with good amenities and fast-paced action. A delightful cove midway between Grand Bay and Cap Malheureux is **Pereybere**.

Sea breezes are more common on the east coast, bringing bracing air to the beaches from **Roches Noires** to **Poste Lafayette**. The **Belle Mare** area is renowned for the white sweep of sands at **Palmar**, while the beach at **Trou d'Eau Douce** narrows as it extends to Mahebourg. By boat, from the Touessrok Hotel at Trou d'Eau Douce, it is a 20 minute ride to the **Ile aux Cerfs** where there are restaurants and a boat house by the jetty, and miles of undisturbed, beautiful beaches on the rest of the island. South of Mahebourg are the beaches at **Point d'Esny** and **Blue Bay**. *Filaos* embrace the beach here which, with its white sand and deep, clear blue lagoon, is fine for bathing.

There are also beaches around the peninsula in the southwest, dominated by the 556 metre-high Morne Brabant, where twin Beachcomber hotels are located. At **Flic en Flac** there is the beach at the Pirogue Hotel and sands fringed with the ubiquitous casuarina trees.

Not all the beaches on Mauritius are idyllic or natural however. Those without hotels close to them are unkempt and some hotels have actually created their own sandy coves, such as has been done effectively at the Touessrok Hotel and at Paradise Cove.

Hotels

The beach hotels in Mauritius have achieved the happy amalgamation of luxury accommodation and informal beachside living. The hotels and beaches are not separated by walls or fences but are joined by gardens of ornamental palm trees, bougainvillaea and exotic plants, to create the perfect holiday resort atmosphere. Many hotels have restaurants actually on the beach, for barefoot dining, and most beach hotels offer free watersports as part of their holiday package.

Eight of the top hotels in Mauritius are managed by two groups whose competitiveness assures the highest standards are maintained, with the paying customer being the beneficiary of their rivalry. There is much local discussion as to whether the **Royal Palm** (of the Mauritius-owned Beachcomber group) or **Le Touessrok Sun** (of Sun International of South Africa) is 'the best' hotel of them all. There are two other contenders for top honours; hotels with a livelier style than either of them – the **St Geran Sun** and the Beachcomber's **Shandrani**.

The trio of Sun International Hotels is completed with the west coast **La Pirogue Sun**, which has its equivalent in the Beachcomber Hotel's **Trou aux Biches** resort. The other top Beachcomber Hotels are the **Brabant** and **Paradis** Hotels. The independently owned **Belle Mare Plage Golf Hotel** and Resort is also among the best.

The medium range of beach hotels includes a variety of styles, from the bonhomie of the **Club Méditerranée** to the professionalism of the resort hotels around Grand Bay (the best districts for the pleasure-loving), the secluded beach life of **Kuxville** in the north and **Villas Pointe aux Roches** at Riambel in the south. Details of individual hotels and restaurants are given in Part Two.

Restaurants

With their demanding clientele, the top hotels have restaurants to satisfy the most discerning diner. The **St Geran** is renowned for the presentation of its dishes while **Trou aux Biches** has a high standard of cuisine in its beach restaurant. A number of recently opened Chinese restaurants in Port Louis and Quatre Bornes also promise fine dining. In Curepipe, the grand **Au Gourmet Relais Gastronomique** serves meals to match its name while the **Gold Crest Hotel Restaurant** of Quatre Bornes offers European, Indian and Mauritian cuisine of quality, both in content and service. Dining at **Le Bateau Ivre** in Pointe aux Canonniers has a certain cachet with predictable expense while **L'Assiette du Pêcheur** in Grand Bay is more modest but sensational for seafood. Both are open for dinner. For a good lunch in a charming ambience in Curepipe, look for my favourite, **Le Gaulois**.

Port Louis, apart from its Chinese restaurants such as **Lai Min**, is not a place for an evening meal since most of its restaurants are closed by dark. Its choice of places for lunch, however, is unrivalled elsewhere in the island and is remarkable for any city of its size. The **Carri Poulé** excels in Indian dishes of originality while **La Bonne Marmite** has a varied local and international menu. **La Palmeraie** is French in food and service. Inexpensive fare is to be had at **Tandoori**, by the Victoria Square bus station, which does not serve Tandoori dishes but local delicacies such as venison, hare and turtle. The visitor need have no fear of having to put up with bland 'tourist' food, although it is available for the queasy.

New, and very popular, in Port Louis for lunch is **Le Café du Vieux Conseil**, an old courtyard. At Domaine les Pailles, a short drive from Port Louis, are some restaurants of top standard which have changed the eating habits of the capital's bon vivants as they are open for dinner as well as lunch. They are the **Clos Saint Louis** (French), **Indra** (Indian) and **Fu-Xiao** (Chinese), with the **Canelle Rouge** (Creole) open for lunch only.

Hospitality

If you have received hospitality which you want to return, an invitation to dinner at your hotel or at one of the major restaurants would be appreciated. The Lai Min Restaurant in Port Louis has a set celebration menu which makes an occasion special, and the restaurant at the Gold Crest Hotel in Quatre Bornes is top class for a business dinner. An evening at Domaine les Pailles' choice of restaurants would be a much appreciated way of saying thank you.

You will not normally be invited to a private home until the relationship has blossomed beyond casual acquaintance, by which time you will know what token gift (such as chocolates) to take in appreciation. Lower income Mauritians will be spontaneously hospitable if you visit their homes unexpectedly, preparing wonderful local dishes and overwhelming you with kindness. If alcoholic drinks are part of your host's way of life, a bottle or two of local rum or wine would be an acceptable contribution to the occasion. Offer to pay for beer, too, if you sense finance is a problem; it will be accepted without feelings being hurt.

Any present from your home country would also be welcome, especially small items for the children. Because of the diversity of their cultural and religious background, Mauritians are tolerant of a stranger's ways as long as you're sincere; don't feel inhibited in case you make a social gaffe.

Eating

Just thinking about the food I've eaten in Mauritius makes my mouth water, from the crusty French bread rolls served with local coffee for breakfast to the aphrodesia of *palmiste* heart of palm salad, and the beguiling taste of *fish vindaye* for lunch, then dinner snacks of *roti* with *brèdes*, Chinese soup from a street stall and golden webs of chicken *catless* available at a certain Muslim eatery in Port Louis. For me, Mauritius is worth visiting for the food alone.

If you have your meals only in your hotel, you'll wonder what I mean. However exceptional its standards, by definition a hotel catering for tourists has to serve international dishes that are familiar to guests and with a taste that is tolerable to nervous palates. The adventure of eating in Mauritius is for the streetwise since so many delicious – and cheap – dishes are available from pavement hawkers or in noisy dives. Of course, the culinary skills of Mauritian cooks are to be found in private homes too, and not only in the wealthy ones. And there are also restaurants which specialise in Mauritian ('Creole') food or European dishes with a local zest.

The influences of Mauritian cuisine were African and Indian, with a dash of French. The recipes of slaves and indentured labourers have been blended with French ingenuity to produce Creole cooking which is uniquely Mauritian. The Chinese influence has been confined to particular dishes, such as *Mine* (pronounced *min*), Chinese spaghetti, and the ever popular fried rice.

Street corner cookery is fascinating to watch as well as to taste. Mauritians are addicted to snacks and from early morning the gutter cooks are crouched beside their charcoal fires. At the Immigration Square bus station I once saw a youth in shorts sitting behind his mobile stall with ribbons of prepared dough draped over his bare thigh. He was nonchalantly dabbing chillie filling into each strip before folding the dough into the triangular packets that are *samoosas*. His companion was using his hands to shape dough mixed with ground *dholl* (split peas) and green chillies into small balls for deep frying to make the golden *gateaux piments*.

There is a street corner in Port Louis (at the intersection of Bourbon Street and Ollier Street, although it does change) which is renowned for its *dholl purées*. These are like thin pancakes, made from wheat flour dough and ground split peas and cooked on a griddle. They are served plain, or rolled around a spoonful of *rougaille* (tomato mixture) or *brèdes* (greens), and wrapped in paper. The cooked purées are piled high in mobile glass cases, with more brought by a boy on a bicycle from a nearby kitchen as supplies run out.

The Indian-originating purée, with its African/French filling, is an example of the successful blend of culinary traditions. *Rougaille* is a tomato-based filling often made with *pommes d'amour*, the tiny cherry tomatoes that are grown and eaten all over the island. *Brèdes* are part of the daily diet of Mauritian country dwellers, cooked either plain or with meat or fish. They are green leaves – such as watercress, spinach, the leaf of tuber plants, Chinese cabbage – tossed with onions, garlic and red chillies in hot oil until the water has dried out.

I found the snacks on sale at street corners were not as fiery as I expected. The *gateaux piments* are mildly spiced *dholl* croquettes. *gateaux bringelles* (aubergine fritters) are another wayside delicacy with flavour-packed batter which, when fried alone by the tablespoonful, gives what are commonly known as *bhajias*. A ground mixture of ginger and garlic, chillies, salt, pepper and coriander, mixed with vinegar and water, is often added to the batter for piquancy.

The sweet tooth is catered for with many Tamil specialties, such as *gateau batate*, a wafer-like pastry of sweet potato and coconut. There is fruit, too, especially the small pineapples dextrously peeled into spirals, with the stem remaining as a handle.

More substantial meals are also available from street sellers, such as *poisson vindaye*, served in a paper bag. This is slices of seasoned, fried fish coated with a masala (cooked mixed paste) of mustard seed, green chillies, garlic and turmeric, often eaten cold with bread. *Achards légumes*, pickled vegetables which have been cooked *al dente* and mixed with spicy paste and vinegar, are also sometimes eaten with bread.

The menus in the streets of Port Louis change after dark, when only the city dwellers remain and the office and port workers have gone home. Bowls of Chinese *bouillon* (soup) are sold with a choice of fish balls or other additions, including chopped chives. *Mine* (spaghetti) is available with lashings of sauce, freshly fried in a wok over a charcoal stove. Fried rice with chicken is another favourite.

All street eating costs little since office and shop workers on small salaries are the main customers. Some workers carry their lunch with them in plaited reed baskets, dainty square boxes suspended from a string handle with a cover concealing the contents. These containers, called *tentes*, are made from vacoas leaves. They are sold in the markets and make unusual souvenirs.

Mauritians do not only eat in the street. There are inexpensive eateries in all the towns, where the typical dishes will be meat, chicken or fish served either as *carri* (curry), *daube* (stewed with potatoes and peas) or *kalya* (cooked with saffron and ginger/garlic). These will be served with boiled rice or slices of bread, accompanied by a side salad, usually of grated carrots and grated cucumber with lettuce.

Snacks, called *gadjacks* by my Creole drinking companions, are also served in bars on small saucers, like Spanish *tapas*, to accompany drinks. The range is generous from *rougaille ourite* (octopus in tomato) to *croquettes volaille* (chicken bites).

Home cooking will depend on the status of the family but all will use the freshest ingredients obtainable every day from the main markets or on a twice weekly basis from plateau town markets. Vegetables abound and are arranged so attractively in Mauritian markets that the housewife finds them hard to resist. While local fruits, such as papaya and mangoes, are also available, fruit imported from South Africa, such as apples, oranges and grapes, is at times easier to buy.

Snoeck rougaille (salted fish in tomato) is a frequent standby if fresh fish is not available, and shrimps or lobster are also sometimes served in rougaille. *Camarons* (freshwater crayfish) served with watercress salad are a favourite with Franco-Mauritians. Wild boar, hare and venison are still available out of the hunting season because of cold storage facilities. Goat (*cabri*) is sold in the meat markets in the way that mutton is sold in Europe and is delicious in curry. The exotic *palmiste* (for which miniature palm trees are especially cultivated to yield their hearts) is sometimes served boiled instead of in salad, with a Creole (red) sauce.

Drinking

A popular Mauritian drink is *alooda*, sold on the streets and in markets by energetic salesmen praising their own product. It consists of dissolved, boiled china grass (*agar agar*) and sugar, which has been strained and allowed to set and then grated, to which is added water, milk, rose syrup and soaked *tookmaria* (falooda) seeds. The mixture is refrigerated and served cold in tall glasses. Local beer is excellent and inexpensive (Rs13) in a corner bar, or retail, but higher in hotels and restaurants. There are several local rums, of which connoisseurs rate *Rum of Mauritius*, in its plain glass bottle with stencilled red labelling, as the best. It is also known as Goodwill. Don't be surprised if your Mauritian host deliberately spills a little of a new bottle on the floor before pouring drinks. It is a custom to appease the other spirits. Under a new regulation, drinking in village shops or liquor stores is officially only permitted on Mondays to Saturdays, 16.00–19.00, and on Sundays, 10.00–12.00. Since wines are also produced locally, as are local versions of spirits such as gin, whisky and brandy, the tippler is as well served as the gourmand.

Beer

At the beginning of the sixties, Pierre Hugnin listened to the suggestion of a friend from Tahiti that he should start a brewery. At the time, 18,000 hectolitres of beer were imported into the island annually. While going into the figures for the project, Hugnin had the well water at his proposed site in Phoenix analysed and found it ideal. He set up Mauritius Brewery Ltd (MBL) and issued a prospectus inviting the general public to subscribe. The response was negative as, in those days, Mauritians were not interested in investing in local industries. Hugnin contacted shopowners to raise capital, as foreign investment was refused, and in 1963 MBL was granted the first development certificate. It was the beginning of a new era of industrialisation in Mauritius.

The first Mauritian beer – called Phoenix – was brewed in August 1963. With beer seen as an acceptable drink in multi-religious Mauritius, MBL launched a second beer, Stella, two years later and began to distribute Guinness, which it eventually brewed under licence from 1975. Phoenix (5% vol) has become synonymous with beer for Mauritians and is the company's best seller. The Stella brand was succeeded in 1993 by Stella Pure Gold light beer (3.5% vol). MBL also produce Blue Marlin, a stronger beer (6% vol) and Phoenix Export, a premium brand (5% vol).

Mauritius beer has won many international awards for its quality, the most recent being gold medals for Phoenix (1989) and Blue Marlin (1993).

Mauritius sugar is used in production (where other breweries might use maize or rice) since it produces a beer that is more digestible. Top quality hops come from the UK, for bitterness, and from Germany, Yugoslavia and Czechoslovakia. The staff has grown from 30 in the beginning to more than 475 now, and the brewery has a production capacity of 320,000 hectolitres. The company has diversified into other areas, including a distribution company in Rodrigues and a company manufacturing decorative glass objects out of broken glass.

The beer itself has a clean and refreshing taste with lots of flavour. I prefer Phoenix but Blue Marlin has the body and richness of a formidable beer that commands respect. Try the beer at an uninflated price in a corner grocery store or Port Louis pub to savour it the way Mauritians do. (Mauritius Breweries Ltd, Pont Fer, Phoenix, tel: 686 6535, fax: 686 7197, telex: 4283 BEER IW).

Spirits

Over 150 years ago, a commentator on Mauritius complained, 'The facility with which spirits, especially arrack of inferior quality, are to be procured is more fatal to the soldiers than exposure to the sun, or any other effect of the climate'.

The place of arrack, an alcoholic spirit distilled from toddy extracted from the spadix of the coconut palm tree, has been taken by rum in today's Mauritius. Actually, rum-making in the island dates back to 1639, following the introduction of sugar cane by the Dutch, when it was made from cane juice even before people knew how to extract the crystals. Alcohol is now the most successful by-product of sugar, obtained from turning sugar molasses into fine spirit.

There are many rums produced in Mauritius, including the mellow *Rum of Mauritius* and the romantic-sounding *Green Island Rum*. At the Beau Plan sugar estate situated in the north of the island, sugar has been grown by the Harel family since 1838. Their two sugar mills average 80,000 tonnes of sugar every year. In 1934, the company decided to go into distilling, diversifying before it was government policy, and Grays Refinery Ltd and Grays Bottling Plant Ltd (Beau Plan, Pamplemousses, tel: 243 3642, telex: 4827 GRAYS IW) were founded.

Now five million litres of high quality spirits flow annually from the new complex built close to the 200-year-old original sugar factory. The technically advanced refinery is the only one of its kind in Mauritius, putting Grays to the forefront of spirit producers. The four column plant, together with a copper pot still, produce an alcoholic's dream of spirits, ranging from heavy rums and liqueurs to light gins and extra neutral spirit. The daily output at full capacity is 20,000 litres of pure alcohol.

The Grays' insignia, which looks like a Viking vessel with oars and full sail, appears on a variety of whisky, gin, brandy, cane spirit and rum bottles, including *Mainstay Dry Cane Spirit* and a rum 'of the highest possible quality' called *Old Mill Rum*. Its delicate *Vieux Rhum De L'Ile De France* has been matured in oak casks for over 10 years, and is available in Europe.

Vodka and liqueurs are made according to the company's own recipes as well as under licence. *Whisper*, *Nicholson Gin*, *Napoleon* brandy and *Bardinet* liqueurs are elaborated from imported components. Over a hundred Mauritians are in the Gray's team and in 1985 the company was awarded an International Gold Medal for quality alcoholic beverage.

Wine

In a tasting of rosé wines from South Africa, France and Portugal conducted by a wine writer in South Africa a few years ago, a bottle of *Château Bel Ombre* featured well. It was determined by half the tasters as being South African in origin and by others as from Southern France or Portugal. Everyone was flabbergasted when they learned it came from Mauritius. E C Oxenham & Co Ltd (Autoroute St Jean, Quatre Bornes, tel: 454 1646, fax: 454 1663), the company that produces *Château Bel Ombre*, has even been praised in the Paris newspaper *Le Monde*.

The absence of vineyards in Mauritius has led sceptics to dismiss Oxenham's wines as being obtained through the fermentation of Mauritian fruits. Not so. The wine is made from grape must, concentrated for travel, and imported into Mauritius in plastic blow-packs.

Edward Clark Oxenham, a descendant of British colonials, was a pioneer who tried to grow grapes on his farm in Rodrigues. He failed, but with help from the Pasteur Institute of Paris started to produce wine from dried grapes and local fruits in 1931. He moved to Mauritius and in 1932 founded the company that now bears his name. On his death in 1948, his four sons carried on the business.

In 1963 a new start to wine production was made with the importation of grape juice from South Africa (for white and rosé wines) and from Italy and later Spain for red wines.

Mauritian white and rosé wines can be drunk young, but the red is stored in oak vats to mature. Selected white wines are 'champagnised' by the carbonated method to produce two 'country sparkling liquors': *Decramon* – somewhat sweet – and *Montrevel*. There is also *Kirvel*, which is sparkling with a fruit flavour to resemble a Kir Royal cocktail, although it is deep gold rather than pink in colour.

The Oxenham range of locally produced wines begin with *Eureka*, the everyday wine of Mauritians, through the pleasant and inexpensive *Rosé Chaptalin*, to finer wines with the *St Nicholas* label, as well as vermouth. They also produce fruit wines, such as lychee wine, which are in great demand. The company also bottles some South African wines locally as well as importing wines from France and Germany for the domestic market.

For the past five to ten years, according to the company's wine marker, Patrick Oxenham, Mauritians have changed to drinking drier wines, a demand the company is meeting with a production of 2.5 million litres annually. It also bottles wine for some of the major hotels under the hotels' own labels and its wines have won prizes in numerous exhibitions since 1935.

Wines produced in Mauritius have the added attraction for the drinker of their low retail price, although hotel or restaurant markup can increase the price by as much as five times.

Basic drinking is done in corner bars, many of them housed in solid 19th century buildings with thick granite walls and little comfort. Rum is sold by the peg, with the barman coming to your table with a glass and pouring the measure in front of you. Payment is

made to the cashier who overseas the operation and makes a note of
every drink you consume, with the help of commentary in Creole
from the barman. You pay when you leave. These are lively, convivial
places with snacks – *gadjacks* – on sale at the counter and lots of
noise. They are safe for visitors even if they look a bit disreputable.

EVENING RELAXATION

Nightlife
For most tourists, nightlife will centre around their hotel since the
hotels themselves are isolated on the coast and far from whatever
local action there is. Nightly hotel entertainment is of good (but not
international) standard, either with bands for dancing, floor shows
with local artistes, discotheques and occasional concert parties and
fashion shows organised by the hotel's 'animation' staff. One hotel
has monthly lectures on astronomy. Many feature special performances of the island's unique and very suggestive folk dance, the
séga. My list is only to give an idea of what is available, since the
séga performance may be on other nights as well.

Disco freaks who want to meet young Mauritians enjoying themselves should head on Saturday nights to The **Palladium**, an extra-

Entertainment

Hotel	Location	Tel.	Dancing	Séga Show
Ambre	Belle Mare	419 2554		Saturday
Belle Mare Plage	Bella Mare	415 1083		Monday
Canonnier	Pointe aux Canonniers	263 7999	Nightly	Saturday
Grand Gaube	Grand Gaube	283 9350	Nightly	Friday
Maritim	Balaclava	261 5600	Nightly	Friday
Mauricia	Grand Bay	263 7800		Wednesday
Merville	Grand Bay	263 8621	Nightly	Friday
Paradis	Morne	683 6775	Nightly	Wednesday
Pirogue Sun	Flic en Flac	453 8441	Nightly	Wednesday
PLM Azur	Mont Choisy	261 6070	Nightly	Saturday
St Geran Sun	Belle Mare	413 2825	Nightly	Wednesday
Shandrani	Plaine Magnien	637 3558	Nightly	Tuesday
Sofitel Imperial	Flic en Flac	453 8700		Monday
Touessrok Sun	Trou d'Eau Douce	429 2451	Nightly	Friday
Trou aux Biches	Trou aux Biches	261 6562	Nightly	Tuesday
Veranda	Grand Bay	263 8032		Monday
Villa Caroline	Flic en Flac	453 8411		Saturday

ordinary building with a mock Roman villa façade, on the left at Trianon, just before the St Jean's church roundabout on the drive from Port Louis. You'll need your own transport or a pre-arranged taxi since there are no buses at night. There are other discos near tourist resorts, as well as a popular one in Vacoas, another upstairs in the commercial centre of Rose Hill, and one in Quatre Bornes.

Music

Unique to Mauritius are the music and the dance known as *séga*, pronounced *saygar*, which have evolved from the spontaneous dances of African and Malagasy slaves. At night, after a days toiling in the canefields, slaves used improvised instruments to create a primitive music to which they could dance and forget their woes.

They were passionately fond of dancing, especially to the beat of a goatskin tambourine, called a *ravane*, and the throb of a *tantum*, a kind of bow with a gourd fitted to it, which was plucked in time to the drumbeat. The girls danced to songs composed and sung by their admirers while the spectators encouraged them with hand clapping, foot stomping and chanting. Songs were also song about the slaves' plight and were highly critical of their masters. The more impassioned the lyrics, the more heated the music and the more tempestuous the dancing.

What makes *séga* unique is the combination of musical influences it has absorbed over the centuries, until it has assumed its own immediately recognisable beat. Like the *ka-danse* or *zouk* music of the French West Indies, also sung in creole *patois*, it has a similarity to Latin American music in its jaunty rhythms.

Modern exponents of *séga* include an electric guitar in place of a homemade string instrument. Drumming is vital and the skins of drums have to be heated from time to time to keep them tight during playing. A container (sometimes wooden of fashioned from a gourd) with pebbles inside it is shaken like the maracas. This is called a *coco*. A triangle beaten with vigour adds a carillon voice echo, just as a cowbell does in *ka-danse*.

Discotheque	Location	Tel.	Dancing
Blue Mauritius	Rose Hill	464 4097	Wed/Fri/Sat
Climax Club	Grand Bay	263 8737	Fri/Sat
Magnum 44	Black River	683 6768	Saturday
Number One	Grand Bay	263 8434	Saturday
Palladium	Trianon	454 6168	Nightly except Monday
Sam's Disco	Vacoas	686 5370	Nightly except Monday
Le Top	Quatre Bornes	n/a	

A *séga* dance is a courtship drama, beginning slowly with couples dancing apart from each other. As the beat intensifies, they shuffle closer together, hips swinging in time, but they never quite touch. The girl will sink to her knees at the cry of *en bas*, leaning back in the manner of a limbo dancer passing under a pole, with fluid, sensual movements. Her partner extends his body over her, still not touching, as they both shimmer and shake, while the music races to a crescendo. The climax reached, the music slows and the partners retreat.

It is sublimely provocative as a dance with a wonderful, joyful music that seizes spectators with an urge to join in, which they are encouraged to do at hotel performances. The uninitiated soon find it easy to dance to the simple, samba-like rhythm. At hotel shows, the men will wear the traditional costume of skin-tight breeches, while the women are sensational in a billowing skirt, snugly fitting the hips.

Sometimes it is possible to witness impromptu *séga*, with improvised instruments and hand clapping, and bottles of rum being passed around to fuel the participants. On the beach at night with a flaming torch to provide light, it is easy to imagine how *séga* was in slavery times, and to get caught up in the orgy of music and dance.

Séga is closer to its original form, both in music and dance, in Rodrigues where its exponents – mostly the mountain-dwelling descendants of slaves – have been isolated from external influence. The traditional homemade instruments are used, and the beat seems wilder. It is mostly the women who dance, often for hours, while the men succeed each other at short intervals.

The dance starts with a heavy thumping of feet by both partners. This is accompanied by a swaying of the hips, gently at first, but gradually becoming more animated as the music gets livelier. The woman remains at the same spot, occasionally wheeling to the left and right, goading her partner who twists and turns close to her.

The orgiastic courtship theme of the dance comes from the days when women in Rodrigues were in short supply so they had the pick of the men. In *séga* they taunt them unmercifully until choosing the one they want at the dance's climax.

Romance

The beauty, laughter and fine physique of Mauritians of both sexes inevitably attracts the attention of the romantic. Mauritius is an island founded on love; people making love across the racial barriers have given the island its wonderful mix. Their heritage has endowed Mauritians with an uncomplicated approach to sex. The visitor with an urge for romance will find it. However, AIDS has arrived in Mauritius. Posters warnings of the dangers of AIDS/SIDA (the French acronym) appear in public places.

Getting Married

In keeping with the romantic ambience of Mauritius, the island has become a popular place for visitors to get married – not to Mauritians, but to each other. Wedding packages are a feature of the overseas tour operators who sell holidays in Mauritius, and the local representatives make all the arrangements.

According to a brochure of Sunset Travel (306 Clapham Road, London SW9 9AE, tel: 071 498 9922, fax: 071 978 1337) 'a special licence will be arranged for you to allow you to be married within two days of arrival but a visit to the Ministry in Port Louis is necessary before your wedding day to obtain special dispensation under Mauritian law ... Divorced ladies must allow a minimum 300 day gap between the divorce and new wedding date, or a pregnancy test taken locally must be negative'. The cost is put at £170 with various extras such as a bouquet (£10), champagne and photographer (£90).

It is possible to arrange a wedding independently. Vital is a certificate issued under the authority of the Prime Minister to the effect that the couple are not citizens or residents of Mauritius. This is obtainable on application (at least 10 days before the date of the proposed wedding) to the Registrar of Civil Status, 7th Level, Emmanuel Anquetil Building, Port Louis (tel: 201 1727). The documents needed for the application are two photocopies of each birth certificate and two photocopies of the pages showing the issuing authority and personal details of each passport, and any other documents in case of proving divorce, or demise of former spouse. This certificate has to be produced to the Civil Status Officer at the time of publication, and the marriage may be celebrated on the day immediately following the day of publication.

Gambling

There are eight casinos in Mauritius, six of them within hotel compounds. There is also one in Curepipe and another in Port Louis. The hotel casinos feature charming female croupiers to spin the roulette wheel or run the games of blackjack and baccarat; they also have slot machines. Stakes are low, but dress standards call for more than beachwear. The casinos are generally open from early evening for playing the slot machines, but only from 21.00 for gambling at the tables. On Sundays, they open about 15.00, when they are popular with wealthier residents, particularly the Chinese.

The chance of gambling has increased with the opening near Port Louis of the **Grand Casino du Domaine**, at Domaine les Pailles. In a sumptuously furnished salon in a replica of a large Creole house, similar to those built in Curepipe with terrace enclosed by bay windows, are eight roulette tables, six black jack tables, 58 one-armed bandits and 30 electronic poker games. It is open seven days a week,

13.00–03.00 for the slot machines, 21.00–03.00 for the tables, and from 15.00 on Sundays.

The locals' love of gambling has been met by the long established **Casino de Maurice** in Curepipe and by **L'Amicale de Port Louis**. The entrance to the latter is appropriately seedy. It is in the side road (Anquetil Street) that leads to the waterfront from Royal Street by the ONU bar. Taiwanese fishermen roll around the entrance and there are trolleys selling Chinese and Creole food on the street corner close by.

The atmosphere of genuine lowlife is continued in the wooden stairway to the first floor and the peeling red, white and blue paint-work of the walls with handwritten signs about opening times. The first sight on entering the lobby leading to the casino room is more reassuring: tubby policemen in uniform gazing with avuncular eyes on the insatiable gamblers crowding around the gaming tables. The clients are mostly local, Chinese with other Mauritians, and seamen. Tourists are occasionally to be seen as members of a group on a conducted night tour.

There is no pressure on patrons to gamble and entrance is free. There is a cocktail bar in one corner with drinks priced higher than other bars in the vicinity. A notice regrets the management's inability to provide free tea due to rising costs. Another one cautions about using obscene language.

Ornately shaded lamps hang over the tables with a torch suspended from each to be switched on by the croupier in case of power failure. At most tables bets are made by placing money (minimum stake is Rs5) on the numbered square of one's choice. The winning square (according to the roll of dice or deal of domino) is illuminated by the croupier.

The games played at L'Amicale are all Chinese: Van Lak, Chinese Dominoes, Big and Small, Vindaye De Poisson. If you don't under-

Casino	Location	Tel.
L'Amicale de Port Louis	55 Royal Street, Port Louis	242 3335
Belle Mare Plage Hotel	Belle Mare	415 1083
Casino de Maurice	Teste de Buch Street, Curepipe	675 5012
Grand Casino du Domaine	Les Pailles	212 4225
Brabant/Paradis Hotels	Morne Brabant	683 6775
La Pirogue Sun Hotel	Flic en Flac	453 8441
St Geran Sun Hotel	Belle Mare	413 2825
Trou Aux Biches Hotel	Trou aux Biches	261 6619

stand, one of the policemen will be happy to explain. Some of them have worked there on extra duty for nearly twenty years.

THE ARTS

The arts flourish in Mauritius despite a lack of appreciation and encouragement from the outside world. Local authors and poets who want to be published have to pay for the printing of their own works unless they can find sponsorship from foreign cultural organisations. Several slim volumes of verse, *belles-lettres* and travelogues by local authors are to be found hidden away in local bookshops. Robert Edward Hart, who died in 1954, was Mauritius' most renowned poet, awarded the OBE and the French *Légion d'Honneur*. His house at Souillac is now a museum.

Shelf-loads of books, mostly in French, have been written about Mauritius. The island has been the setting for novels, too, the most famous being the pastoral French novel, *Paul et Virginie*, by Bernadin de Saint Pierre, which was first published in 1773 and is still in print, with English translations available in bookshops. Its sentimental tale of love and heartbreak is remarkable for the accuracy of its nature notes and description of an idyllic Mauritius when it resembled a garden of Eden.

Joseph Conrad set a short story, *A Smile of Fortune*, in Mauritius and Sir Walter Besant, a teacher in Mauritius from 1861 to 1867, used the island as a setting for two novels, *My Little Girl* and *They Were Married*.

The Alliance-Française (Bell Village, tel: 208 8648) is very active in its encouragement of the arts and the French language, so much so that the British Council which slumped into inactivity was revived at the end of 1987 with the appointment of a new representative. (British Council, Royal Road, Rose Hill, tel: 454 9551). Modern novelists in Mauritius are writing in French. Former Port Louis town clerk, Somdath Bhuckory, writes in French, English and Hindi and has been acclaimed for his promotion of Hindi literature in Mauritius as well as for his own poetry.

There are some local folklore and dramatic societies which occasionally perform cultural shows of their own devising and plays. The old opera house in Port Louis (Municipal Theatre, tel: 212 1090), built in 1822, has been lovingly restored and is a fine setting for local drama, although seldom used. The Plaza Theatre (Royal Road, Rose Hill, tel: 424 1145) is part of the Beau Bassin-Rose Hill town hall complex, a baroque 1920s creation by Coultrac Mazérieux which has become a prestigious venue for Mauritian and foreign cultural activities.

An art gallery at the Beau Bassin-Rose Hill town hall complex is named after the Mauritian artist, Max Boullé, and often features exhibitions by local artists' groups.

In Port Louis there is the **Galérie d'Art de Port Louis** in Mallefille Street, just behind the Mauritius Institute, which holds a new exhibition of local artists' work every month. It is open 09.00–16.00, Mondays to Fridays, and 09.00–12.00 on Saturdays. More professional work is to be seen at the commercial art gallery in Quatre Bornes or at the gallery in Grand Bay.

Contemporary architecture in Mauritius mostly finds expression in new hotels since new houses tend to be standard, cyclone-proof concrete boxes. Examples of colonial architecture such as Government House in Port Louis are sometimes overwhelmed by the modern monstrosities erected next to them. The Curepipe market building, with concrete culverts upturned like gigantic organ pipes, is a most remarkable example of modern public architecture. More pleasing is the rustic style of the recently built Royal Palm, Touessrok and Casuarina Village Hotels which are a tribute to the ingenuity and design of the Mauritian architect, Maurice Giraud.

SPORT

Watersports
Most beachside resort hotels provide watersport facilities free of charge to their guests. This usually includes (limited) waterskiing and windsurfing, as well as kayaks, pedallos and snorkelling. Some have glass-bottom boats for lazy fish and coral watching, and also dinghy sailing. Beach games and water polo can be arranged. Of course, where watersports are free, there can be a considerable demand, so it is really subject to availability. It also means that otherwise peaceful lagoons are fairly busy. If you're not staying in a beach hotel there is a boathouse, appropriately roofed with an upturned boat, on the Ile aux Cerfs, where equipment can be hired by non-residents.

The popularity of **windsurfing** and the ideal conditions for it have resulted in many competitions, including World Championships, being held in Mauritius. Windsurfing instruction is available and equipment can be hired at beachside boathouses. Sailing shoes should be worn to prevent coral cuts. **Waterskiing** in the sheltered waters of the reef-protected lagoons is also available at a cost, with patient instruction for beginners.

Snorkelling is an incredible experience since so many fish can be seen close to the beach without even having to go by boat to the reef. It is easy to forget the powerful effect of the sun while floating with head and nose down in the water, so snorkellers are advised to protect exposed skin to avoid sun burn. Full shoe fins should be worn. Equipment, when it's not free, can be hired. If you want your own, try the Quay Store at 3 Kennedy Street, (PO Box 436), Port Louis, tel: 212 1043 or Aquasport Ltd, 2 d'Entre Casteaux Street, Port Louis, tel: 212 2206. Fishing and diving equipment is also available.

For **surfing**, the Bay of Tamarin used to be popular as the rollers coursed in through the break in the coral reef. I recall watching a lone surfer perform fantastic feats there a few years ago. Now conditions have changed and a hotelier lamented recently that no spectacular surf has been seen there for some time.

Aqualung **diving** lessons are given in hotel swimming pools and if you are fit and have the aptitude there will be a quick progression to shallow sea dives. The diving school at La Pirogue Sun has a classroom with audio-visual aids for theoretical training for beginners. Dives and equipment are charged for. A two or three week holiday would be enough time to learn the basics and make dives under supervision to depths of about 25 metres. Since there are amazing gardens of coral in depths of seven metres and enough fish to make you feel you've been let loose in a tropical aquarium, this is adequate to begin with. The west coast is ideal for diving all year round while the east coast is at its best from September to May.

Hotel dive centres organise deeper dives to 25 and 40 metres for qualified divers with brevet and log book. There, the coral gardens give way to canyons and in the faster flowing water there will be shoals of large, ocean-going fish such as sharks, barracuda, king fish and marlin. There are even forests of rare black coral. Popular dives are to *Whale Rock*, reached by boat from Trou aux Biches or Merville, which has a dramatic seascape at 27 metres depth, and the *Cathedral* archway and cave off the coast of Flic en Flac. Off the southeast coast of Blue Bay is *Roche Zozo*, a spectacular underwater rock accessible only in summer. Off Round Island, there is a submerged crater at 25 metres.

In summer a wetsuit is not necessary for diving to a maximum of 20 metres but a lightweight suit would be desirable beyond that depth. A wetsuit jacket and trousers for those diving twice a day during winter, or deeper than 20 metres, is recommended.

Beginners are enchanted by the friendliness of some of the fish, which can be fed by hand, although they should watch out for the red and white striped Lionfish, slow-moving and conspicuous, with a painful and poisonous sting in its feather-like fins. Stonefish, immobile among rocks and coral, have poisonous dorsal spines; sharks and barracuda should be treated with respect. Spear fishing is prohibited. Advice on diving can be obtained from the Mauritius Underwater Group, Railway Road, Phoenix, tel: 696 5368, or from the Mauritius Scuba Diving Association at Villas Caroline, Flic en Flac, tel: 453 8450. In Rodrigues, check La Licorne Diving Centre, English Bay, Port Mathurin, tel: 831 1959.

A unique experience (unless you have tried it in Tahiti or the

Bahamas) is the **Undersea Walk** from Grand Bay. You don't have to be able to swim as you literally walk along the sea bed, with a helmet like an upturned bucket with glass windows over your head and air pumped in. Even the most aquaphobic, or elderly, types can enjoy this underwater guided tour of the reefs and feeding fish, especially as you are actually only a couple of metres below the surface. You could make contact with Robert Barnes, who organises the undersea walks, through the Royal Palm Hotel, Grand Bay, tel: 263 8353.

Sailing
Full day sailing programmes can be booked through tour operators or hotel boathouses. Some outings combine sailing with shore excursions to otherwise inaccessible spots. An individual can join a group at a fraction of the cost of a private yacht charter. Sailing regattas are held annually. Grand Bay is the main centre for yachting and the Grand Bay Yacht Club (tel: 263 8568) has a temporary membership scheme for visitors. Sailing cruises are available on the schooner *Isla Mauritia*, a 19th century, 32m-long tallship, the last existing vessel of her class, operated by Yacht Charters Ltd, Royal Road, Grand Bay, tel: 263 8395, fax: 263 7814.

Deep sea big game fishing
Big game hunting for sport in the world's savannahs and forests has been superseded by the rage for deep sea fishing. Nowhere is this more apparent than in Mauritius, which offers the best big game fishing in the world – at the best prices, too, when compared with such places as South Africa. With hotels devoted to the needs of the deep sea angler and predator fish who obligingly feed close to the shore, where the bottom falls away to 700 metres, the island is ideal for sports fishing.

The season is from October to March although it can be extended from September to May. The best chance of catching a big one seems to be during the January to March peak. Bookings for fishing trips at the height of the season are best made well in advance; otherwise they can be made locally on arrival.

Mauritius holds several world records for the weight of fish caught including the tail-walking battler, the *blue marlin*. Only one hooked marlin in five is ever boated, which adds to the excitement for the angler. Live bonito fish are used as bait.

Other fish which can be caught, if only after strenuous battles, are *black marlin*, occasional *striped marlin*, *sailfish*, *yellow fin tuna*, the smaller *skipjack tuna*, the dolphin known in Mauritius by the Spanish name of *dorado*, and the fast-running *wahoo*, as well as *baracuda* and *shark*. Sharks are not usually sought but are sometimes caught, with *hammerheads* and *makos* giving the hardest fight.

Modern deep sea fishing boats, well-equipped and designed for fishing competitions, may be booked through most of the beach hotels or tour operators. The largest fleets are on the west coast, at the fishing hotels of Black River and also at the fishing centres at La Pirogue Sun and Trou aux Biches Village Hotels. Domaine du Pêcheur (Anse Jonchée, Vieux Grand Port, tel: 631 9261, fax: 631 9261) offers a chance to fish the plentiful waters off the east coast and includes one night's accommodation in a six or nine hours charter fee.

Mauritians are proud of their beautifully built teak fishing craft which ride big swells with ease and comfort for the anglers on board. Six hours is the minimum charter time (nine in the peak season) and boats can be shared by up to three anglers. All charter boats are equipped with tackle; reels are Penn International or Shimano 130, 80, 50, 30lbs. Lighter rods are also available for bait fishing the smaller skipjack tuna. If you have your own jig or trolling lure, your skipper will willingly let you try it.

Not only are the boats and their tackle good, but so are the crew. The skippers know where the fish are and how to handle their craft to the angler's advantage during the long battle to boat the catch. The high-powered boats are fitted with special seats in the stern into which anglers are strapped for safety, since the fight can be tough and risky. A hire of six hours costs from Rs6,000 for a fully equipped boat, or from Rs7,000 for nine hours. Boats have two-way radio telephones and the skipper will cheerfully alert press and photographers if the angler is returning with an exceptional catch.

Hotels which specialise in fishing expeditions, or which have on-site facilities for the resident and non-resident deep sea angler are:

Beachcomber Fishing Club, Morne Brabant
Tel: 683 6775, fax: 683 6786
Black River Sport Fishing Organisation, Auberge de la Rivière Noire
Tel: 683 6547
Corsaire Club, Royal Road, Trou aux Biches
Tel: 261 6267, fax: 261 6611
Domaine du Pêcheur, Anse Jonchée, Vieux Grand Port
Tel: 631 9261, fax: 631 9261
Hotel Club, Rivière Noire
Tel: 683 6552, fax: 683 6318
La Pirogue Big Game Fishing, Flic en Flac
Tel: 453 8441, fax: 453 8449
Sofitel Imperial Big Game Fishing, Wolmar
Tel: 453 8700, fax: 453 8320
Sportfisher, Royal Road, Grand Bay
Tel: 263 8358

Hunting

Hunting is a status sport in which only wealthy or well-connected Mauritians take part. The traditional season for deer hunting is June to September and the popular area is around Plaine Champagne and Case Noyale in the southwest. *Miradors*, seats raised high on stilts where the hunter sits while deer are driven by beaters into his range of fire, proclaim hunting country.

Visitors can hunt at Domaine du Chasseur (Anse Jonchée, Vieux Grand Port, tel: 631 9261, fax: 631 9261) in the southeast corner of the island, where 1,500 Javanese deer live in a game reserve of 2,350 acres. Because the deer herd has to be culled to keep its natural increase within the ability of the reserve to sustain it, organised hunting is a form of conservation. The basic rate starts at Rs3,500, rising according to the size of deer shot; the fee for a companion is Rs1,000. Guns – Manlicher 30.06, Parker Hale, Savage Sauer 308 – are provided; cartridges cost Rs50. Trophies can be arranged. All hunters are accompanied by skilled guides. The shoot is conducted by stalking, or in the traditional manner with dogs and beaters, the hunters themselves perched in *miradors*. Wild boar and hare are hunted year round.

Golf

The Gymkhana Club at Vacoas (tel: 696 1404) has an 18-hole golf course (a legacy of colonial days), to which visitors are welcome by temporary membership. Clubs can be hired by arrangement with the caddy master and golf lessons are available. There is a nine-hole course designed by Gary Player alongside the lagoon at the St Geran Sun Hotel. The Beachcomber hotels of Paradis/Brabant, Shandrani and Trou aux Biches Village also have nine-hole courses. Use of the golf courses, and clubs, is free for holders of the hotels' privilege cards.

In 1994, the first international 18-hole golf course in the Indian Ocean region opened on the east coast at the Belle Mare Plage Golf Hotel and Resort (tel: 415 1083, fax: 415 1993). Designed by Hugh Baiocchi, Tony Falkson and Alan Barnard from South Africa, it has been created on 158 acres of deer reserve, prime virgin land with hundred-year-old plant species and dotted with bougainvillaea and flamboyant trees and with numerous water spots and lakes. On Saturdays a tournament is arranged for clients of the hotel, founder members and residents of Mauritius.

No green fees are charged to hotel guests, but you will be asked for your handicap certificate, or to take a test with a professional, before being allowed to play on the course. There is also a nine-hole course at the hotel for all types of players, as well as teaching by professionals. Clubs are available for hire and all charges can be added to your hotel bill. There is a dress code: Men must wear collared shirts with tailored trousers or tailored shorts with long socks. For women, collared shirts with skirt below knee length, or long shorts or tailored trousers.

Tennis

Tennis, usually free, is available at many of the island's major hotels. Some hotels have floodlit courts for playing during the evening, when it is cooler. The Port Louis Tennis Club is located in the Champ de Mars (tel: 212 0727). Hard court tennis is available at the Gymkhana Club in Vacoas (tel: 696 1404).

Horse riding

The Beachcomber hotels at Morne Brabant have a small stable with horses available for guests.

Near the Club Méditerranée off the Grand Bay to Port Louis road, there is the Club Hippique de Mont Choisy, Marc Raffray, Pointe aux Canonniers, tel: 263 8211, with stables. There is another, the Club Hippique de Maurice, at Allée Brillant, Floreal, tel: 696 4387.

In the Domaine les Pailles (tel: 212 4225, fax: 212 4226) complex near Port Louis, the 'Ecuries du Domaine' opened in 1993 for horse lovers to practise their sport, with experienced riders being able to enjoy a ride in the natural setting of the Guibies Valley, accompanied by a qualified instructor. Lessons are held in the paddock for children and riders wanting to improve their style and technique. Riders have to provide their own jodhpurs, or trousers or jeans, while riding hats and boots are provided by the *Ecuries*.

Football

Football is Mauritius's major sport – there is *no cricket* – and is played by amateur teams throughout the island. There is even a lawyers' side that regularly plays matches with the top teams. There are football stadia in the main towns for local league matches, including a massive new one which seems to be in the middle of nowhere, at Belle Vue, north of Pamplemousses. Unofficial games are played with passion wherever there is a space large enough. The Mauritius Football Association is at Chancery House, L Geoffroy Street, Port Louis, tel: 212 5771.

Horse racing

From the first week in May to the end of November, it is the horse racing season in Mauritius, with 24 to 26 race days, most of them on Saturdays, at the Champ de Mars race track. It is in a striking setting with a backdrop of gaunt mountains like a natural amphitheatre for the drama played out on the vast plain.

A white fence has been erected around the track as people used to dash across in front of the horses. Tickets are required to enter the grandstands on one side but entry to the arena surrounded by the track is free. There are dozens of canvas-covered stalls in the centre at which to lose money throwing darts at a chart or drink beer and eat snacks. There are also bookmakers' stalls actually resembling stables.

The Champ de Mars has been a racecourse since the Mauritius Turf Club was founded by an English army officer, Colonel Edward Draper, in 1812. Colonel Draper held nearly every office, except that of governor, in the administration. He oversaw the building of the circular track of 1,450 yards in length on what was then the army parade ground. Only horses belonging to the English garrison were ridden by young army officers at first, until the French settlers showed interest and entered their own horses. By 1837, horse racing was firmly established. The club has 450 members. Visitors, if suitably attired in jacket and tie or safari suit, can enter the members-only area as members' guests, as long as they have a permit issued in advance. (Mauritius Turf Club, Eugene Laurent Street, Port Louis, tel: 212 5836.)

As there is no thoroughbred breeding in Mauritius, race horses are imported by the Turf Club, mainly from South Africa and occasionally from the UK, France and Australia. The club allots them to the 10 registered racing stables under strict conditions. There are usually about 170 horses in training. Jockeys come mostly from Australia and South Africa and a few apprentices also ride alongside the professionals. Seven races are held each meet with a maximum of 10 runners a race.

Saturday afternoon at the race track adds gaiety to the atmosphere of Port Louis with the grandstands and public areas always crowded. It is possible to stand at the rails and watch the horses thunder by, enjoying the excitement of the meet without taking part in the prodigious amount of betting that goes on. Three different sweepstakes are organised on each race and the tote system of betting was introduced in 1991. The race meet makes Saturday a jolly climax to the working week of the capital.

Mauritius for Business

HOW TO MAKE MONEY IN MAURITIUS

Mauritius is 'the right location for the right investor', according to the title of a booklet issued in 1993 promoting industrial investment in the country. Mauritius is no longer a country looking for any kind of investor, due to the success of two-and-a-half decades of diversification and industrialisation. For instance, an entrepreneur wishing to set up a labour-intensive industry is not the right investor for Mauritius any more; he should look to Madagascar instead.

To make money in Mauritius now, the investor needs to anticipate the requirements of the next century, and how to cooperate with Mauritians in supplying them. That means the mysteries of the modern world, such as informatics, software development, computer-aided publications, and all the support systems needed for items that probably have not been invented yet. For the entrepreneur with the right idea, there is money to be made in Mauritius.

Unlike many developing countries desperate for foreign investment, Mauritius has already proved that foreign investors, and the country itself, can benefit. The officials know the formalities and don't antagonise the potential investor until he wants to strangle them with their own red tape.

'We don't like red tape', said an official of the Mauritius Export Development and Investment Authority, engagingly known by its acronym, MEDIA. 'Files are handled quickly'.

MEDIA was inaugurated by the government in 1985 to provide a professional service for both buyers and investors visiting Mauritius, to identify new market outlets for products manufactured in the EPZ (Export Processing Zone), and to plan and coordinate industrial promotion activities in order to attract the right type of enterprises to the EPZ. It is an organisation of both government and private sector officials making a concerted effort to promote the industrialisation of the country. Its activities are independent of government and it works with the potential industrial investor, or with an established manufacturer, as part of his team. Its main office is at 25 Pope Hennessy Street, Level 2, BAI building, PO Box 1184, Port Louis, tel: 208 7750, fax: 208 5965, telex: 4597 MEDIA IW.

According to MEDIA's promotional booklet, the organisation is 'the friend of the industrialist, and the services the Authority provides to both potential investors and industrialists who have already invested on the island are hard to beat. The individual attention given to the business community has now become proverbial'.

Its services include:
- assistance in identification of investment opportunities
- organisation of visits and meetings with the various economic operators on the island
- identification of joint-venture partners
- assistance in site location and factory buildings
- assistance in obtaining various clearances before a factory starts its operations
- identification of market outlets for Mauritian products.

Besides the enabling environment created by the government, Mauritius also offers a balanced package of fiscal incentives.

Incentive scheme	Fiscal incentives
Export Processing Zone	• Corporate tax of 15% throughout • Dividends tax free for 20 years • Complete exemption from customs duties on machinery and equipment, spare parts and raw materials • Free repatriation of profits, dividends and invested capital • Exemption from payment of half the normal registration fee on land and buildings by new industrial enterprises • Companies employing a minimum of 50 workers can also import a 25-seat bus or above, duty free
Pioneer Status Enterprise Activities involving technology or skill which will enhance industrial and technological development of Mauritius	• Corporate tax at the rate of 15% for 10 years • Tax exemption on shareholders' dividends for a period of 10 years • Exemption from payment of duty, levy and sales tax on scheduled materials and equipment
Strategic Local Enterprise Projects of national interest promoting industrial and technological advancement of Mauritius	• Corporate tax at the rate of 15% for whole life of company • Tax exemption on shareholders' dividends for 20 years
Modernisation & Expansion Enterprise Investment in new techniques involving CAD/CAM, automation equipment and environment friendly activities	• Customs duty exemptions on production equipment • 10% tax credit (spread over 3 years) on new investment (Rs10 million minimum) for modernisation/expansion, within 2 years of issue of certificate • Investment allowance and capital allowance on capital

expenditure incurred: total allowance of 125%
during the life time of the equipment
- An enterprise investing in pollution control
and environmental protection technology
benefits from an initial allowance amounting
to 80% on capital expenditure incurred.

Industrial Building Enterprise
Building with floor space of not less
than 1000m^2 for use by
manufacturing enterprise

- Corporate tax at the rate of 15% for the
whole life of the company
- Tax exemption on shareholders dividends for
a period of 10 years
- 50% exemption on registration dues for land
purchase

Small and Medium Enterprise

- Exemption from payment of customs duty,
import levy on production equipment
of aggregate CIF value not exceeding
Rs5,000,000.

MEDIA Overseas Branches

UNITED KINGDOM
MEDIA Office
c/o Mauritius High Commission
Elvaston Place
London SW7
Tel: 071 225 3331
Fax: 071 225 1580

SOUTH AFRICA
MEDIA Office
1st floor, Block 4
Lancaster Gate
Hyde Park Lane
Hyde Park
Sandton 2146
PO Box 47 133
Tel: 11 325 0340/1
Fax: 11 325 0401

UNITED STATES
MEDIA Office
c/o Embassy of Mauritius
4301 Connecticut Avenue
Suite 441, Washington DC 20008
Tel: 202 244 1491
Fax: 301 530 7423

FRANCE
Bureau de la MEDIA
118 rue de Vaugirard
75006 Paris
Tel: 1 45 44 62 14
Fax: 1 45 48 75 22

GERMANY
MEDIA Office
c/o GFE
Grunner Weg 13
D-5100 Aachen
Tel: 241 155 533
Fax: 241 155 646
Telex: 832177 GESP D

INDIA
MEDIA Office
506 Delamal Towers
211 Nariman Point
Bombay 400 021
Tel: 240 529/283 2074
Fax: 283 2079

The whole country is in fact an Export Processing Zone, and
MEDIA constructs factory buildings which are leased out to

industrialists. The annual rental in 1993 was approximately US$30 per square metre.

The presence of commercial banks in the countryside is extremely useful to the Export Processing Zone as the entire country is now a free zone. All commercial banks extend both short term and long term credit to manufacturing establishments. Another bank which has played a crucial role in the industrialisation process is the Development Bank of Mauritius, Ltd, which advances long term loans to industries. The interest rates vary between 10 to 13%.

Besides the commercial banks, the Stock Exchange of Mauritius, offshore banks, and the Mauritius Leasing Company (Fon Sing Building, Port Louis, tel: 212 0262, fax: 212 6465) all contribute substantially to the economic development. Although the Stock Exchange (6th Floor, Les Cascades Building, Edith Cavell Street, Port Louis, tel: 212 9541) is of recent origin, it is playing an important role in mobilising funds on behalf of companies listed on the Stock Exchange. Similarly, the offshore banking sector is authorised to provide loans in foreign exchange to the EPZ sector at competitive rates. The Mauritius Leasing Company provides financial leases up to 100% of the value of production equipment for a period of three to seven years.

Mauritius has entered the offshore business with company formation as well as banking, and is seen as an excellent jurisdiction for asset protection planning. As with the MEDIA strategy to help entrepreneurs, a one-stop authority has been set up: the Mauritius Offshore Business Activities Authority (MOBAA). This supervises all offshore activities in Mauritius. Offshore legislation covers offshore exempt companies, offshore ordinary companies, trusts, fund management, insurance, banking and shipping.

Companies can be incorporated, granted exempt status and issued with an offshore certificate within one week. The MOBAA application fee for exempt-status companies is US$250, with an annual licence fee of US$250. Disclosure of beneficial ownership is not required and annual accounts do not have to be filed with the authorities. Directors do not have to be resident in Mauritius. The MOBAA application fee for ordinary companies is US$500, with an annual licence fee of US$1,500. Accounts have to be audited and submitted to the MOBAA. Foreign trust laws are recognised and MOBAA's charge for registering a trust is US$250.

Mauritius has double tax treaties with France, Germany, India, Malaysia, South Africa and the UK. Offshore companies can take advantage of those treaties and may obtain a certificate of fiscal residence from the Mauritian tax authorities stating that a company is resident in Mauritius for the purpose of tax for a particular treaty; elect to pay a rate of domestic tax.

THE BUSINESS BEAT

The visiting entrepreneur will find it unbelievable that although all the offices, ministries and banks are located in Port Louis there is no business hotel in the city. Many have been proposed in the past, and for the future but nothing seems to happen.

The alternative, if you must stay in Port Louis – and it is certainly more convenient than shuttling in and out by car all the time – are the city guesthouses. My favourite is the Chinese-run Bourbon Tourist Hotel above a shopping arcade in Jummah Mosque Street. Rooms are air-conditioned with shower/toilet and some have telephones, with calls placed through the barman. The City Hotel (formerly Ambassador) in Sir S Ramgoolam Street, has seen better days. Both have rooms starting at Rs350.

The nearest international-standard hotel suitable for business visitors is the **Gold Crest** in Quatre Bornes. This has the advantage of being equidistant between Port Louis and Curepipe and central for getting to anywhere on the island, including the golf course at Vacoas and the west coast beaches. It has large, air-conditioned rooms, each one with writing desk, two armchairs, private bathroom, room service, radio, TV and IDD telephone, as well as telex, photocopying and secretarial assistance. There is a conference room with presentation equipment, a good club-type bar and a top restaurant. Taxis and buses are available at the door and there are restaurants and supermarkets within minutes' walk in the orderly town of Quatre Bornes. (Gold Crest Hotel, tel: 454 5945, fax: 454 9599, telex: 4690 CRESTEL IW.) The special business tariff starts at Rs800 for a single, inclusive of government tax.

For those who have to stay in Curepipe, there is the **Continental Hotel**, above the Currimjee shopping arcade (tel: 675 3434, fax: 675 3437, telex: 4389 CONTEL IW), which looks rather worn. Single bedrooms with air conditioning and bathroom, radio and telephone start at Rs725 with an additional 10% government tax and 10% service charge.

The closest beach hotel to Port Louis is the **Maritim**, about 20 minutes' drive away in Balaclava, Terre Rouge (tel: 261 5600, fax: 261 5670, telex: 4720 TURTLE IW). The needs of business guests there are recognised with conference rooms and facilities, computer rental availability, secretarial service and help with local contacts such as government departments, offshore business and banking consultants. However, it is primarily a package tourist hotel, very popular with German clients. Expect to pay from Rs3,000 for a single.

Other beach hotels within 30 minutes of the city are also used by business visitors, but the accent in them is essentially on pleasure rather than creating a business environment. An exception is the **Royal Palm** in Grand Bay (tel: 263 8353, fax: 263 8455, telex: 4653) where the rooms have work desks and the hotel has a real concierge, a helpful and efficient attitude of service, and a serenity that makes it ideal for business – but then room rates start at Rs5,650, single.

The business beat during the day will involve visits to Port Louis offices. It's better to walk to appointments within the city since it is quite compact and most offices and the main commercial area are around the Place D'Armes. Traffic congestion and one-way streets make driving short distances impractical. Since the pavements are uneven, mostly granite slabs in need of repair, walk carefully. Traffic does stop at marked crossings to allow pedestrians to cross.

Restaurants in Port Louis for business lunches are La Bonne Marmite and Carri Poulé. There is absolutely nowhere to go for 'Happy Hour' drinking unless the Rocking Boat Pub at La Bonne Marmite decides to stay open. About 10 minutes out of town is the Domaine les Pailles complex boasting four restaurants, with the French, Indian and Chinese ones just made for a quiet discussion over a good meal. In Curepipe, La Nouvelle Potinière and Au Gourmet are good for lunch. There are some speciality restaurants suitable for business entertaining on the coast which I've described in the guide to the various districts. Local business people, while keeping to office hours, are quite prepared to discuss business at any time.

Business assistance

There is a fully equipped office available for rent by the hour or for up to a week at 22 Sir William Newton Street in Port Louis. This is run by **Service Bureau** (tel: 212 5450, fax: 212 0505), an all round secretarial service that has been operating for 20 years. Typing and word processing, photocopying, telexing, office staff selection, temporary staffing and quick printing can be arranged here. In collaboration with professionals such as chartered engineers, accountants and lawyers, the bureau can also offer assistance during the implementation stage of any new product, including loan negotiation, feasibility studies and government applications.

A company that specialises in assistance in the setting up of companies is **International Management (Mauritius) Ltd**, (IMM), located at Les Cascades, Edith Cavell Street, PO Box 60, Port Louis, tel: 212 9800, fax: 212 9833. A member of the Eurotrust International Group, with shareholders including the major Mauritian company, Rogers Group, IMM helps clients to set up, manage and administer offshore entities including exempt and ordinary companies, and to liaise with the MOBAA (see earlier in this chapter). IMM carries a stock of ready-formed shelf companies and can obtain name approval for new companies within two working days. IMM also provides consultancy services to clients wishing to be onshore rather than offshore and to set up a physical presence in Mauritius, and helps to obtain residency permits for them.

There are two **courier companies** represented in Mauritius: DHL and TNT. DHL Worldwide Express is based at 14 Mgr Gonin Street, tel: 208 7711, fax: 208 7714, telex: 4737 DHLMRU IW. The agents for TNT are Cargo Express at 40 Farquhar Street, Port Louis, tel: 208 5021, fax: 208 0401, telex: 4416 FREIGHT IW.

The Mauritius **Chamber of Commerce and Industry** (MCCI), at 3 Royal Street, Port Louis, tel: 208 3301, fax: 208 0076, telex: 4277 CHACOM IW, was founded in 1850 and now has 400 members, with the payment of subscription fees according to turnover. The minimum fee is Rs4,000 for a turnover up to Rs10,000,000 or for firms not yet operating, with fees rising by stages to Rs10,000 for a turnover above Rs50,000,000. Affiliated to the Chamber are the Chinese Chamber of Commerce, the Indian Traders' Association and the Mauritius Chamber of Merchants.

The Chamber's activities include constant dialogue with government, trade fair and mission organisation, serving as an information centre; provision of intelligence via publications on air/sea cargo manifests, ships' arrivals, motor car registration, trade enquiries and commercial news; and defending the economic interests of Mauritius by participating in the activities of the EEC. It also operates a full telex and telefax service for its members. There is a consultancy service for small businesses and computer and system analysis courses are held. Every year the Chamber issues an annual report, essential reading for anyone interested in doing business in Mauritius.

Business visa

Business visitors to Mauritius do not need a special visa (as long as they are nationals of countries for which no normal visa is required – see Visa Section in Red Tape chapter.) A proper business visa does not exist. However, business visitors staying longer than three months will require a work permit.

Mauritius kestrel

Mauritius for Nature

The destruction of the endemic flora and fauna of Mauritius started with the island's discovery by the Portuguese. By the late 19th century, man's effect was apparent and the government began to buy back land from the French concession holders to try to conserve it. In the 1930s, certain areas were declared as national (later nature) reserves to be protected from all development. However, conservation happened too late to save those species of flora and fauna that began vanishing soon after the first humans arrived in the 16th century.

The beginning of Mauritius was actually the molten lava that began to bubble up from the ocean's floor some 13 million years ago, building up huge blocks of basalt. It pushed above sea level about 7½ million years ago, throwing up high mountains that time and weather have eroded to their present heights. The mountain ranges of Grand Port, Moka and Black River date from that period. Later, the light grey rock that can be seen throughout the island was scattered over the landscape by volcanic activity on an axis from northeast to southwest, creating such areas as Bassin Blanc, Trou aux Cerfs and the Kanaka crater.

The volcanoes have now been dormant for 200,000 years, allowing life to evolve. The first plants were lichens, but as the rock weathered into soil, other plants took root, brought to the island as seeds caught in the feet and feathers of birds, or washed up on the shore by the sea.

Birds, bats and insects found their way from other lands, either deliberately or blown accidentally by the wind. Floating logs brought snakes and lizards. The new plant and animal arrivals adapted themselves to the terrain. Birds, such as the renowned dodo, lost the power of flight since there were no predators from which they had to escape. Others developed a distinctive plumage and became unique to Mauritius.

Man's settlement began with an orgy of destruction. Forests were cut to provide timber for construction and export, and to clear land for crops. The dugong, which lived in the mouths of rivers and inspired mariners' tales of mermaids, disappeared along with the dodo, the tortoise and other trusting animals. They were replaced by invaders: rabbits, rats and goats, which speeded up the ecological changes.

NATURE RESERVES

The dense forest and undergrowth that stretched from the mountain tops to the shore, covering the scars of evolution, has survived only in traces around Black River Gorge, Bel Ombre and the Kanaka Crater. The coastal palm savannah has been reduced to a few hectares,

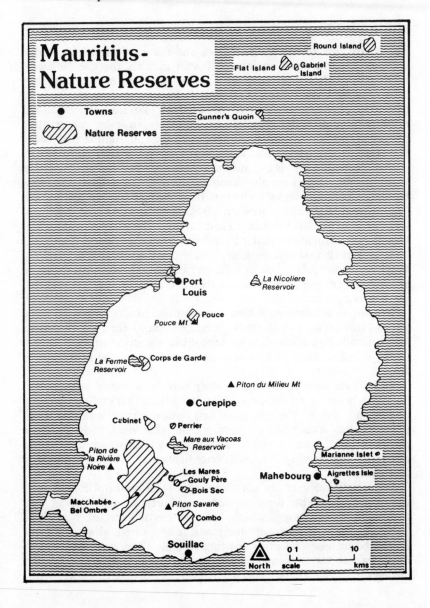

Mauritius-
Nature Reserves

● Towns

Nature Reserves

Round Island

Flat Island Gabriel Island

Gunner's Quoin

Port Louis

La Nicoliere Reservoir

Pouce
Pouce Mt

La Ferme Reservoir Corps de Garde

▲ Piton du Milieu Mt

● Curepipe

Cabinet ⊘ Perrier

Mare aux Vacoas Reservoir

Piton de la Rivière Noire ▲

Marianne Islet ⊘

Les Mares Gouly Père
Bois Sec

Mahebourg ● Aigrettes Isle

Macchabée - Bel Ombre

▲ Piton Savane

Combo

Souillac ●

North scale   kms
0 1   10

leaving interior forests to form the nucleus of the 4,500 hectares nature reserves. Their conservation is difficult due to lack of funds and trained personnel.

As well as being managed to encourage the regeneration of native species, nature reserves have to be maintained and policed. No structures, firearms, animals or rubbish dumping are allowed within their boundaries. No person, says the law, shall be in a national forest between 18.00 and 06.00. Permission has to be obtained from the Forestry Department (adjoining the Botanical Gardens in Curepipe) to visit them.

At sea level the forest is palm savannah while at altitudes of up to 250m, trees such as ebony, *bois d'olive* (*Elaeodendron orientale*), *bois de natte* (*Mimuspos maxima*) and *bois de fer* (*Stadtmania sideroxylon*) are most common. Re-afforestation to save threatened trees is a slow process since it may take two or three centuries for the trunk of a tree to grow to a diameter of 25 centimetres.

The nature reserve most popular with hikers, where most of the remaining endemic birds can still be seen, is the Macchabée-Bel Ombre Reserve that comprises Macchabée, Pétrin, Plaine Champagne, Bel Ombre and Montagne Cocotte forests. Pétrin and Plaine Champagne have porous soil with heath-type vegetation, and various species of *Pandanus* thrive where the soil is marshy. The transition between upland and lowland forest can be seen in the Bel Ombre reserve, while there is mossy forest in the high altitude Montagne Cocotte area, which has heavy rainfall and strong winds. Corps de Garde and Pouce are mountain range reserves.

The smallest reserve (1.5ha) is Perrier, between Curepipe and the Mare aux Vacoas reservoir. This is of interest beyond its size not only for its large number of endemic species but also because it shows an intermediate stage between lowland and upland forest.

Nature reserves

Aigrettes Isle	Gouly Père
Bois Sec	Macchabée – Bel Ombre
Cabinet	Mares (Les)
Cocos Isle (off Rodrigues)	Marianne Islet
Combo	Perrier
Corps de Garde	Pouce (Le)
Flat Island	Round Island
Gabriel Island	Sables (Sand) Island (off Rodrigues)
Gunner's Quoin Island	Serpent Island

CLIMBING AND HIKING

It is possible to explore the nature reserves independently although permission has to be obtained from the Forestry Department. Nature

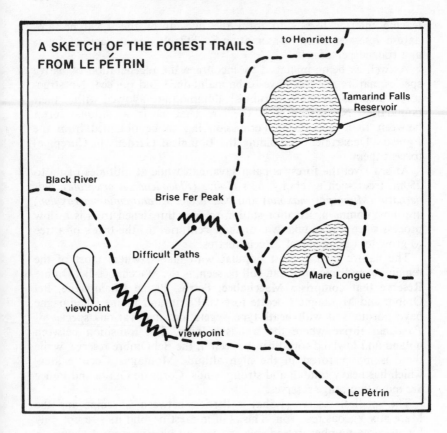

A SKETCH OF THE FOREST TRAILS
FROM LE PÉTRIN

to Henrietta

Tamarind Falls
Reservoir

Black River

Brise Fer Peak

Difficult Paths

Mare Longue

viewpoint

viewpoint

Le Pétrin

trails as such are not clearly defined and visitors may find it easier in organised groups. Hiking tours to such places as the Coloured Earths at Chamarel, La Nicolière artificial lake, Bassin Blanc natural lake, Black River Gorges and Combo Forest, as well as across the Ile d'Ambre (Amber Isle) are arranged by MauriTours.

At Le Pétrin, at the junction of the road from Mare aux Vacoas to Grand Bassin, there is a large signboard with a map of the trails that begin there, either north towards the Mare Longue Reservoir or up past Tamarind Falls and on to Henrietta. Westward, the trails go up to the Black River mountain range and to Brise Fer Peak at 622m. Stout walking shoes are generally all that the hiker needs. The hilly parts are difficult and require at least average fitness.

Confronted with so many mountains within easy reach, even the non-climber might be tempted to reach a summit or two. With a strong pair of boots, a water bottle, a bar of chocolate as a snack and a light, windproof anorak, it is possible, since only a few of the mountains are really tough to climb. Black River Peak, for instance, is a longish mountain ramble through jungle paths, hot and tiring, but requiring no special skill. An attempt on Corps de Garde peak can be frustrating, however, because it's easy to lose one's way.

There are three books which climbing enthusiasts will find useful. In 1873, Colonel Nicholas Pike, the US consul in Mauritius, published his personal experiences of adventures and wanderings in *Sub Tropical Rambles in the Land of the Aphanapteryx*. (His title refers to the red tailed, flightless heron that became extinct in the 19th century.)

A century later, Alexander Ward wrote *Climbing and Mountain Walking in Mauritius*. Robert R V Marsh produced a follow-up to this book, *Mountains of Mauritius, A Climber's Guide*, a 123-page volume which, unfortunately, is reported to be no longer available at local bookshops, so you will have to start a climb at the Mauritius Institute Library reference section. The book describes 30 climbs that any person of little more than ordinary fitness can complete in just about half a day.

FLORA

The forests of Mauritius retain only token remnants of the great, ancient trees found by the Dutch. The ebony, *bois d'ebène* (*Dios-pyros tessellaria*), does still exist and is now a protected tree. Mauritian ebony is the blackest wood in the world. The early settlers felled large trees that could have been a thousand years old and exported them as logs to Europe.

Teak and colophane were common in the forests and although colophanes are now rare, groves of them are to be seen in the Macchabée area. In the Royal Botanical Gardens at Pamplemousses there is a *bois colophane batard* (*Protium obtusifolium*). The tambala-coque with its silver-coloured trunk and prop-like roots (*Calvania major*), has become rare, too; some trees remain in the Macchabée forest.

Despite the many indigenous trees and tree orchids which have vanished, over 10,000 plant species remain. Over 150 species are endemic to Mauritius and 40 to Rodrigues.

The rarest plant in the world comes from Rodrigues. This is the *café marron* (*Ramosmania heterophylla*), a member of the coffee family. It was believed extinct until one bush was discovered on Rodrigues in 1980. A fence erected to protect it attracted the attention of the curious, who realised the plant must be valuable but didn't know why. The rumour spread that the plant's leaf, when brewed in a tea, was a remedy for hangovers and venereal disease.

The bush, having withstood browsing animals, insect infestations and windburn, now became the target of *tisane* (tea) makers and was almost destroyed. In 1986, some cuttings were sent to Kew Gardens in London to see if the plant could be grown in their laboratories. One of them took root.

Screwpines, known locally as *vacoas*, of the *Pandanus* family, can be seen throughout Mauritius, especially in marshy areas. The tree is easily recognized by its clusters of spiky leaves springing from a trunk that has exposed props for roots. Its long leaves are dried and used in basket making. The blue latan (Latania loddigesii) is another palm endemic to Mauritius, similar in appearance to the *vacoa* but distinguishable by its blue-tinged stem.

While the early settlers culled the forests of the islands, they also introduced plants from abroad that have now become prolific. Bamboo (actually a grass, one of the three dozen grass species in Mauritius) grows both in the wild and in residential areas where it has been tamed to form hedgerows.

Most common of the imports is the casuarina (*Casuarina equisetifolia*), called *filao* locally, which resembles a pine and is to be found close to beaches throughout the island. It was introduced from Malaysia in the 18th century, and is a useful tree both as a windbreak and for its wood (known as iron wood), which is good for fires and is used for making matches.

Along the east and southeast coasts are seen mangroves (*Rhizophora micronata*), growing in brackish swamps, the only trees in Mauritius that live in salt water. Its roots arch out of the ground in a tangle, or lie partially submerged. The seedling has a long root which digs itself rapidly into the mud so it can resist the wash of the sea. Another tree recognisable by its roots is the banyan (*Ficus benghalensis*), an import from India, which grows to a huge size and sports roots dangling from its branches to the ground.

On the savannah and thorn scrubland of the lowlands, the long stem, rising above spiked leaves, of the agave is distinctive, as are the aloes (*Furcraea foetida*). The aloe comes from Africa. Although it resembles a cactus, with its spiny, sharp, pointed leaves, it belongs to the lily family. Its succulent leaves are full of juice, used as an ingredient in beauty preparations. It has a red flower and is sometimes known as shoot of paradise, or the healing plant. It is cultivated for its strong fibre, from which sacks are made.

The plateau regions were planted with eucalyptus which has spread rapidly since being introduced to dry up swampy areas. A frequent sight is the traveller's tree (*Ravenala madagascariensis*), which attains a height of eight to ten metres, with leaf-stalks spread out like a lady's frilled fan. A beautiful tree when tended, it grows wild and straggly in Mauritius with its leaves torn by the wind. It really belongs to the banana family and gains its name because water (to refresh travellers) can be found at the join of its leaves with the stem.

In December, the roads are covered with scarlet petals which fall from the flamboyant tree (*Delonix region*) which blossoms from

November to January. Also called poinciana, it is remarkable for its fiery appearance when in full flower, and for its heavy pods, which hang down when its branches are bare.

Flowers frequently seen, as well as the nursery-cultivated anthurium/andreaneum, are poinsettias, oleanders, hibiscus, and bougainvillaea of every hue. Even roses, carnations, sweet peas and delphiniums are to be found in the higher plateau areas. There are 60 different varieties of orchid.

Mauritius has its own national flower, called the trochetia (*Trochetia boutoniana*), which is endemic to the island but seldom seen, although it has been reported on the south face of Trois Mamelles Mountain. It is a delicate rose-pink, bell-shaped blossom that hangs down from a nobbled stem crowned with leaves, and is called locally *Bouche d'oreille*.

Fruits

Small, sweet strawberries grow wild in the forests while larger ones are cultivated and offered for sale at stalls by the side of the highway from Port Louis to Quatre Bornes. Bananas grow everywhere throughout the year. Mangoes, the majority of the maison rouge variety, are plentiful. Lychees are abundant from November to January.

Jamalac (*Eugenia malaccensis*) is a spongy, wet, fleshy fruit, either white or red. Pomegranate (*Punica granatum*) grows from mid-winter to mid-summer, becoming bright red when it is ripe. Carambole (*Averrhoe carambola*) is an acid fruit which, when cut in slices, appears like a starfish. The round and long bilimbi is of the same family. It does not grow on the tips of branches but on the stems, as does the jackfruit. This is a versatile fruit which can grow as large as a sack of rice, weighing over 40 kilos. It has a green, gnarled skin. The pulp and nuts can be eaten cooked as a vegetable, while the yellow flesh enveloping the nuts is a fruit tasting like lime and pineapple. The wood of the tree is used in furniture and in building.

In spite of this abundance, it is surprisingly difficult to buy local fruits, yet apples and oranges imported from South Africa are easily obtainable from street vendors.

Further information

The best places to see samples of the flora of Mauritius are the botanical gardens of Pamplemousses and Curepipe. Port Louis is blessed with several small gardens, including the Company Gardens off the Chaussée in the city centre, and the Robert Edward Hart Gardens on the south side of the harbour. In Beau Bassin are the municipal Balfour Gardens. The garden of Government House at Le Réduit is an example of a formal garden in a tropical setting.

Books on the flora of Mauritius are limited. There is a detailed guide to the plants at the Royal Botanical Gardens at Pamplemousses, written in 1976 by the Conservator of Forests, A W Owadally. In 1877, J G Baker produced *Flora of the Mauritius and the Seychelles*. A more recent (1981) publication is *Fleurs et plantes de la Réunion et de l'ile Maurice* by Th Cadet.

(*The notes on Flora and Fruit have been adapted from a contribution by Yogeshwar Raghoobeer.*)

FAUNA

The value of Mauritius' wildlife has been acknowledged by laws passed to protect species, even if funds to do so are limited. It was the island's wildlife which first attracted the early colonists. Tortoises, for instance, presented an ideal source of fresh meat; they could be turned over and laid on their backs until needed. There were so many tortoises, the early settlers could walk on them from one to another. Now there are none save imported ones.

The only mammal in Mauritius when it was discovered was the fruit bat or flying fox (*Pteropus rubricollis*) whose cousin, the Rodrigues fruit bat (*Pteropus rodericensis*) was, until recently, in danger of becoming extinct. Popularly known as the golden bat, it is an appealing creature to look at, with a fox-like face and large eyes. Soft golden fur covers its head and it wraps its body of darker brown fur in a cape made up of its velvety leather wings. It is vegetarian, spending its days hanging upside down in groups and its nights gliding across valleys in search of trees with ripe fruit. There are thought to be 200 to 300 of them but successful efforts are being made to breed them in captivity to create new colonies in the wild.

The Mauritius fruit bat is more common but, since it is much appreciated in fruit bat curry, its existence could be threatened, without encouragement for it to breed. It can be seen in the Black River Gorge area and in the Savannah and Grand Port Mountains.

The Gorge, Chamarel and Case Noyale areas are also the habitat of the macaque monkey (*Macaca trustrus*), a native of Southeast Asia. This was probably first introduced by the Portuguese from Malaysia in 1528 and again by the Dutch in 1606. It has caused much damage to the native flora and fauna by feeding on plants and birds' eggs.

Other animals were introduced by the Portuguese in 1528 as emergency food stocks. The wild pig (*Sus scrofa*) became a resident then, being a descendent of the Portuguese domestic pig. It survived elimination by hunters through its ability to detect man from a great distance. Wild goats (*Capra hircus*) were introduced, as were dogs. Unintentional visitors who jumped ship were the brown rat (*Rattus norvegicus*) and also the black rat (*rattus rattus*), although this is not so common.

A hedgehog-like animal arrived from Madagascar in the early

1880s. Known locally as *tenrec* (*Centetes ecuadatus*), it is tailless, brownish in colour and largely nocturnal. This species has no prickles and is a sought-after delicacy. Hare is more frequently found as a dish. In this case it is the black-naped hare (*Lepus nigricollis*), introduced by the French from India in 1750. It thrives especially on Gunner's Quoin. Wild rabbit (*Oryctolagus cuniculus*) was brought by the Dutch from Java in 1639. Released on Round Island in 1840 it has created disturbances in the ecology there.

The Dutch also brought in deer (*Cervus timoriensis russa*) from their colony in Java so they could have a ready supply of meat and some sport hunting them. Herds descended from them are to be seen in the Black River District, and in areas such as Savanne their breeding is encouraged for meat. The mongoose (*Herpestes griseus*) is a recent import (1900) from India. This short-legged, brown, furry animal with red eyes and a long, bushy tail was supposed to keep down the rat population but also destroys game birds.

If there were more snakes in Mauritius, the mongoose would destroy them, too. Those to be seen are the Indian wolf snake (*Lycodon aulicus*), known locally as *couleuvre*. Pale brown in colour with chocolate and gold markings, it is not poisonous but can be aggressive if disturbed. There are two boa-type snakes (*Bolyeria multicarinata* and *Casarea dussumieri*) remaining from the three indigenous snakes on the island at the time of settlement. Both of them are confined to Round Island where they are unique in filling a gap in the evolutionary cycle, having 'broken' as opposed to fixed jaws. There are thought to be only 70 to 80 remaining of the aboreal type and attempts have been made to breed them in captivity. The ground one was last seen in 1976 and may already be extinct.

At the time of settlement there were also 15 species of lizards, of which three have become extinct. There are three species of green lizard of the *Phelsuma gekkonidae* family, which are native to Mauritius. These geckos are the brightest coloured lizards in the world, active by day and living in palm and banana trees. They feed on fruit, nectar and insects. There are 2,000 species of insects and butterflies. Three of the butterflies are unique to the island: the citrus, ficus and sailor varieties.

Birds
The most interesting of the birds are the endemic, those species that were created in Mauritius itself by evolution and cannot be found anywhere else in the world. Only nine of a known 25 endemic birds remain and only the pic-pic (*Zosterops borbonica*) has adapted itself to man's presence and become common all over the island. It is a small gregarious bird that lives off insects picked from plants or caught in flight, moving in flocks of six to 20. It is conspicuous by its white rump.

Of the birds that have disappeared, the most famous is 'the ghastly dodo' as a zoologist in Mauritius described it. The dodo (*Raphus cucculatus = Didus ineptus*) was seen by the Dutch in 1681 but was extinct by 1692. Like a large turkey in size, it was related to the pigeon, plump, with wings that became atrophied through lack of use. It had downy feathers and a crooked beak with which it could crush the hard seeds that were its diet. Its plumpness and docility made it an ideal candidate for the clubs and cooking pots of the Dutch, although its flesh was not really to their liking.

The Dutch list of birds on the island when they arrived includes turtle doves, herons, parrots, owls, swallows and wild geese. They hunted them gleefully. Captured parrots were persuaded to call other parrots to attract them within range to be slaughtered.

The flightless *Aphanapteryx* was also annihilated, but the pink pigeon (*Columba nesoenas mayeri*) survived because of its diet. Its favourite food was the white fruit of an evergreen shrub called the *fandamane* (*..phloeia mauritiana*), which has a narcotic effect. After eating it, the pigeons flopped to the ground in a daze, making them an easy target for the Dutch gourmands. However, after eating pink pigeon pie, the Dutch foodies also fell into a stupor and quickly learned to leave the pigeon alone.

The dark blue and mauve Dutch pigeon (*Alectroenas nitidissima*) was not so lucky. The last one to be shot fell to the gun in 1826 at Savanne, surviving as a specimen in the Institute Museum in Port Louis. However, sightings of the species continued until 1850. One Dutch sea captain recorded with pride that his sailors shot 150 in an afternoon. The solitaire of Rodrigues (*Pezophaps solitarius*), a relative of the dodo, was exterminated in about 1760.

The remaining endemic birds are all extremely rare and are protected species, except for the pic-pic, mentioned above, known in Creole as *zozo maniok*. A spectacular endemic bird with a scarlet head and throat is the cardinal or banana bird, the Mauritius fody (*Foudia rubra*). This frequents the forested remnants of the indigenous scrubland although it is sometimes seen around Vacoas and Curepipe. Another, the flycatcher (*Terpsiphone bourbonnensis*), has a lovely song and is a tame, inquisitive bird found in forests.

The cuckoo shrike or *cuisinier* (*Coracina typicus*) haunts the native forests around Black River Gorge and Bel Ombre. It hunts insects and occasionally robs the nests of birds such as the pink pigeon, whose eggs it sucks. Even rarer is the parakeet or *grosse cato verte* (*Psittacula echo*) which should not be confused with the introduced green parrot. Its habitat is also the forests of Black River Gorge. The Merle or blackbird (*Hypsipetes olivacea*) is omnivorous, eating fruits, insects and small lizards, and is quick to sound the alert when disturbed.

The olive white eye or *oiseau a lunettes* or *yeux blancs* (*Zosterops chloronotos*) is related to the much more common pic-pic. It inhabits scrub at higher altitudes, living on nectar and occasional insects. It has a conspicuous white circle around its eye.

The pink pigeon, another inhabitant of the native forests around Black River, had become very rare by 1974, when only 30 individuals were known. Strenuous efforts to rear it in aviaries have resulted in about 180 being bred in ten years. In 1984, 22 birds were released in Pamplemousses Gardens so they could live in the wild. People decided otherwise, either killing them for fun or the cooking pot. It remains the world's rarest pigeon and Carl Jones, whose efforts to rear it in the aviary at Black River have been so successful, believes it could be doomed since its gene pool is now too small.

One of the rarest birds of any kind to which Carl Jones has turned his attention is the Mauritius kestrel (*Falco punctatus*). At the aviary close to its habitat of the native forests in Black River, kestrels are being hand-reared with the aid of science in an effort to save this endemic bird from extinction. Their number was down to four in 1974, but now there are more than 200 in existence. Some have made the Domaine du Chasseur in the Bamboo Mountains of the southeast their home, where they can be seen swooping in for the mice fed daily to them by the warden to supplement their diet.

Indigenous birds, that is those which are natural to Mauritius but are found in other countries as well, include the oceanic birds nesting on Round and Serpent Islands. The Trinidade petrel (*Pterodroma arminjoniana*) is the most interesting, found elsewhere only on an island off Brazil. Tropic birds (*paille-en-queue*) with their long tails of white or red (*Phaethon lepturus* – the white – or *rubricauda* – the red) are found on Round Island, Gunner's Quoin and in some river gorges.

The island's common birds, with the exception of the pic-pic, were all introduced from overseas and include the red-whiskered bulbul (*Pycnonotus jocosus*), sometimes called the Persian nightingale. A pair of birds which escaped from a cage in 1892 are said to be the ancestors of all the bulbuls on the island. Other cage birds that escaped and have bred in open country are the waxbill (*Estrilda astrild*), the rock dove (*Columba livia*) and the ring-necked parakeet (*Psittacula krameri*) which escaped from a cage in 1886.

The Indian house crow (*Corvus splendens*) is spreading from the Plaine Verte area of Port Louis, having been introduced there in the late 1960s. The mynah (*Acridotheris tristis*) came two centuries before to control locusts. From India in 1860 came the house sparrow (*Passer domesticus*), which can often be seen enjoying a dust bath. The yellow fronted canary (*Serinus mozambicus*) was imported during French times as a cage bird from Africa.

Some 45 species of birds live in Mauritius. Many of them can be seen in aviaries at the Casela Bird Park in the Black River district or flying freely from the Royal Botanical Gardens at Pamplemousses. A full description appears in *Birds of Mauritius* by Claude Michel, published in Mauritius in 1986. A larger work on the Mascerene Birds, edited by A W Diamond, has been published by the Cambridge University Press.

UNDERWATER

The marine life of Mauritius has also suffered from man's arrival although it is an additional attraction for visitors. It is easy to visit coral gardens in depths of seven to 20 metres through hotel diving centres. The range of fish to be seen, especially those engaging in antics like the boxfish with their curious sculling action and the trumpet fish with darting movements, is fascinating.

The appeal of the reef is enhanced by the variety of the coral which is among the most beautiful in the world. Because of the sunlight which filters through sea of the right salinity and temperature, the coral thrives better in the waters of Mauritius than elsewhere. There are notable coral gardens at the southern corners of Mauritius, off Morne Brabant and Blue Bay. Underwater walks are organised from Grand Bay (see under Watersports in the chapter on Mauritius for Pleasure.).

Shell collecting has been so rapacious since the 1960s that a limit has been imposed on the number of shells a visitor can take from the island. To meet the demand, shells are imported from the Philippines to be sold to tourists who want something pretty as a souvenir, not a genuine rare shell. The rarest and most valuable shells in the world, such as the several varieties of conus, *Lambis violacea* and *Cyproe onyx-nymphal*, have been found off Mauritius.

There is an extensive collection of shells at the Mauritius Institute Museum. A model of the rare cone (*Conus milneedwardsi*) can be seen among the exhibits. This was brought up in a fisherman's basket net from a depth of 40 fathoms, off the coast of Black River. Also exhibited is a giant clam (*Tridacna gigas*), the largest lamellibranch ever evolved.

It is possible to find shells on the beaches but these will be dead and rather dull. Shells sold by beach vendors will probably have been treated with a coat of varnish. Live shells have to be found on the sea bed. The days when a local housewife could quite easily find a beautiful tiger cowrie to take home as a darning 'mushroom' have passed. Helmet shells, once exported to Italy to be used in making cameos, are also rare now.

Cone and cowrie shells, while delightful, can be deadly if of the *Conus aulieus, geographicus, marmoreus, rattus, textile* or *tulipa* species. Poison injected from their sharp ends can bring death within

150 minutes, with no known antidote. 105 species have been recorded. Harp shells, four species, with ribs resembling the strings of a harp, are attractive to collectors, especially the double harp (*Harpa costata*), which is not found outside Mauritian waters. There are 135 species of mitre shells (*Mitridae*), which are spindle to oval-shaped and notched in front. Murex shells such as *Murex tenuispina* with its elongated, jagged stem, are popular. The purple fluid secreted by them was used in ancient times as a dye.

Starfish are common and the presence of the crown of thorns (*Star achantaster*) is destructive to coral. An excellent specimen of the very rare *Acanthocidaris curvatispinis*, which is known only in Mauritius, is on display at the Institute Museum. The collection of *echinoderms* there also contains a remarkable specimen of *Chondrocidaris gigantea*, exhibited in a special show case as it is considered to be the most beautiful sea urchin in the world.

Protected plants
All indigenous orchids (*orchidées*)
Ochna mauritiana (*bouquet banané*)
Hornea mauritiana (*arbre a l'huile*)
All *Diospyros* species (*ebène*)
Sideroxylon grandiflorum
Cordyline mauritiana
All *Tambourissa* species (*bois tambour*)
All *Trochetia* species (*boucles d'oreilles*)
Erythroxylon laurifolium (*bois de ronde*)
All indigenous ferns (*fougères*)

Protected wildlife
Deer *Cervus (rusa) unicolor*
Hare *Lepus nigricollis*
Partridge *Francolinus spp*
Quail *Perdicula spp*
Wild guinea fowl *Numeda spp*
Wild pig *Sus spp*

The hunting season for the above game species begins on the first Saturday in June and extends until the first Saturday in September.

Protected species
Gecko *Phelsuma guentheri*
Gecko *Phelsuma guimbeaui*
Mauritius bulbul (*merle charpentier*) *Hypsipetes olivacea*
Mauritius cuckoo shrike (*merle cuisinier*) *Coracina typicus*
Mauritius flycatcher (*coq des bois*) *Terpsiphone bourbonnensis*
Mauritius fody (*oiseau banane*) *Foudia rubra*

Mauritius kestrel (*crécerelle*) *Falco punctatus*
Mauritius parakeet (*grosse cateau*) *Psittacula echo*
Mauritius pink pigeon (*pigeon des mares*) *Nesoenas mayeri*
Mauritius white eye (*oiseau lunette*) *Zosterops chloronotos*
Red-tailed tropic bird (*paille en queue a brins rouges*) *Phaethon rubri-cauda*
Rodrigues bat (*chauve souris*) *Pteropus rodericensis*
Rodrigues fody (*cardinal jaune*) *Foudia flavicans*
Rodrigues warbler (*fauvette*) *Bebrornis rodericana*
Round Island snake *Bolyeria multicarinata*
Round Island snake *Casarea dussumieri*
Serpent Island skink *Cyrtodactylus serpensinsula*
Telfair skink *Leiolopisma telfeirii*
Trinidade petrel *Pterodroma arminjoniana*

Pink pigeons, one of the rarest species in the world

Collecting Mauritius

TREASURE HUNTING

Mauritius does not have a great trove of antiques and artefacts to show for its 350 years of settled history. Old buildings have been torn down by people and cyclones or allowed to disintegrate as they become too expensive to maintain. The furniture and collectables have been plundered by the more appreciative (and wealthier) French from Réunion and shipped away to grace homes there. Its history survives in the flagged streets and cobbled roads of Port Louis (where they haven't been tarred over), behind the shuttered louvres of French colonial mansions, and in the wide walls of Victorian warehouses, now turned into Chinese grocery stores.

Treasure

In October 1987 a Frenchman arrived in Mauritius on board a vessel equipped for underwater exploration. He announced he was leading an expedition to locate wrecks of the 16th and 17th centuries and that he intended to prepare a marine archaeological map of them to present to the government.

Since his name was Eric Surcouf and he confessed to being a descendant of the celebrated corsair, Robert Surcouf, Mauritians assumed a treasure hunt was underway. Surcouf's purpose, he said, was to recover what was in the wreck he located and to donate it to form a marine museum in the island. For Mauritians, the name of Surcouf and treasure are inseparable.

Robert Surcouf was real, the most famous corsair of his time; his treasure remains a legend. From 1793 to 1802 a total of 119 prizes were brought into Port Louis by corsairs. The booty was valued at £2,500,000; most of it was traded with neutral ships. However, in 1799, Surcouf captured the East Indiaman *Kent*, a large vessel of 1,200 tons. Legend insists he dumped his rich haul of treasure from the *Kent* somewhere in the vicinity of Port Louis habour rather than hand it over to the French.

If Surcouf and his fellow corsairs (pirates) did leave treasure on the sea bed or buried on shore, no one has admitted to finding any. Nevertheless, wrecks abound and relics have been retrieved from the reef-fringed lagoons.

The site of the wreck of the *St Geran*, a vessel of the French East India Company which sank near the Ile d'Ambre (Amber Isle) in 1744, was known by local fishermen in 1966. By the time marine archaeologists explored it scientifically in 1979, it had been stripped. Perhaps treasure was taken, too. Its bell is in the naval museum at Mahebourg. (The wreck of the vessel forms the climax of St Pierre's novel, *Paul et Virginie*.)

In the late 1960s a treasure hunter spent years trying to find some £10 million of corsair's treasure supposedly buried near Tombeau Bay. Rumours persist and some old French-Mauritian families are said to have maps...

Antiques

There is almost nowhere in Mauritius where a visitor can buy colonial antiques. The idea of foreigners taking out antiques (that were, in any case, imported into the island) is anathema to the people who care. Chinese antiques, however, are available for purchase, having been imported especially to sell to tourists.

Furniture of the French East India Company period of the 18th century is particularly prized in Mauritius and some fine examples are to be seen. There is a collection at Eureka, the French-style colonial home that serves as a museum in Moka.

In Curepipe, there is a shop, *Ville-Valio*, in the arcade under the Continental Hotel which offers brass pots and occasional antiques for sale. More interesting is a scruffy shop without a name near the Mandarin Hotel in Floreal, close to the Chung Yum Tack Floreal Store. Among the dusty bric-a-brac when I visited were two wind-up gramophones with the kind of horn the HMV dog listens to. One was priced at Rs4,000, the other at Rs3,000.

Real antiques can be acquired by commissioning a local enthusiast to look for them. I discovered the name of one expert who deals in antiques as a hobby by asking a professional tour guide. I recommend that strategy for someone determined to purchase a piece of collectable Mauritius.

Philately

Mauritius holds a special place in the affections of stamp collectors since the first stamps issued there are now one of the greatest rarities in the philatelic world. At the end of 1993, at an auction in Zurich, someone paid the equivalent of US$3.3 million for 'the crown jewel of philately', an envelope – 'the Bordeaux cover' – with two stamps on it, sent from Mauritius to a Bordeaux wine importer in 1847. This is the only cover known with the two values (one penny and two pence) of the Mauritius 'Post Office' series.

Mauritius was the first British colony to use adhesive postage stamps, and was, in fact, only the fifth country in the world to issue stamps, in 1847.

Postal services under the British began on January 11 1811, only a month after the island's capitulation. In 1834, an organised postal service was set up inland with the introduction of a weekly stage/mail coach between Port Louis and Mahebourg. In 1840, the first adhesive stamps recording prepayment of letter postage were issued in the UK. In December 1846 an ordinance was passed by the council in Mauritius authorising the issue of stamps there.

The first 1,000 postage stamps (500 at a penny value and 500 at two pence) were produced by Joseph Barnard, a watchmaker and jeweller of Port Louis, who engraved the dies onto a copper plate and laboriously printed the stamps one at a time, direct from the engraving. Despite his skills as a craftsman, the results were very primitive compared with the famous penny blacks of Britain. They also contained an error. Instead of the words POST PAID he engraved POST OFFICE in the vertical left hand margin.

The stamps were released on September 21 1847, and on the same day Lady Gomm, the Governor's wife, used a considerable number of the orange-red penny value on invitations to a ball at Le Réduit. Only 15 1d stamps and 12 of the blue 12d value are believed to exist.

Joseph Barnard was instructed to produce further stamps in 1848. To facilitate printing, he engraved each stamp 12 times on the printing plate. The result when printed was that no two stamps were identical, although this issue had the correct words POST PAID on them. These stamps, which were in use until 1859, are also highly prized among collectors.

After 1859 mass produced stamps, printed in Britain, were issued. However, stocks of more frequently used stamps were often exhausted before fresh supplies could arrive from London. Consequently, the lower value stamps that were still available were surcharged, thereby creating more stamps of interest to philatelists.

The first pillar boxes were erected in Port Louis in the early 1860s. Special date stamps for mail collected from them were used in the period 1885 to 1926 in Port Louis, Beau Bassin, Curepipe, Mahebourg and Rose Hill. Examples of such cancellations are rare.

Other historical events have also given Mauritius stamps special value. The first airmail flight from Mauritius to Réunion took place in 1933. The first use of aerogrammes in Mauritius was on December 27 1944. In 1952, the Postal Authorities inaugurated a second class airmail service, air parcel post and insured air letter service. In 1972, the first airmail service to Rodrigues was launched.

Philatelically, the late Victorian era up to the Second World War was a time of dullness in the stamps of Mauritius. The fate of the dodo might have descended upon the collectability of Mauritian stamps but for the introduction of designs displaying the attractions of the island.

Since independence this practice has improved. Moreover, the respectability and appeal of the stamps has been preserved by restricting the number of commemorative issues each year to five and by limiting their production to realistic figures for commercial use. The stamps are all colourful yet artistic and feature themes connected with Mauritius.

Used postage stamps and first day covers can be seen on sale in the windows and shops selling tourist souvenirs in Port Louis and Curepipe, and stamps can be bought at the post office. The philatelist is catered for by Mr Prakash Purmessur, a specialist in rare Mauritius stamps, who has a shop in the grounds of the Eureka House Museum at Moka (tel: 433 4951).

A fascinating booklet, reading like a detective story, about the 'Post Office Mauritius' stamp and its legend, together with a short survey of the stamps of Mauritius, was published in 1990 by the Editions de L'Océan Indien. I found a copy in a Grand Bay supermarket in 1993 for Rs35.

TREASURE VIEWING

Museum collections

Eureka House at Moka is an independent museum featuring antiques, furniture, old lithographs and other objects from private collections. There are also public museums with collections of natural history, naval, historical and literary items, which come under the aegis of the **Mauritius Institute**.

This was set up in 1880 'to establish and incorporate a Public Institute, a Public Museum and a Public Library, for the purpose of promoting the general study and cultivation of the various branches and departments of Arts, Sciences, Literature and Philosophy and for the instruction and recreation of the people'.

The result was the building in the Chaussée, next to the Company Gardens, of a two-storeyed building, opened in 1884 on the occasion of the Inter-Colonial Exhibition. The Institute has now grown into a complex that includes a Natural History Museum, an Historical Museum, a Memorial Museum and a Public Library. It is run by the Ministry of Education, Arts and Culture with the help of an Advisory Council. The Institute building is itself a national monument.

The lower floor of the Institute Building in Port Louis is occupied by the Natural History Museum. The nucleus of its collection is the bequest to the nation by Julien Desjardins in 1885 of his specimens of marine fauna and birds of the Mascarene Islands. Other bequests followed, including that of the shells collected by Elize Lienard. Through its research over the years the museum has become the centre for documentation and exchange in the various fields of natural history in the Mascarenes.

In 1950, a laboratory was set up to provide research facilities and assist the maintenance and restoration of the Institute's collections. Valuable specimens of marine fauna, land molluscs and plants have been acquired and a number of modern exhibition cases installed.

The **Historical and Naval Museum** is at Mahebourg, housed in an old French country house, built around 1722 and itself having an interesting history. It was in this building that the two wounded commanders of the English and French squadrons, the Admirals Willoughby and Duperre, were treated during the naval battle of Grand Port in August 1810.

The museum was opened in 1950. Its collection of naval relics was created in 1934 and located in Port Louis until 1942. Also on display are pieces of furniture and objects of local historical interest, old maps, stamps, engravings and water colours depicting the scenery and customs of Mauritius in the past.

The only Memorial Museum which exists in Mauritius is the **Robert Edward Hart Museum** at Souillac. This charming seaside bungalow built out of coral was the home of Mauritian poet, Robert Edward Hart (1891–1954). It was opened in 1967 and contains a collection of the poet's memorabilia.

The treasure of the Institute lies in its **library**, a collection of books begun with the bequest of Sir Virgil Naz, an eminent Mauritian lawyer, and formally opened in 1903. It is housed above the Natural History Museum, reached by a stairway at the back of the building, and is free and open to the public.

In 1905, a reference library of works of local interest on the Mascarenes, Madagascar, and the Indian Ocean was created. This collection has been added to regularly and can be studied in the room at the back of the lending-library section. The library of the Royal Society of Arts and Sciences, stored in the building since 1885, is also open for study. In 1947 an oriental language section was added.

The **National Archives**, once stored in Port Louis, are now housed in conditions not conducive to their preservation on an industrial estate at Coromandel.

Historical sites and monuments

Since 1944, ancient monuments and places of historical interest have been preserved. In 1985, a new act substituted the word 'national' for 'ancient'. The **National Monuments Board** was set up to advise on what should be designated a national monument as well as on how private interest in national monuments could be fostered.

A monument is described as 'any structure or remains of a structure ... the preservation of which is a matter of public interest for aesthetic, archaeological, architectural, artistic, historical, scientific or traditional reasons'. Ecclesiastical buildings used for ecclesiastical purposes are not included.

In the Port Louis district, no less than 66 national monuments have been designated (a list is available from the Director of the Mauritius Institute). The Rum Warehouse Building near Immigration Square has been deproclaimed and dismantled but a new national monument, the old wooden home of Sir Seewoosagur Ramgoolam, has been added to the list. While some of the Port Louis monuments are buildings, such as the General Post Office, Fort Adelaide, Line Barracks, Trou Fanfaron Police Station and Government House, others are statues and tombs. There are 62 other national monuments throughout the country.

Despite the listing of buildings and statues for preservation, the names of many historical areas are not being retained. Streets with colonial or evocative names have been renamed for indigenous politicians and contemporary figures. For example, in Port Louis, Washerwoman's Row has become Seetulsingh Street, Cattle Walk Street is now Solim Street and Crooked Lane has become Bouchet Street. The landmark Place D'Armes is preserved in peoples' minds by that name, despite its new designation as Place Sookdeo Bissoondoyal.

Inexpensive Mauritius

KEEPING COSTS LOW

This chapter is short because most of Mauritius is inexpensive for the prudent visitor. Unfortunately, low budget travellers are not the kind Mauritius wants. The economic success of its tourist industry depends on high-spending package tourists, not bargain hunters.

However, there is an acknowledgement by the MGTO that not all the world's travellers are wealthy, or actually want the champagne breakfasts and free watersports of the island's resort hotels. There is the thought, too, that the independent traveller spends more money in more places in Mauritius than the packaged tourist. So the MGTO has produced a booklet, issued every year now, giving the tariffs of 'Budget Hotels, Bungalows and Boarding Houses'. The 1993 edition has grown to list 82 establishments, of which the lowest cost Rs80, single, or Rs125 double, bed and breakfast. (It was Pension Labourdonnais, Mon Plaisir, 52 impasse Stevenson, Quatre Bornes, tel: 424 1197). Others ranged from Rs125 to Rs500 for a single, and, for a double with B&B, from Rs250 (Tandoori Hotel, Port Louis, tel: 212 2131) to Rs800.

David Sullivan of Cleveland, Ohio, one of the few from the USA to visit Mauritius (under 2,000 a year find their way there) commented on this chapter:

'I agree that travelling cheaply is very possible in Mauritius. Everything is available at two very different price levels (eg: transport from airport to Pereybere can be taxi for Rs500–1,000, or bus for Rs40). General rules: strenuously avoid taxis, except for the inexpensive and good "taxi trains", eat street food and Chinese, bargain down prices for everything, including hotels, stay cheaply in places like Grand Bay, or camp by public beaches.'

The biggest cost of a holiday in Mauritius is getting there. After that, travel by buses, staying in guesthouses, and eating – and drinking – where Mauritians do, can keep the visit within the tightest budget. However, it is not a country where visitors can sponge off the generosity and gullibility of locals. A stranger is no novelty to be feted lavishly, but a visitor who does not look and act like a tourist will not be overcharged.

Lost cost living need not be uncomfortable. The cheapest places to stay are in Mahebourg, Port Louis and Curepipe. Accommodation will be basic, in small rooms with a common toilet and shower. The place will be reasonably clean and the proprietors, being Mauritians, will be anxious to see you enjoying your stay. If not, find another guesthouse.

There are no campsites on the island with toilets, showers and water supply. Since every available plot of land seems to be in use, finding a suitable site to pitch a tent takes time. However, most of the public beaches have water and toilet facilities with shade trees nearby. Mauritians themselves sometimes camp under the *filaos* for a few nights.

In Rodrigues, a tent is the only accommodation outside the main town of Port Mathurin. It is possible to spend two weeks hiking around the island, camping each night by a new beach or in the mountains, although there are no formal facilities. Basic supplies can be obtained from the Chinese-run village shops.

Self-catering accommodation does exist in Mauritius but mostly in the tourist areas, such as Grand Bay, where it is at special (high) tourist rates. In Grand Bay prices can reach Rs20,000 for self-catering accommodation for a month. The equivalent in the Black River district, on the beach, would be less. Individual contacts, through Mauritian friends, could result in the renting of a privately-owned beach bungalow (*campement*) when it is not being used by its owners.

Although self-catering sounds fine in theory, the extra expenses could make it more costly than boarding house accommodation. You will need food and supplies and unless there is a well-stocked shop within walking distance, or a good bus service to the nearest town, you will need a car. And car hire is expensive.

The cheapest way to travel is by bus. Since passengers conduct themselves in an orderly manner and don't treat your lap or the open window by your shoulder as seating space, this is reasonably comfortable. It is often possible to visit a beach during the day by bus and return in the afternoon to eat and live cheaply in town.

Shopping can be inexpensive, especially clothes made in Mauritius for export, which can be bought from wayside vendors. You can bargain successfully for quantity. There are supermarkets with imported goods which will be cheaper than in village shops. For fresh vegetables, every town has a market at least twice a week, and villages have shops and kiosks where fruit can be bought cheaply.

Eating at street stalls is a tradition in Mauritius and the food is well prepared and unlikely to cause health problems. If a cheap eatery is crowded, it's OK. The customers are just as likely to be senior civil servants as labourers. (Similarly, in an expensive restaurant, your fellow diner is just as likely to be a bank teller as a company chairman.)

Only by venturing into strange places can the visitor hope to make discoveries that will lead to an inexpensive holiday. There is usually a low-cost option for everything. However attractive a beach hotel or restaurant looks, a snack or drink there is going to cost more than at the grocery store. It will probably taste better, too, in the village shop, with Mauritians for company instead of other tourists.

To prove the point, I found the Shop Owners' Association price list for drinks served in the bar of a village grocery store. In 1994, prices were as follows:

Drink		Ordinary	Chilled
Phoenix beer	(bottle, 650ml)	Rs13	Rs14
	(chop, 330ml)	7	7.50
Export	(chop)	11	11.50
Blue Marlin	(bottle)	14	15
	(chop)	7.50	8
Guinness	(bottle)	16	17
	(chop)	8.50	9
Malta		5.50	6
Rum	(measure)	2.50	
	(bottle)	35 (on premises)	
	(bottle)	31 (off premises)	

Help

Medical/Dental

Wherever you are staying, the management will recommend the nearest doctor or dentist for an emergency. The largest hotels have a nurse and small dispensary on their premises, and a roster of doctors on call. Medical facilities in Mauritius are excellent, with private clinics and public hospitals available if a doctor advises hospitalisation. The standard is the equivalent of major countries and the cost of treatment will be a lot less than private treatment in Europe.

This list of hospitals and clinics was provided by the Tourist Office.

Important Hospitals
Dr Jeetoo Hospital (ex-Civil)
Volcy Pougnet Street, Port Louis. Tel: 212 3201

Moka Eye Hospital
Moka. Tel: 433 4015

Princess Margaret Orthopaedic Hospital
Candos. Tel: 454 3031

Sir Seewoosagur Ramgoolam National Hospital
Pamplemousses. Tel: 264 1661

Private Clinics
Clinique du Bon Pasteur
Thomy Pitot Street, Rose Hill. Tel: 464 7238

City Clinic
Sir Edgar Laurent Street, Port Louis. Tel: 241 2851

Clinique Darné
G Guibert Street, Floreal. Tel: 686 2307

Clinique Ferrière
College Lane, Curepipe. Tel: 676 3332

Clinique de Lorette
Higginson Street, Curepipe. Tel: 675 2911

Clinique Mauricienne
Réduit. Tel: 454 3061

Clinique du Nord
Coast Road, Tombeau Bay. Tel: 247 2532

Clinique de Quatre Bornes
Stevenson Avenue, Quatre Bornes. Tel: 425 0423

Pharmacies, well stocked with European/US proprietary medicines, are also open in the evenings in the towns, and there are dispensaries and health centres in most villages. There is a Social Hygiene and Venereal Diseases Clinic at Maillard Street, Port Louis, and at Dr Bouloux Health Centre, Cassis, tel: 212 0811.

Police
To call the police (or fire or ambulance) in an emergency dial 999.

If reporting theft of property covered by insurance, ask the police for a copy of your report to substantiate your insurance claim.

Crime against tourists is low-key, often the result of foolishness on the part of the tourist. Normal precautions should be observed. Hotels provide safe-keeping facilities.

Police Headquarters, Line Barracks, Port Louis, tel: 208 1212.

Weather
For weather information, you need only dial 96.

Drug and Alcohol Addiction
If you have a problem, there is a hotline for help: 212 6284. Counselling takes place from 09.00 to 16.00, Monday to Friday.

Environment
There is an SOS service on the environment at 212 5050. Stray dogs, as a menace, can be reported to 464 5084.

Airport
If you need to leave in a hurry, you can check flights, or alert the emergency services, on 637 3531.

Consular help
Embassies, High Commission and their consular offices do not exist as 'minders' or information bureaux. Whereas consuls will help in an emergency, repatriation to your home country at your government's expense is not one of the services generally provided. It is not necessary to register at your consulate unless staying in Mauritius for an extended period.

Complaints

Complaints to achieve redress ought to be made while you are in Mauritius, not after you've returned home. Go to the top and make your complaint in a reasonable manner. Keep copies of any documentation submitted. Usually your comments, if justified, will bring about an acceptable solution.

Letters of complaint to the Mauritius Government Tourist Office (E Anquetil Building, Sir S Ramgoolam Street, Port Louis, tel: 201 1703) marked for the attention of the general manager, will be investigated, especially as the MGTO prides itself on Mauritius being a 'no problem' destination.

The National Transport Authority (Barrack Street, Port Louis, tel: 212 9502) has an inspectorate to investigate complaints about transport, particularly the taxi service.

140

Giant waterlilies, *Victoria amazonica*, in the pond at the Royal Botanic
Gardens, Pamplemousses

PART TWO

A GUIDE TO THE DISTRICTS AND ISLANDS

INTRODUCTION
This section describes the nine districts of Mauritius based on the traditional boundaries. The final section covers the islands.
1. Port Louis
2. Pamplemousses
3. Rivière du Rempart
4. Flacq
5. Grand Port
6. Savanne
7. Black River
8. Plaines Wilhems
9. Moka
10. Rodrigues and Island Dependencies of Mauritius

Hotels and restaurants
Although many of the hotels and restaurants are mentioned elsewhere, I have described here those I was able to visit according to the district in which they are located. The full address and other details of each are included in a separate list in the Appendices.

The hotels and restaurants seem to fit naturally into one of these broad categories: (a) those catering for tourists, (b) those which are enjoyed by Mauritians as well as by tourists, (c) the cut-price establishments which tourists would not normally patronise.

To describe in one word the general 'feel' of a place, I have used one of three numbers or terms, thus: 1 = *Grand*, 2 = *Medium*, 3 = *Basic*.

This does not necessarily match up with (a) (b) and (c) categories mentioned above, because not all places catering for tourists are by any means *Grand*. Many tourists come from neighbouring Madagascar and Réunion and stay very happily in places away from the beach that fall into my *Basic* category. These would be ideal for the visitor on a limited budget.

Some establishments are exceptional for some reason, perhaps offering a *Grand* experience in the *Medium* price range, whereas some places that I grade *Basic* might be charging *Medium* rates. I've tried to clarify that in the notes. The room rates supplied by the MGTO and by hotels themselves are called 'public rates'. This means they are the rates announced to the general public and actually bear little connection with the rate a guest actually pays. Although no charter flights come to Mauritius, most people who stay in the *grand* or *medium* category hotels come on some kind of package deal that includes flight, hotel room and one or two meals. They don't pay anywhere near the public rates. Even independent travellers choosing to stay at a *grand* or *medium* hotel will be able to secure rooms at a rate lower than the public one, as long as they ask.

Because prices change without notice, where costs are given they should be regarded as approximate.

Hotels
1. *Grand*   A deluxe hotel with lots of frills priced at least from Rs2,500 single per night, and for some properties that are very grand, over Rs5,000 single per night.
2. *Medium*   A wide range of acceptable hotels, some with lots of facilities, priced from Rs800 to Rs2,500 single, per night.
3. *Basic*   No frills but fun, ranging from boarding houses with shared bathrooms to beachside bungalows, priced from Rs150 to Rs800 per person per night.

Restaurants
1. *Grand*   Wonderful food, excellent service and splendid decor or location. You pay for it, too.
2. *Medium*   Either the food or the service is good but not necessarily both.
3. *Basic*   Cheap, enjoyable food but basic service and amenities.

*Exchange rate in February 1994: Rs26 = £1; Rs18.65 = US$1.

THE DISTRICTS

Port Louis

Port Louis looks best from the sea. It is a booming city that combines new buildings with old, contrasting with the spires and peaks of the threadbare mountain range behind. In the centre is Pouce, poking 811 metres into the sky like Jack Horner's thumb. On its left is Pieter Both, a peak named after a Dutch notable who drowned in the bay, distinguished by the boulder balanced precariously on its tip.

To the right the city's boundary extends along a switchback of daunting crags: Snail Rock, Goat Rock, Spear Grass Peak and Quoin Bluff. The sheer sides of Signal Mountain (323m) dominate the western flank of the town. Also included within the district are Plaine Lauzon and the mouth of the Grand River Northwest.

Solid Victorian warehouses and modern concrete towers, like sawn-off skyscrapers, crowd the flat expanse of the city. Houses claim the land right up to the foothills of Pouce Valley, leaving open spaces only on the plain of the Champ de Mars and the isolated 86 metre high hill in the middle of the city, on which perches the battered vulture of a fort called the Citadel. Tall Royal Palms have somehow survived the city's growth to form an avenue of greenery leading from the waterfront up the centre of the Place D'Armes to Government House.

The settlement's earliest name was Turtle Bay, so called by the Dutchman Matelief de Jonge in 1606 because of the great numbers of turtles and land tortoises 'as fat as pigs' which he found there.

It was officially named as Port Louis in 1722 by M Denyon, the commander of the first party of French settlers. The name was chosen either to honour the then young King Louis XV (1715–1774) or to link the settlement with Port Louis in Brittany from which, at that time, French seamen sailed for India. When Mahé de Labourdonnais arrived here in 1735, however, the harbour was still being called Port North West.

In 1735 dense vegetation covered the area, except for land cleared between where the theatre now stands and the *Chien de Plomb* at the bayside, which was the ships' watering-point.

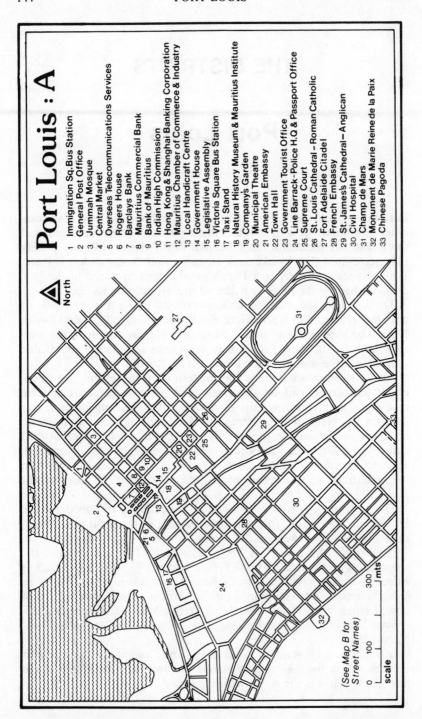

Port Louis : A

1 Immigration Sq. Bus Station
2 General Post Office
3 Jummah Mosque
4 Central Market
5 Overseas Telecommunications Services
6 Rogers House
7 Barclays Bank
8 Mauritius Commercial Bank
9 Bank of Mauritius
10 Indian High Commission
11 Hong Kong & Shanghai Banking Corporation
12 Mauritius Chamber of Commerce & Industry
13 Local Handicraft Centre
14 Government House
15 Legislative Assembly
16 Victoria Square Bus Station
17 Taxi Stand
18 Natural History Museum & Mauritius Institute
19 Company's Garden
20 Municipal Theatre
21 American Embassy
22 Town Hall
23 Government Tourist Office
24 Line Barrack - Police H.Q & Passport Office
25 Supreme Court
26 St. Louis Cathedral – Roman Catholic
27 Fort Adelaide Citadel
28 French Embassy
29 St. James's Cathedral – Anglican
30 Civil Hospital
31 Champ de Mars
32 Monument de Marie Reine de la Paix
33 Chinese Pagoda

North

(See Map B for Street Names)

scale
0 100 300 mts

There were sixty mud huts thatched with palm leaf in this clearing, the homes of the French East India Company staff. Soldiers lived in makeshift shelters of straw. The stream running down from Pouce Mountain formed a swampy gully dividing the plain in two. The right side, as viewed from the sea, became the residential area while the left was given over to commerce.

A statue of Mahé de Labourdonnais stands overlooking the harbour he created. This is a national monument, erected in 1859 at the entrance to the Place D'Armes (now named Place Sookdeo Bissoondoyal), where it is isolated on a roundabout in the midst of a daily scrum of traffic. Nearby, a stone set into the patch of lawn at the foot of the palm trees commemorates the 250th anniversary of his founding of Port Louis. City status was conferred on the town by Queen Elizabeth II in 1966.

Port Louis is the seat of government and the most populous town in Mauritius, with 15% of the island's population. Those with French pretensions call it **Por' Louie**; those with English affectations say *Port Loo-iss*. Most people compromise and pronounce it *Port Loo-ee*.

It is a city of boundless charm that has preserved a village soul, perhaps because the crowds of people who descend from the plateau towns during the day to work, leave the city alone at night. Its streets are empty then, echoing with the sound of recorded music from wedding parties in upstairs halls, the click of dominoes from Chinese club rooms, or the call of the *muezzin*.

Viewed from the Citadel hill or from Signal Mountain – unfortunately out of bounds now for security reasons – the layout of the city is uncomplicated: rectangular street blocks as far as the eye can see. There are only a few patches of green, no great river courses through it, and the surrounding mountains are invariably parched, showing their sharp features beneath a thin covering of scrub.

The Port Louis Through Road is just that, cutting through the city, straight along the waterfront, linking the south of the island with the north. On one side of it are the **harbour**, deep water docks, modern warehouses, bulk fuel storage tanks and containers. A new container terminal was built in 1980 on reclaimed land. Boats can be hired on the waterfront to tour the harbour and, on ships' open days, to visit vessels tied up at the docks.

On the other side of the road is the **city**. It is a pleasant place to walk since balconies overhanging the streets provide shade from the sun or shelter from the rain. Many of the pavements are flagged with the original blocks that have served pedestrians since before there were motor vehicles, first introduced in 1903. There are so many new office blocks going up, you'll often have to step into the road to avoid the building sites. And of the 70,000 motor vehicles registered in Mauritius, most seem to be in Port Louis, except on Sundays when the streets are quieter.

Facing the **Place d'Armes**, Government House is at the far end of the old parade ground. On the left is an Egyptian-looking bust on a plinth honouring Emmanuel Anquetil, syndicalist and politician, 1885–1946. There is also a taxi stand here with Mercedes and large Japanese cars, and drivers who delight in carrying tourists.

On the next patch of grass, the bust in chocolate-coloured stone is of Renganaden Seeneevassen, politician (1910–1958), whose funeral attracted more than 50,000 people. The statue in the next square of lawn is of Sir John Pope Hennessy. He was the most outstanding governor of the latter part of the 19th century (1883–1889), sympathetic to calls of Mauritius for Mauritians. Opposite him is a statue of Sir William Newton, a lawyer and fiery champion of reform, which bears the inscription '*ses compatriotes reconnaissants*'.

The roads at each side of the Place D'Armes' lawns have been named Duke of Edinburgh Avenue (on the left, facing Government House) and Queen Elizabeth Avenue (on the right). The old thoroughfares of Royal Street and Chaussée meet in front of Government House. The Chaussée, originally a causeway of rough stones constructed over a swamp, was rebuilt in 1779 by a French engineer. The trickle that remains of Pouce Stream runs down a concrete gully under the small **Chaussée Bridge**.

A statue of a matronly Queen Victoria stands at the entrance to **Government House**, with a statue of a nearly forgotten man, Sir William Stevenson, governor 1857–1863, in the forecourt behind her. He claimed the same privileges for Mauritian officials that British ones enjoyed.

Government House dates back to 1738 when Labourdonnais built the ground floor and the wings that form the forecourt's sides from stone. In General Decaen's time, wooden upper storeys were added, just before the British arrived in 1810. Although no longer the home of the governor, the building is at the centre of government since, together with the office block adjoining it and the Legislative Assembly Chamber behind it (built in 1965), it is part of the parliamentary complex. It is used for offices now and is not open to the public.

The road (Intendance Street) beside the government buildings leads past the Treasury (designated as a national monument) into Gillet Square (Place Foch), with its incongruous Parisian wrought-iron street lamp preserved on a traffic island. Across the road is the **theatre**, its magnificent colonnaded front a sharp contrast to the mediocre buildings around it. French architect Pierre Poujade designed it and Governor Farquhar laid the foundation stone in 1820. It was opened in 1822 with a production by a Creole amateur troupe of *La Partie de Chasse de Henri IV*. It is said to be the oldest theatre in the southern hemisphere.

The days of its popularity as an opera house have passed and it is now only by chance that you'll be able to see inside since it is invariably closed and shuttered. The interior has been restored to evoke its days of grandeur with an awning suspended from the ceiling to give a false dome on which have been painted a dozen happy little cherubs and the names of European composers. The crest of Mauritius is above the stage.

It is worth visiting the theatre whenever it's open just for the atmosphere – which will probably be better than the production.

City Hall, built in 1962, is a few yards away up Koenig Street, on the right. Outside is a concrete block tower without walls, with steps spiralling up its interior to the clock at the top. This represents the fire towers formerly used by watchmen to overlook the town's wooden buildings. There is a library in City Hall open to the public.

Opposite is the **Emmanuel Anquetil Building** with its pigeon-patrolled plaza, post office and tourist office.

The Police Station and Supreme Court (a listed building) are on the right side of Pope Hennessy Street with the **Cathedral Square** on the left. Now used as a car park, the square contains the remains of a fountain dating to 1788, an obelisk, and what appears to be a statue of a medieval king, St Louis, erected in 1896.

The Roman Catholic **Cathedral of St Louis** is the third church on this site. Built in 1932 in awesome twin-towered imitation gothic, it replaced the previous one, demolished in 1925. An earlier church dating from 1756 was destroyed by cyclone. The **Episcopal Place**, a 19th century mansion with airy verandas more suited in style to the tropics than the cathedral, stands beside it.

The Luna Park Cinema, the largest in Port Louis, is in the next block of Pope Hennessy Street. Other cinemas in the city are the Classic, the Rex and the Majestic, which show movies dubbed in French, and the Venus which, like the Luna Park, features Hindi movies.

On the left, at number 25 and easily overlooked because of its overgrown garden, is the oldest hotel in Mauritius, the **National**, built in 1925. In 1948, it was described by a visitor as being 'greyish white with ancient paint ... the ground floor consisted of one long room, or hall, flagged with black and white marble'. Incredibly, it looks exactly the same now as it did 45 years ago.

The original Franco-Mauritian owners have been replaced by a Chinese family who have been there 30 years, running the long-room restaurant at an unruffled pace. The original reception desk serves as a bar counter with drink bottles (and a dust-coated model of a dodo) on shelves behind it. The owner sits there writing down orders. His wife comes out from the kitchen from time to time, looks at the orders and wanders back to cook them. A doll-like girl drifts around declining to take orders, waiting on tables according to a system of priorities known only to herself.

The atmosphere is that of a treasured, run-down private club that seems decades behind the rest of the city. The menu contains routine

Chinese dishes with extras such as venison steak and salad. Portions are small. The restaurant is only open for lunch. It is a rare glimpse of pre-boom Mauritius, a place that seems to have more ghosts than guests, since it no longer functions as a hotel, all its rooms being closed 'for repairs'.

Behind walls and railings in side streets nearby are Creole mansions where life probably goes on in the same bygone manner. At number 36 in Pope Hennessy Street there is the **Rossignol Hotel**, a newish Chinese-run guesthouse with 21 rooms (with toilet/shower), costing from Rs250. There is a restaurant downstairs.

People still promenade in the **Champ de Mars** as they did in the 19th century, although joggers and children have taken the place of crinolined ladies and their beaux. There is a statue of King Edward VII in the centre (with birds nesting in the crook of his arm) and the tomb of Malartic (governor, 1792–1800) at the far end of the road. The obelisk erected in 1846 snapped in a cyclone in 1892 and was subsequently repaired.

The **Shree Vishnu Kchetra Temple** is in a tranquil location in St Denis Street, which runs parallel to the Champ de Mars, one block from it. It serves Hindus and Tamils. Shoes have to be removed and left by the bench a few yards inside the gate. The older Hindu temple is simply laid out with bright paintings and statues and places for offerings of coconuts and incense. Worshippers toll the bell to wake the gods.

In the same compound is a new Tamil temple, a single, spartan room. An ancient, sacred peepul tree (*Ficus religiosa*, known as a bo-tree in Sri Lanka) is in the garden with a plaque recording its planting by Pandit Chandan Mishra, a former *parajee* (priest). The temple is closed for five minutes at midnight when it is considered a dangerous time to disturb the gods.

The Anglican **Cathedral of St James** is in a garden block, with its entrance on Poudrière Street. As a cathedral this is a disappointment, since it looks more like a small New England mission church with its single, cream-plastered spire.

It was built in 1828, incorporating the two-metre-wide walls of the original building, a French powder magazine. Its stoutness made it a useful hurricane shelter in the last century. Inside it has a wooden ceiling and wood-panelled walls with commemorative tablets set in them. There are 12 columns in the portico at its entrance. Services in English are held on the second and fourth Sunday every month; except during times of worship, the cathedral is closed. In the same leafy compound is **St Mary's Hall**, a traditionally styled church building with ornate red-painted wooden shutters and doors.

On the north side of the Champ de Mars, at the corner of Dr Eugene Laurent and Corneille Streets, is the **Lam Soon Temple**, which is actually two temples. The newer one, built in the 19th century, is in the foreground, a curious adaptation of British colonial architecture to Confucian Buddhist needs, the columns of the veranda painted red and gold and the interior devoted to worship. The centre altar is extravagantly carved while the interior walls are simple. Lists in Chinese showing the names of the temple's sponsors are posted on the exterior walls.

The ancient custodian makes a point of telling visitors the temple is independently run and depends on offerings for its upkeep, indicating the offertory box. Once you've put something in, you're invited to walk through to the more dilapidated wooden temple beyond. Its frail female keeper bangs a gong to announce your visit, but the transistor radio keeps playing pop music and the neon light she switches on chases away the atmosphere of the gloomy interior.

This temple doubles as a commercial enterprise, not only selling incense sticks and flags but also soft drinks and pickles. Business, according to the old custodian, is brisk on race days. The temple is open from 06.00 to 14.00 every day.

On the right down Church Street, at its junction with Suffren Street, is a typical Port Louis grog shop. Its conversion from a solid granite block store to a bar has involved little more than installing a counter, some shelves and, long ago, a coat of whitewash. The Viking boat insignia of Grays Bottling Company is displayed on one wall and I used to think the place was called Grays until a regular told me it is known as **Jolie Madame**, after its original owner.

There are *gadjacks* in plenty here 'to cut the rum', including squid steak and roast eggs. Chinese-run, it now opens only from 16.00 to 19.00.

The shortage of bars in Port Louis has a precedence in history. In 1722, there were 125 drinking shops known to the police. The French governor, Ternay, found this excessive and closed all but 30, eventually reducing that number to four.

Beyond the cathedral, Church Street becomes Sir William Newton Street and links up with Desforges Street, which is now known as Sir Seewoosagur Ramgoolam Street after the country's first Prime Minister, who was Governor General when he died in 1985. The **City Hotel** (formerly the Ambassador) is here, an attempt at the European concept of a hotel with concierge, reception and hotel staff. The rooms, however, are small and gloomy and not very welcoming. Double rooms have baths, single showers. *Basic* category. There is a restaurant.

In the same street, in the block between Pasteur and Jummah Mosque Street, is **Providence**, a Muslim-run eatery that stays open until after midnight. A cook stands outside frying *gateaux piments* in an enormous wok. The entrance is blocked on one side by a counter of take-away delicacies such as the hamburger-like chicken *catless*, *tikkas* (fried chicken on a skewer) and sausage-shaped **kabobs** with meat and vegetable filling.

The other side of the narrow entrance is taken up by baskets and shelves of long, crusty loaves. It is always crowded but inside, up three steps, is a dining room divided into half-a-dozen cubicles, with a large table and benches in each. Step outside to the loo, and you will find yourself in a neglected courtyard of solid grey granite blocks, the kind of place that reeks of history. The menu is whatever hot dish is available from the kitchen or snacks from the counter. Soft drinks only. It is a lively place where the erratic service improves when they know you.

Other eateries open late in the evening, possibly until 22.00, are to be found at the Plaine Verte end of Ramgoolam Street, but none have quite the panache of Providence. Pharmacies open late in the evening are also to be found along here. This street is especially crowded at Christmas time, with vendors selling plastic gifts and toys from pavement stalls. It is one of the main shopping streets for locals with many fabric and clothes shops.

Upstairs at number 53 is the **Flore Orientale** restaurant, which has window tables overlooking the street and the courtyard of a white, wooden Creole house opposite. There is an informal cocktail bar here and 11 tables with a menu offering *medium* category priced Chinese specialities such as golden fish balls as well as squid and venison.

The road up to the **Citadel** used to be called Ti-Mountain Street because of its small hill. It is now a continuation of Jummah Mosque Street. A French post existed here in the 18th century but the fort, commonly known as the Citadel, was begun in 1835 and named after Queen Adelaide, wife of William IV. It was built by the British who were worried that the French settlers would revolt against the abolition of slavery.

Its solid, dark-grey stone walls and two-tiered rooms, built around a central barrack square, are a depressing sight. It was abandoned for over a century until brought to life in the 1980s with open-air sound-and-light shows, recreating the history of Mauritius, and pop concerts. If you ever go there at night, wrap up warmly. Coaches take tourists there to look at the view over the city, and there are plans in 1994 to open it to the public with a restaurant and bar.

The best of the *basic* guesthouses in Port Louis, the **Bourbon Tourist Hotel**, is in Jummah Mosque Street. Located above shops opposite Chinese warehouses, it offers 16 twin-bedded rooms with shower and toilet. The rooms are bright and large and the atmosphere is friendly and welcoming. Although it's noisy during the day, at night all is quiet, unless wedding celebrations erupt with firecrackers and dance music from one of the upstairs halls nearby. There is a first floor restaurant and bar in case of emergency, but since the hotel is on the edge of the Chinese Quarter there are plenty of places for eating in the area. Continental breakfast is served in the rooms. The rates are from Rs350 per night.

In the same block, on the corner with L'Homme Street, is an
Indian foodstall which does a roaring trade during the day. Especially
good is the *poisson vindaye*.

The **Palais d'Or** a few doors further down, is a Chinese restaurant
that can be raucous at nights, with some *basic*-rate guest rooms
attached. Jummah Mosque Street leads into Royal Street and gives a
view of the splendid 'wedding cake' architecture of the **Jummah
Mosque**.

The mosque extends an entire block, its white towers and friezes
imposing grace on the clutter of lock-up shops beneath its balconies.
Its huge teak doors are priceless, ornately carved and inlaid with ivory.
Tourists can only glimpse the marble-cloistered mysteries within. The
muezzin's call from the minaret before dawn is the signal not only for
prayer but for the cacophony of the city to erupt. This mosque, built
in the middle of the last century, is the island's most impressive. It
opened when Muslims (inaccurately called Arabs in those days)
formed an exclusive merchant group in the neighbourhood.

Now this section of Royal Street is the centre of the city's Chinese
Quarter of stores, warehouses and restaurants, its shops bright with
the plastic and chrome knick-knacks much in demand by modern-day
Mauritians. Each door opens off the street into a retail/wholesale
business of some kind. There are small, not very pleasant, eating
places in side streets and a hint at night of an inscrutable underworld
which, although it won't affect the visitor, lurks behind closed shutters.

In E Anquetil Street, leading to Royal Street, there are some local
eateries as distinctive as their names, such as **Restaurant Everyday** and
Hotel Dingdong. The corner where the street joins Royal Street is the
place for street food at night, with stools to sit on while enjoying
Chinese soups and *mine*. The corner of the next block is for rice and
chicken with an African touch.

In Royal Street, there are a few places open in the evenings, all
within a radius of 50 metres. The **Lai Min** restaurant (*medium*) has
undergone many changes in the 45 years of its existence. Now run by
the son of the founder, it has been upgraded gradually from a postwar eating house into a smart, air-conditioned restaurant. There is a
takeaway counter at the ground floor entrance, open daily from 09.00
to 22.00, selling grills, fast food, pastries and soft drinks. Upstairs is
an arts and crafts showroom with handmade model ships, sea chests,
Chinese fashions and beach wear.

The restaurant is open for lunch and in the evenings from 18.00 to
22.00. It specialises in quality Chinese food, with both Cantonese and
Szechuan dishes prepared by expert chefs from mainland China. The
celebration banquet, with menu card especially prepared for a party
and T-shirts as gifts, is a ten-course feast. Diners who manage to
survive the baptism ceremony of drinking seven different Chinese

liqueurs lined up in front of them, win certificates. The record is 52 downed by one guest in an after-dinner session!

On the opposite side of Royal Street is my favourite pub in Port Louis, a joint known as **Hotel Onu**. The name is an acronym but none of the patrons know what for. It is an old building with flagstone floor and granite block walls, at the junction with Anquetil Street. It's not a hotel at all but a streetside tavern with doors wide open to the road. It reeks of atmosphere and is a friendly, safe place, with the barman and his bottle boy ever alert to hustle out foreigners if a fight is about to break out.

The Onu isn't for the squeamish and it can get boisterous. However, it is a wonderful place to observe the streetlife of Port Louis. It closes around 20.00, unless there are enough customers to keep it open. Prices seem flexible until a customer is regarded as a regular. The two badly painted murals, of a couple dancing *séga* and a wistful Paul and Virginie, add a touch of glamour.

The Chinese casino, **L'Amicale de Port Louis**, is on the other corner of Anquetil and Royal Streets. This is open 19.00–02.00 every night and on Sundays from 13.00. A block away, at the corner of Anquetil and Queen Streets, there is one of the new *medium* category Chinese restaurants that have opened since 1986.

Kwang Chow is on the first floor, and specialises in Cantonese cuisine. Starters are displayed on a table and the manager will help a novice customer find a main dish on the menu. I recommend anything with grandmother's sauce. This place is popular with Mauritians of all walks of life. There is a cocktail bar and a TV set and a private dining room if required. It is open from 11.30 to 23.00, closed 15.00–18.00.

For a contrast, if you're a sailor or can find one to take you in, don't miss the **Merchant Navy Club** at the harbour end of Rivière Street. The lights from the veranda of this colonial mansion shine across its garden, vivid in the darkness of the street, offering a welcome to seafarers of all nationalities and rank. Although its facilities are for the benefit of seamen only, visitors may sometimes obtain permission from the Resident Welfare Officer to look around.

The club is not a mission. It opened originally in 1857 as the Mauritius Sailors' Home, becoming the Merchant Navy Club a century later. It is a local society with no connection with other clubs elsewhere. It is subsidised by a percentage of the Port Welfare dues.

It is famed among mariners as one of the best of its kind in the world. The setting is perfect, tranquil sanity in the midst of the heat and bustle of the port. The premises spread the width of the entire street block, with a lounge bar and veranda, a restaurant for snacks, rooms for table tennis, billiards and darts, loggias and garden alcoves, badminton, volleyball and outdoor movies. It is open every day (except January 1) from 09.00 to 23.00 hours.

Not far from here, at the Farquhar Street end of Corderie Street, is another establishment in a colonial building, the **Namaste**. Located behind the market, this restaurant is astonishingly good value in the *basic* category. Its block walls are decorated with dark brown ply-wood, the chairs are chrome imitation of cane work, and the tables are formica topped. Anywhere else it would be trendy, here it con-centrates on serving quick, cheap lunches. The menu is written on the cardboard insert from a shirt pack. There are bottles of tap water on the tables. Meat or chicken or fish are served with a plate of rice and a side salad in separate dishes. It is closed in the evenings.

The **Immigration Square Bus Station** is close by, at the end of Pasteur Street, still known by city denizens as Hospital Street, because of the hospital that was in the square. It is difficult to know which bus queue to join but other passengers are helpful. Buses go to the north of the island from here.

The attraction of the **Tan Yan** bar in Farquhar Street is being able to sit at a table by the open door of this old building, and watch people hurrying between the bus station and the market. It's a scruffy place (*basic*), open only during the day. There are floor to ceiling shelves behind the bar counter which a small boy scales like a squirrel if you order something from the top shelf.

The **market**, in the block between Queen and Farquhar Streets, spills out into Farquhar Street with vendors' stalls in the gutters sell-ing colourful, Mauritius-made underwear and beach shorts, and fruit imported from South Africa. The meat and fish market is on the right, in the block that leads to the new highway that was Quay Street.

The stone and ironworks of the market are listed as national monuments, but the market buildings themselves are temporary shelters which catch fire occasionally. In 1981, half the market was burnt down. The wrought iron work above the entrance has the initials VR (Victoria Regina) intertwined in it.

The vegetable market houses stalls with carefully arranged piles of exotic fruit and vegetables, including little bundles of soup ingre-dients. Adjoining this is a veritable souk, a bustling bazaar of narrow, crowded passageways through stalls selling everything from T-shirts to salted squid, from seashell earrings to spice powder, and from postcards to the popular alooda drink. I was warned about pickpock-ets in here but the atmosphere isn't threatening and it is a popular place to hunt down souvenir bargains. The market is open all week, Sunday mornings included. There are also some souvenir shops in Farquhar and Queen Streets.

Across the throughroad that has been constructed out of Quay Street, at the other side of the Central Market, is the **General Post Office**. It seems very much a Victorian widow of a building, at odds with the modern world racing by.

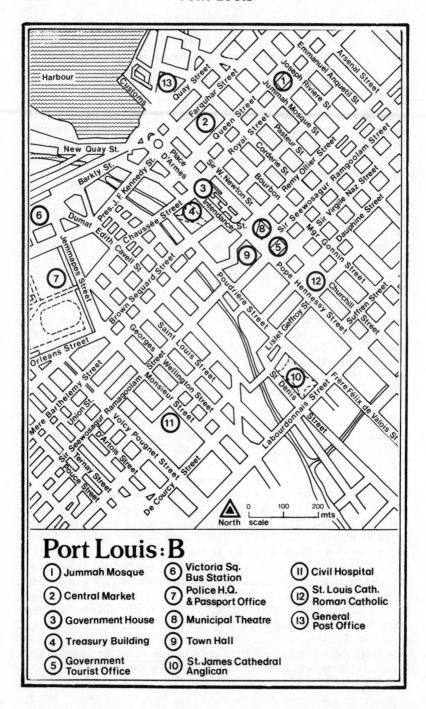

Port Louis:B

1. Jummah Mosque
2. Central Market
3. Government House
4. Treasury Building
5. Government Tourist Office
6. Victoria Sq. Bus Station
7. Police H.Q. & Passport Office
8. Municipal Theatre
9. Town Hall
10. St. James Cathedral Anglican
11. Civil Hospital
12. St. Louis Cath. Roman Catholic
13. General Post Office

On the next corner (Queen and Newton Streets), up a flight of stairs, is **Snow White**, a cosy restaurant with red tablecloths and smartly dressed, keen waiters serving mostly Chinese, but some European dishes. Open from 09.00 to 17.00 (closed Sundays), it's mostly lunchtime business in this *medium* category place.

Shamrock is on the corner of Royal and Corderie Streets, with views of Pouce Mountain and the city. This is open until 21.30, so serves dinner as well as lunch, with the accent on Chinese cooking. *Medium* range. Another, much older, Chinese restaurant that opens until 19.00, is the **Paloma** in L'Homme Street. *Basic* to *medium*, closed Sundays.

The entrance to the **Underground** is in Bourbon Street, with a van selling pastries outside it. Inside, a corridor leads down a few steps to a snack bar in a semi-basement. A gallery around the snack bar constitutes the restaurant. The Underground caters for lunchtime trade only, mostly office workers. In the *medium* price range, there is only an à la carte menu, while sandwiches and snacks are served 'underground' – underneath the gallery.

La **Bonne Marmite** claims to be a café, pub and restaurant and with a young man at the door to welcome you and guide you to the section you want, it is effectively all three. Located in the street (Newton) at the side of the government offices, it has a snack bar (café) on the ground floor.

Behind this is the **Rocking Boat Pub**, skilfully designed to project the ambience of a European drinking den with low lighting, dark decor and a cocktail bar with stools for the steadier drinkers. There is even a dart board. Draught beer and bar snacks are available. I wonder, though, how it can be called a pub when it closes at three in the afternoon, except when there is a special evening event in the city to keep it open.

The restaurant **Bonne Marmite** is upstairs in a grand room with attentive, if sometimes confused, staff and an occasional appearance from the lady owner. There are table d'hote and à la carte menus. It is a good setting for an impressive dinner but it's only open at lunchtime, except on special occasions. *Medium* price range with *grand* possibilities.

On the other side of the Government House complex, in Intendance Street, there is another combination of places to eat at **La Flore Mauricienne**. You enter through a pavement café, complete with umbrellas, moody waiters, and customers who sip soft drinks and hope their friends will see them. Downstairs is a self-service restaurant with arrogant staff. There is also an elegant dining room, where the accent is on European cuisine and clientele, and two rooms to keep tour parties out of the way.

The basement cafeteria is painted a strident green and equipped with triangular yellow trays on which to balance your food. There are usually three *plats du jour*, being variations of fish, chicken or meat. Wine is available by the glass, or small bottle. Patronised by regulars, it has a cliquish atmosphere. Lunch service only, *basic* to *medium* category. The restaurant itself is *medium* to *grand*, lunch only.

Probably setting a new trend in Port Louis for alfresco meals with a *grand* touch but almost *basic* in price, is the **Café du Vieux Conseil** in Old Council Street, a restored cobbled lane just opposite the Municipal Theatre. You can sit under umbrellas made in Madagascar in the courtyard, or at tables along one side. The menu is designed for impecunious gourmets with specialities like crêpes filled with smoked marlin or asparagus (at Rs70 in 1994) and a set meal of salads from the self-service salad bar, sirloin steak with Bearnaise sauce and sweet of the day or ice cream and coffee, for Rs200 (plus 10% government tax). Tea is only Rs15. There is a bar and the Café is open on Friday and Saturday evenings as well as for weekday lunches.

For a contrast, imported fast food has also reached the city, with a Pizza Hut in Newton Street, open daily 10.30–21.00.

Long famed as a favoured place for visitors, the **Carri Poulé** is in the Place d'Armes, on Duke of Edinburgh Avenue, close to the waterfront. A hostess greets visitors who are served professionally by stewards dressed in starched white shirts with frilly fronts and white bow ties. There are three dining rooms. The first has a bar with stools and tables placed by the pillars that divide the room. The second and third are to accommodate groups as well as individual diners.

There are specialities every lunchtime with a buffet twice a week (usually on Wednesdays and Fridays). The à la carte menu is extensive, with well-prepared Indian dishes that have a Mauritian touch, not the stereotyped offerings of European 'Indian' restaurants. There are even diet dishes. Wine is available by the glass. The overall impression is reassuring for the visitor both in service and cooking. *Medium* to *grand* and worth it. It's closed in the evenings except Fridays and Saturdays and on special occasions.

Across the road from the Carri Poulé, at the other side of the Place D'Armes, was the government printery, torn down for a modern building with only a relic of its Victorian horse trough to commemorate days of yore. Behind it in New Moka Street, now known as President John Kennedy Street, is **Rogers House**, a complex of airline offices, including Air Mauritius, and foreign missions with a Mauritius Telecom office on the ground floor. The **Victoria Square Bus Station** is off Dumat Street, where buses leave throughout the day for Curepipe and the plateau towns.

There are a number of *basic* category snack bars around the bus station, all serving low-cost meals, such as **Moontaza, Bistro Champs Elysées** and **Teenagers**. The **Chez Ah Nee** is a tavern for serious drinkers, with snacks on display under glass at one end of the counter.

At the corner of Victoria Square and Jemmapes Street is the **Tandoori Tourist Hotel**, with small rooms (each with shower and toilet) above a restaurant. There are more rooms for rent downstairs, in a bungalow which has a sitting room. Rates are from Rs175 with breakfast, and are negotiable for a long stay.

The **Tandoori Restaurant and Snack Bar** is deservedly popular. Open until the last bus leaves around 20.00 hours, it features a daily-changing menu with a dozen different dishes, often including venison (*cerf salmi*), tortoise and hare, but nothing tandoori at all. There is a good selection of wines, properly stored.

Behind the noisy snack bar is a backroom restaurant with brightly painted murals of waterfalls and flamingoes and red-clothed tables in a more tranquil atmosphere for appreciating the food. The cooking, and the service, in this Indo-Mauritian restaurant is 'country style', honest and pleasing. The owner, Mr Narrainen, is usually present and establishes a good rapport with visitors. I found the Tandoori was the best restaurant in the *basic* category (but not the cheapest) in the whole of Mauritius.

A block behind the Tandoori are the imposing walls of **Line Barracks**, whose foundations go back to the early days of the French occupation, when they housed 6,000 men, as well as rebel colonists after the French Revolution. A police station, police headquarters, the traffic branch and the passport and immigration offices are now there.

Nearby in Edith Cavell Street is another cheapie restaurant, **Luxor Palace**. This is unusual because of its dining gallery suspended above the snack bar, only a few feet from the ceiling. You have to lower your head as you grope for a place to sit at one of the shared tables. There is even a tiny bar counter in the corner, although the area is no bigger than a ship's cabin. The waiter is bent double as he serves dishes of chicken, meat or fish, either as *briani* (mixed with rice), *daube* or *kalia* (stews), with bread and grated cucumber/carrot salad. Beer is available. Good value, *basic* range.

There are some striking buildings in Edith Cavell Street, such as that of The Electric Motor Car Company, which is as dated as its name. Small wooden mansions from the French period are to be seen inland, especially in the block between Poudrière Street and St George Street.

In Sir Celicourt Antelme Street, off the Chaussée, is the French-inspired **La Palmeraie**, noticeable by its dark green doors, pavement shrubs in tubs, and its three different table d'hote menus displayed outside. A passageway leads to a charming restaurant set out in the covered courtyard between two houses. The walls are white pebble-dash, the woodwork dark green and the ceiling bamboo. The waiters, who wear white shirts and black bow ties, are alert; the food is French. The usual problem: only open for lunch and not at weekends. *Medium*.

Chaussée Street has shops and offices on one side, and the **Company Gardens** and the Mauritius Institute on the other. The Company Gardens derives its name from its connection with the French East India Company in the 18th century, when it was created from the marshland around the Pouce Stream. It was taken over in 1791 by the town council. For ten years after the fire of 1816, which destroyed half of Port Louis, it was the site of the town market. Its importance as the city becomes more built up is recognised both by the public, who enjoy the benches in the shade of its trees, and by the municipality.

Although it is less than a hectare in area, the garden seems larger, with its narrow paths, beds of flowers and shrubs, ponds and statues. Five of these are listed national monuments: those of Rémy Ollier, a 19th century journalist and champion of coloured people, who died age 28; Adrien d'Epinay, planter, lawyer and campaigner *against* the abolition of slavery; Léoville l'Homme, poet; Brown Sequard, scientist, and the Indian advocate, Manilal Doctor.

The superintendent of gardens, responsible for the nine gardens maintained by the municipality, has an office hidden at the end of this small city park. Other gardens include the Marie Reine de la Paix Garden Monument, dedicated to Our Lady of Peace. The first Mauritian bishop of Port Louis was consecrated there in 1989. The promenade provides a spectacular view of the city and harbour, looking from the Edward VII Boulevard beneath Signal Hill.

There are also gardens around Line Barracks and on the city's roundabouts and traffic islands. Others are at Champ de Mars, Place d'Armes, and the three sections of Plaine Verte at the northern end of Royal and Ramgoolam Streets. The main garden, where a nursery is also maintained to supply plants and flowers to them all, is the **Robert Edward Hart Garden**, by the harbour.

Some plants in the gardens are indigenous seasonal flowers, others are grown from imported seed. Eight foremen supervise 52 gardeners and 30 labourers. There is a team of nightwatchmen and daykeepers to contain the constant disappearances of plants and the rising levels of vandalism.

The **Mauritius Institute** (see chapter on Collecting Mauritius) building looks out over the Company Gardens at the other side of Poudrière Street. The ground floor Natural History Museum is popular, although its displays of stuffed birds (including a goose-down clad dodo replica), animals and fish are somewhat dowdy. It is closed on Thursdays and Sundays, otherwise open 09.00–16.00 (until 12.00 on Saturdays). Entrance is free.

A winding staircase at the back of the building leads to a first floor gallery that opens into the magnificent library, public admitted weekdays 09.00–16.00, Saturdays 09.00–12.00. Here magazines and newspapers can be read, books borrowed, and the history of Mauritius studied in its excellent reference section.

The bulk sugar terminal at the western side of the harbour is built close to the Robert Edward Hart Garden. The Muslim, Chinese, St George, Western and New Cemeteries are in this district, part of Cassis. There is an enormous head of V I Lenin sprouting from a lawn in the gardens and also a monument commemorating the landing of Commandant Dufresne d'Arsel on September 20 1715, to claim the island for France. The gardens are pleasant for a stroll despite the racket of the port. The **Western Cemetery** has scores of closely packed sepulchres and memorials, two dozen of which are listed monuments because of their historical connections.

The cemetery was moved to this present site at **Cassis** from the middle of Port Louis, where it was a source of infection, during the governorship of Desroches (1769–1772). Cassis derives its name from the cassia plant (*Cassia obtusifolia*) called, in English, Indian laburnum. The **St Sacrement Church** of Cassis became known as the Cathedral of the Poor when its congregation lost its wealthy members to the more salubrious air of the plateau towns.

The industrial estate of Plaine Lauzon is on the outskirts of Port Louis, along the highway to Curepipe. This level tract of land is named after the French commander who used to exercise his squadron of cavalry there. **Signal Mountain** between Plaine Lauzon and the city marks the western end of the mountain range around Port Louis. A beacon used to be kept alight on its summit at night, and flags hoisted there during the day as a guide for approaching vessels.

To the east of Port Louis, on the main road to the Camp Yoloff roundabout, the small church isolated in a triangle of roads is the **St Antoine Chapel**. The suburbs that side of the city include Abercrombie, named after the general who commanded the British invasion of 1810. **Sainte Croix**, nestling below Long Mountain, is famous for its church (a modern-style replacement for the original) with its shrine containing the body of Père Laval, to which pilgrims flock every September.

Vallée des Prêtres, behind Priest's Peak, which overlooks the city, gained its name because a priest had a plantation there. The housing estate of **Cité ca Cure** lies at the foot of the hills rising up to Pieter Both. Seen from the plain by the Cité, those mountain peaks are a haunting sight in the setting sun.

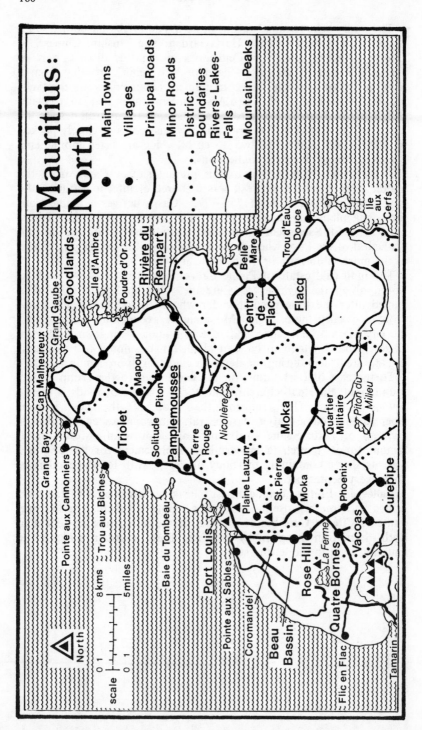

Mauritius: North

Main Towns
Villages
Principal Roads
Minor Roads
District Boundaries
Rivers - Lakes - Falls
Mountain Peaks

North

scale
0   1   8 kms
0   1   5 miles

Pamplemousses

This district in the northwestern part of the island has a population of over 75,000. Its boundary is the mountain range encircling Port Louis, with **Crève Coeur**, behind Pieter Both, as its southernmost village. It cuts through the sugar plantations east of Pamplemousses town and runs northwards to the coast at Pointe aux Cannoniers.

The name Pamplemousses was originally given to this area by the Dutch because of the orchards of shaddock trees (*pampelmoes*, a kind of grapefruit) which they imported from Java and planted there. In Tamil, the fruit has a similar name: *bambolmas*.

Places of interest include the reservoir of **La Nicolière** at 250m above sea level, behind the Nicolière mountain range. The road to the reservoir, where there is a viewpoint over the district, goes through Grande Rosalie and Villebague. **Villebague** is one of the oldest sugar estates, with a château at **Grand Rosalie**, built by Governor Villebague (1756–59). The château, not open to the public, is a copy of the headquarters of the French East India Company in Pondicherry, with 20th century additions which include the side turrets.

The remains of the old sugar factory, a derelict chimney, are listed as a national monument. At **Riche Terre**, just outside Port Louis, the windmill tower is another of the district's listed buildings.

The **Royal Botanic Gardens** at Pamplemousses are only 11kms northeast of Port Louis and are easily accessible by bus from the Immigration Square bus station. The new highway reaches there before disappearing at Mapou.

The highway was originally planned to serve an international airport in the flat lands of the north, but was built despite the abandoning of the airport project. It is of great benefit to the sugar producers, making a smooth drive to and from Port Louis.

The fence and gates at the entrance to the Botanic Gardens are scrolled in wrought iron and gained a first prize in the International Exhibition at London's Crystal Palace in 1862. The gate was a gift from François Liénard, a Frenchman, born in India in 1783, who lived in Mauritius. He was interested in natural history and created a museum in Port Louis that was destroyed in the fire of 1816. There is a listed memorial obelisk to him in the gardens.

Entrance to the gardens is free. There are no official guides, but a small, comprehensive guidebook, published in English or French, is on sale at the gate. It is written by A W Owadally, the Conservator of Forests.

The gardens are open daily from 06.00 to 18.00. Cars are allowed to drive around slowly, except on Sundays when the gardens are popular with picnickers. The entire area covers 90 arpents (93.06 acres or 37.68 hectares), of which a third is an experimental station.

The gardens' origins go back to 1729 when a French colonist acquired about half the present site, then called Mon Plaisir. Labourdonnais bought it in 1735 and created a vegetable garden (to the left of the present main entrance) beside his own residence, to supply vegetables to his household, to the town and to visiting ships. He also built a road from Port Louis to Pamplemousses and had wagons constructed to transport goods, using oxen, instead of slaves, imported from Madagascar.

The garden was also used as a nursery to encourage the growth of plants imported from Europe, the east and South America. Mulberry bushes were planted in the hope of starting a silkworm industry but were replaced by *bois noir* (*Albizia lebbeck*), to be turned into charcoal for use in the manufacture of gunpowder for the island's defence. When, in 1770, the gardens became the private property of Pierre Poivre, the administrator of the island, Pamplemousses became famous. In 1810 they reverted to government ownership.

The British neglected the gardens until James Duncan was appointed director in 1849. He stayed until 1864, introducing many of the palms including the royal palms (*Roystonea regia* and *Roystonea oleracea*) which add a majestic splendour to the main avenue. Thousands of eucalyptus trees were planted in the gardens after the malaria epidemic of 1866, for transplanting in swamps, to dry them out and reduce mosquito-breeding grounds. There are 500 species of plants in the gardens today, of which 80 are palms and 25 are indigenous to the Mascarene Islands. Since 1913 the gardens have been under the control of the Ministry of Agriculture.

Highlights of the gardens are numerous. In his guide, Mr Owadally mentions the talipot palm (*Corypha umbraculifera*) which waits until it is 40 to 60 years old (not a century as folklore has it) to bear flowers. The flowers, with over 50 million tiny blooms, reach a height of six metres above the tree. After waiting so long to flower just once, the tree dies.

In the water lily pond are the huge *Victoria amazonica* lilies from the Amazon. The circular leaves with upturned edges, like giant jewel boxes, float at one end of the rectangular pond. Their flowers open for two days only, from the late afternoon to the following morning. The first day they are cream-coloured with a heady fragrance, on the second they are pink.

Another pond contains the white and yellow flowers of the lotus (*Nelumbo nucifera*) which is held in veneration by Hindus. The betel nut palm (*Areca cathecu*) grows nearby. Its orange fruit contains the betel nut which is sliced, mixed with lime paste, wrapped in the leaf of the vine, *Piper betel*, and chewed. It's a cancer-causing stimulant which depresses the appetite and stains the gums and lips an alarming red.

A corner of the original garden is marked by a boundary stone with a fleur de lys, the royal emblem of France, etched in it. Giant bamboo (*Dendrocalamus giganteus*), which grows up to 30 metres high, acts as a windbreak along the boundary.

The **Château de Mon Plaisir** looks impressive but lightweight, perhaps because it is not the original home of Labourdonnais but an English-built office mansion. The first floor was once an herbarium and museum but is now used as a reception area. There are offices downstairs. This is a listed building, as is the reproduction of an old sugar mill close by. The former Prime Minister and Governor General, Sir Seewoosagur Ramgoolam, was cremated outside the mansion, in front of which are trees planted by visiting royal and political dignitaries.

In the tortoise pen are tortoises first brought to the gardens in 1875 from Aldabra Island to protect them from being wiped out by sea-birds (when young) or being eaten by humans (when older). The stag park contains the *Cervus timorensis russa* deer, first introduced in 1639 from Batavia.

Other animals to be seen at liberty include the indigenous flying fox (*Pteropus niger*), two species of rat (the brown Norway rat and the black arboreal Asiatic rat), and the Madagascar tenrec (*Centetes sp*). The large and beautiful black butterfly with blue windows on its wings is the *Papilio manlius*.

Indigenous birds flying around freely include the black Madagascar moorhen (*Gallinula chloropus pyrrhorrhoa*), with its red bill, and the little green heron (*Butorides striatus rutenbergi*). The small greyish bird in groups with a tip-tip-tip call is *l'oiseau Manioc* (*Malacirops borbonicus mauritianus*). Species of the *Phelsuma* lizards may be seen on palm trees. The *couleuvre* (*Lycodona aulicus*) is a small Indian snake which is secretive and nocturnal, so you are unlikely to see it. It can be aggressive but it isn't poisonous.

There are several monuments in the gardens including a stone slab which the sentimental believe marks the grave of the fictitious lovers, Paul and Virginie. Their creator, Bernadin de St Pierre, is remembered with a bust.

The **Church of St François** at Pamplemousses was built in 1759 and is the oldest in the island. Its cemetery contains the tomb of Abbé Buonavita who was Napoleon's almoner on St Helena. He settled in Mauritius after Napoleon's death in 1821. Adrien d'Epinay is buried here and so is Villebague. Their tombs are national monuments. There is also a monument in Pamplemousses to Prince Ehelepola, exiled in 1825 from Ceylon to Mauritius for plotting to oust the British from the former kingdom of Kandy. It is by the road at Powder Mill Forest, Morcellement, St Andre.

Pamplemousses was the political stronghold of Sir Seewoosagur and the large hospital in the district is named after him.

Among the canefields, with their cairns of stones piled where the land was cleared by slaves, is the village of Calebasses. The Creole saying 'When you are old, we'll send you to Calebasses' came about because of the home for old people there.

The importance of sugar in the district resulted in the island's first railway line, the Northern Line, which ran from Port Louis to Pamplemousses and on to Flacq, being constructed in 1864 to carry the sugar to Port Louis. It stopped carrying passengers in 1956 and was closed down completely in 1964. The **Solitude** industrial estate on the main road from Port Louis to the north is a former sugar plantation where diversification has opened up the area to industry.

The tourist side of the district begins in the elbow of land just north of Port Louis, in **Baie du Tombeau**. Its gruesome name is derived from it being the site of the tomb of George Weldon, an English merchant who was drowned there in 1697. His wealthy widow erected a massive monument, since vanished, which became a landmark for sailors. Treasure hunters are convinced treasure is to be found in this bay.

There is a flourishing village community and tenement block estate as well as a knitting factory and the **Capri**, a *basic* grade 18 room hotel facing the sea. The **Arc en Ciel**, opened in 1975, is the main hotel in the area, 32 dark and gloomy rooms with shower, toilet and air conditioning, by a disappointing beach. *Basic*. The public beach is by the river where there are some bungalows available for rent.

Back on the main road, at **Arsenal**, there is a road turning off to the coast that is seldom used. It passes the village of **Petit Gamin**, a typical community with colourful houses in the midst of sugar cane. Keep on the road as it curves along the coast to emerge from the canefields at **Turtle Bay** (the first marine park in Mauritius) and the **Maritim Hotel**.

A hotel priced in the *grand* category, recently built with a great deal of concrete and green paint, the Maritim stands in 60 acres by the beach. Banjo players stroll its Quarter Deck bar during the Monday to Friday happy hour (17.00–19.00) but the hotel's main attraction is its proximity (12km) to Port Louis. 180 rooms with TV and mini-bar, smallish bathrooms; luxury without too many frills.

Moulin à Poudre, on the main road, was an iron factory in the 18th century. A powder mill was in operation until 1810 when the British turned it into a prison. On the coast near **Balaclava**, at **Turtle Bay**, are the ruins of a French arsenal and further north, at Pointe aux Piments, lie the remnants of the Batterie des Grenadiers. The pension

Au Soleil Couchant is at **Pointe aux Piments**, *basic* grade with six rooms, no air conditioning, upstairs above a beach-type restaurant. The beach is beyond the *filaos* but isn't very suitable for swimming. Rooms can be rented there by the day, at half the overnight rate.

Also at Pointe aux Piments is the **Calamar Hotel**, a charming complex of 25 beachside studios and cottages with one, two or three bedrooms. *Basic* in price and somewhat rustic, there is even a small swimming pool. This would be a good place for a long stay, especially for the business visitor who wants independence and easy access to Port Louis (20 minutes) or Grand Bay (10 minutes). A similar kind of hotel, but more stylish and hence not so homely, is the neighbouring **Villas Pointe Aux Biches Protea Hotel**. Low *medium* in price with 52 rooms with kitchenettes on two storeys, the thatched villas are located around a swimming pool facing the beach. The hotel runs a free bus shuttle service to Grand Bay.

The largest Hindu temple in Mauritius is at **Triolet**. It is an amalgamation of seven temples added to the original **Maheswarnath Temple**, built in 1857. The town is named after Pierre Triolet, a landowner in the days of the French. There is a Yoga Health Centre in this urban community and a Cyclone Refugee Centre.

The beach road runs parallel to the main road, through the extended hamlet of **Trou aux Biches**. There is supposed to have been a small watering hole here frequented by female deer. Hence its name, compared with Trou aux Cerfs at Curepipe, which was used by the males of the species.

A good *basic* category guesthouse with five pleasant rooms, called **Hotel de la Sirène**, is located here, five metres from the beach. There is a small, pretty restaurant with mirror windows so outsiders can't see in; Indian specialities. Along the coast road are some *basic* self-catering apartments and some seafood restaurants.

There is an aquarium centre on this coast road, open daily, with 36 tanks for fish and living coral from the local waters, and with sea souvenirs on sale.

Basic in atmosphere and price is the **Etoile de Mer Hotel**, next to the public beach and close to the aquarium. There are 37 rooms plus four studios and five suites. The units have been fitted into a small area and are bright and cheerful, some with fridge and kitchen. There is an open-air restaurant by the road.

The **Trou aux Biches Village Hotel** that hugs the beach is close by. Guests checking into this Beachcomber hotel are given a map of the property, which consists of 205 air-conditioned guest units in Mauritian-style pavilions (four units to each one), set in 40 hectares of tropical garden. The hotel, in the *grand* category, was built in 1971. It has become so popular it is usually fully booked. It can't increase the number of guest villas so is improving the quality. Every room has a tea-making facility and fridge.

Watersports, except deep sea fishing and scuba diving, are free. There is free use of the nine hole golf course across the road behind the swaying casuarinas. The hotel has two restaurants, a children's club, a disco and a casino.

Perhaps because it is not on the beach side of the road, the **Casuarina Village Hotel** is in the *medium* price range, but the ambience is definitely *grand*. It has dazzlingly white, fairy-tale cottages, round like toadstools, fully furnished with kitchen, bathroom (solar-heated hot water) and one or two bedrooms. There are a freshwater swimming pool, bar and restaurant. Family apartments include a lounge/dining room. Good place for stylish holiday independence, close to the beach and casino.

The coast road continues to **Mont Choisy** where the new **PLM Azur Hotel** (88 rooms, *grand* price range, *medium* ambience) is walled off from the road. Under French management, with a created beach, all rooms in the block have sea views. Bathrooms have bidets.

The French holiday camp, **Club Méditerranée** (192 rooms) is isolated on Pointe aux Cannoniers, with a polite security guard turning away all visitors except those with permits during visiting hours. (Hours are weekdays 10.00–11.00, 14.30–16.00; weekends 10.00–11.00.) The club is known for its non-stop entertainment and guests stay on an all-inclusive plan that includes all meals and unlimited wine. Colonial style bungalows with terrace and balcony are situated in 45 hectares of botanical park, with over 200 species of trees and flowers for guests to enjoy.

The *grand* restaurant, **Bateau Ivre**, in Pointe aux Cannoniers, is renowned for seafood and its ambience of exclusivity. Meat eaters can try **Le Carnivore**, also in Pointe aux Cannoniers, and open evenings only, 19.00–22.30, no Sundays.

For horse riding, there is the Club Hippique close to the Club Med. Self-catering, *basic* category apartments are 200 metres away around the Pointe, where **Seapoint Beach Bungalows** are located. These are apartments in blocks with lounge, dining room and toilet downstairs and two bedrooms and toilet/shower upstairs.

Rivière du Rempart

Rivière du Rempart is a compact district of contrasts, stretching right across the north of Mauritius and including the tourist hot spots of Grand Bay on the northwest coast, the industrial/agricultural area of Goodlands, and the rugged northeast coast around Poudre d'Or. The town of Rivière du Rempart is in the east of the district, originally named Rampart River because its steep banks resembled ramparts.

Grand Bay gapes inland beyond **Pointe aux Cannoniers**, providing a deep and sheltered bay, often as calm as a lake. It is the place for sailing, self-catering accommodation, and a selection of hotels and restaurants that are among both the worst and best in the island. It is the only area blatantly devoted to mass tourism.

Grand Bay is the safety valve of Mauritius – the place where ordinary tourists, and locals, can go to let off steam without having to pretend to be wealthy jetsetters. You can get anything in Grand Bay, but it will cost a little more than elsewhere in the island.

The road around the bay is dotted with restaurants. A few kiosks by the beach sell shells, fruit and vegetables. Despite its image as a tourist resort, the action is not 'non stop'. Restaurants are open only for a couple of hours at lunchtime and a few hours in the evening, never very late. The opening hours of Phil's Pub (11.30–14.30; 18.30–22.30) are worse than those of an English pub. Getting a drink in the afternoon in Grand Bay requires some research.

Phil's Pub is actually one of the most distinguished restaurants in Grand Bay (most of the others are Chinese) as it doubles as **L'Assiette du Pêcheur**, with superb seafood. On the second floor of the Relais des Iles building in the centre of the town, with a grand view of the bay, it is *medium* in price and a popular escape for guests from the nearby upmarket hotels.

Tea (and drinks) are available at the **Café de la Plage**, where customers sit on wooden stools at wooden tables set in the sand in a compound by the beach. It resembles a typical promenade beach café in its laidback atmosphere, and sense of being at the centre of things. *Medium* in price, it is open 11.00 to 22.00 hours.

David Sullivan reported:

'To stay cheaply in Grand Bay walk around with luggage or backpack. Some sharp-looking young locals will offer to arrange your accommodation. Places in town, one or two blocks away from the waterside, cost half or less than the price of anything on the bay. Lots of them available. Bargain down and prices are well within the *basic* range. We found a great place above **La Boutik Dodo** (a little convenience store with beer considerably cheaper than the main street supermarkets) off Mahatma Gandhi street.'

Despite its raffish reputation, quite unjustified really, Grand Bay is a delightful place to stay since it combines local living (lots of fishing and a beach by a town, not miles from one) within walking distance of sophisticated resorts. Taxi drivers are good. One, Boojhawonah Sidick, has a portable telephone (no 4239184) in his car on which I called him to pick up something I had forgotten, and he charged me *less* than I expected, not more.

There are four major hotels in the north of Grand Bay. **Le Mauricia** (formerly Pullman) is a mass of white concrete, a harsh contrast to the soft glint of the azure sea. 188 rooms with seven suites, *medium*.

A different kind of hotel, and consequently with lower, *medium* range rates, is the **Veranda Bungalow Village**, close to the Grand Bay Yacht Club. There are 36 rustic cottages (and a block of 12 rooms) in a garden with its own manicured beach, swimming pool, boathouse and two tennis courts. The difference is the cottage accommodation (with kitchens for self-catering), which are miniature examples of traditional Creole houses – sloping roofs (galvanised iron, though, not shingles), wooden shutters and stable-type doors, all attractively furnished and with open verandas. They are scattered in seemingly random patterns, separated from each other by tiny 'streets', cobbled courtyards and scaled-down public squares. There is an old street lamp here, an antique water tap there.

Special talents have been to work to create the **Royal Palm Hotel**, proclaimed as an oasis of luxury, at **Grand Sable**, adjoining Grand Bay – a grand hotel in every respect. Opened in 1985, the hotel is a delightful mix of 72 luxury rooms and 12 suites, each with private staircase giving direct access to the beach. The suites have a dining room for six people and a personal valet and kitchen service on request, at a rate of no less than Rs20,000 per day for bed and breakfast. The 'ordinary' rooms are furnished with king-size bed, air conditioning, TV with video, radio, telephone and individual safe, desk, mini-bar, large terrace, and bathroom with separate toilet. The furniture is colonial style, wood with lots of brass. It really is a splendid place to stay with the kind of elegance you would expect for just under Rs6,000, the lowest quoted price for a single. Great food and confident service. One of the 'Leading Hotels of the World'.

The Royal Palm is the flagship of the Beachcomber hotel group, sharing facilities such as the casino, golf course and diving school, with Trou aux Biches Village Hotel ten minutes away. It has a business centre and a departure lounge with bathroom, toilets and luggage storage for guests departing on a late flight after check-out time. The design of the hotel, with its blend of thatch, wood, and stonework is impressive. Entrance to the hotel is controlled and it is usually open only to residents and holders of the Beachcomber card.

The **Merville Beach Hotel** has its own private beach. The rock formations in front of it are a haven for the active scuba diver and the hotel has its own diving centre and boathouse. Watersports, including limited waterskiing, and tennis are free. Here are a swimming pool and games room. The hotel has 114 rooms, either in the three-storey block or in luxury cottages, all with double beds, air conditioning, desk facility, telephone, radio, balcony (with sea view), wall-to-wall carpeting and private bathroom. There is 24-hour room service, even in the cottages, and entertainment nightly. It's priced in the *grand* range.

The coast road from Grand Bay to Cap Malheureux passes through **Pereybere**, with its small bay and beach, popular with locals at weekends. There are several *basic* guesthouses and self-catering apartments although restaurants seem to be overpriced. David Sullivan commented:

> 'The popular **Etoile du Nord** (12 rooms, *basic*) was booked up for months; the **Hotel Sylvilla** next door was very nice and offered the cheapest rate we found in town. *Basic*. Scuba and snorkelling equipment can be rented up the road at **Casa Florida** (41 rooms, self-catering studios; *basic*).'

Cap Malheureux is the most northerly point of Mauritius, 22kms from Port Louis. It was there the British landed in 1810, although no monument marks the site. There is a picturesque Roman Catholic chapel on a bluff close to the beach landing place. The view of **Gunner's Quoin** shows the wedge shape by which the island got its name. Visits can be made to the island from Grand Bay. There is a cave on it called **Madam's Hole**, which was used by the British navy in the 19th century for target practice.

Three miles from Pereybere by bus, with a view of Gunner's Quoin from its veranda restaurant, is **Les Mascareignes**, a *basic* rate hotel with 14 rooms. A family-run business, it is especially popular with visitors from Réunion for a no-hassles holiday at a realistic price. Next door, at Beau Manguier, and similar in style, is the **Coin de Mire Village Hotel**, with 14 apartments and studios, *basic* rate, and including a luxury suite with three bedrooms and its own swimming pool.

Despite the hazards of the coast which gave Cap Malheureux its name, the area is popular for holiday villas, some of which can be rented. Kuxville started as one bungalow for rent 20 years ago and has since expanded to eight self-catering units within the **Kuxville** compound, with other rental beachside villas also managed by the German couple who own Kuxville.

There is no restaurant, but there is a romantic spot for lounging under six thatched sun shades on a spit alongside the tiny beach, surrounded by ferny *filaos*. Rates are quoted in deutschmarks and most of Kuxville's clients, from Germany or South Africa, have been returning year after year to its homely atmosphere. *Medium* category. Remains of old sugar mills are to be seen in the canefields. The windmill tower at Cap Malheureux is a listed monument.

Off the northern coast beyond Gunner's Quoin are Flat, Gabriel, Round and Serpent Islands. **Flat Island** has a lighthouse and is visited occasionally by groups on picnics from the Grand Bay hotels. Dr Ayres, writing in a scientific paper published in 1865, said: 'In Flat Island we find the fossilised remains of an extensive forest consisting of stumps of trees closely planted about two feet high, hollow in the centre to the base, and some of them two feet in diameter'.

It is difficult to land on **Round Island** by boat because of strong currents, and a permit is required to do so since it is a nature reserve. The use of a helicopter has made landing on the island easier and special trips can be arranged for nature enthusiasts. The island, which is kidney-shaped, not round, and is about 1.5km^2 in area, is some 22kms from Mauritius. Its flora and fauna are fascinating, as much is rare, having evolved in isolation without the attentions of the early colonists. Two species of snake and some unique lizards live there, as well as sea birds. Neighbouring **Serpent Island**, a large barren rock with no serpents or snakes, also known as Parasol Island, is a sanctuary for birds.

At Anse du Raie, with a bus-stop outside its gates, is one of the best hotel bargains for the affluent: the *medium*-priced **Paradise Cove Hotel** which is grand in style and the only member in Mauritius of the 'Small Luxury Hotels of the World' grouping. Its 64 rooms are all identical in size (44m^2) and sea-facing, built in two and three storey complexes around a small cove with an artificial, glittering white sand beach. There are also tiny private beaches on the ocean. Beach hawkers can only get there by swimming. Lots of luxuries, and being small it has an intimacy – and no ugly scrums for buffets as in some of the larger resorts.

The coastal road along the north of Mauritius turns inland through stone-encrusted patches of cane, touching the coast briefly at St François before reaching the coastal village of **Grand Gaube**. *Gaube* or *goab* is the local word for an inlet or bay.

A stylish property, the **Grand Gaube Hotel**, with the slogan 'Where Mauritius is delicious' is located on a sandy bay at Grand Gaube, one hour's drive from the airport. With occasional thatched roofs breaking the monotony of its blocks of rooms (119 of them), this is a *medium* resort. The bedrooms are compact, each with a separate toilet as well as a bathroom.

The **Island View Club Hotel** is at Grand Gaube. There is a British connection (it has an address in Solihull) in this *medium* category hotel, with 39 double rooms and four family units in a 1.215 hectare site. Most of its clients come through international tour operators, with independent guests who find their way up this far from the airport being accepted on a space-available basis.

The ambience is sunny with a clever use of the limited size of the public areas. The small number of staff means friendly service. The pine-furnished, two-storey rooms in cottages and apartments are equipped with double beds, bunk beds for children, phone, radio and tea/coffee-making facilities. The bathrooms have circular corner bathtubs. Suites are equipped for self-catering. The 1970s-built Paul and Virginie Hotel used to be on this site.

Grand Gaube is somewhat isolated, but the important industrial towns of **Goodlands** is not far away inland. Historic Marine, manufacturers of wooden ship models, is on the St Antoine Industrial Estate. The list of national monuments includes the Transit of the Planet Venus Pillar at St Antoine. Off the coast, the **Ile d'Ambre** is so called because of the ambergris which used to be found there.

The ill-fated *St Geran* sank on the Amber Island reefs with heavy loss of life, and a monument commemorating the wreck was erected at Poudre d'Or in 1944. That name could have derived from gold found in the region or, more likely, from its golden powder sands. Virginie, the fictional heroine of St Pierre's novel, *Paul et Virginie*, is supposed to have been washed ashore on this coast, prompting Mark Twain to observe wryly that it was 'the only one prominent event in the history of the island, and that didn't happen'. Poudre d'Or is a fishing village with a public picnic area and a sturdy building (built in 1864) as a chest hospital. There are excursions to Amber Isle, and camping and hiking are possible.

The road down the east coast passes between cane and tobacco fields to reach **Rivière du Rempart**. This town has many cyclone-proof concrete block houses as well as two old, wooden mansions, one on each side of the road, opposite each other, that have managed to survive all of the progress and storms. Inland, the oddly named village of **Gokoola** derives its name from the town of Gokul, between Delhi and Agra in India.

South of Rivière du Rempart is the bulge of **Roches Noires**, with weekend houses – *campements* – facing the turquoise sea. In summer, this coast is pleasant, but it suffers from strong southeast winds in winter. Pedlars on motorbikes, loaded like an oxcart with goods of every description, pass along the road to sell their wares to women working in the fields who can't go to town to shop. The boundary separating the district from Flacq cuts across the flat lands as the road approaches Lafayette.

Sugarcane cutting

Flacq

To the Dutch goes the credit for naming this district which ranges
from the Plaine des Roches (Plain of Rocks) in the north through the
eastern centre of the island to the Bamboo Mountains in the south.
Its original name was Groote Vlakte (Great Plain), or sometimes,
because of the rice and vegetables grown there, Farmers' Plain, Boere
Vlakte. Vlakte became Flacq during the years of the French.

Much of it was ebony forest. The Dutch began the process of fell-
ing the trees to make a road northwards from their settlement at
Grand Port. The French continued attacking the forests, using the
timber to build ships and houses. The district is now devoted to agriculture and has two of the island's largest sugar estates.

It is the third most populated district of the island with a population in excess of 100,000. Its principal village is **Bon Accueil**, on the
main road (and bus route) to Centre de Flacq. The most easterly
point of the island is **Poste Lafayette**, approached either from Roches
Noires in the north, or via **Poste de Flacq**, a few miles to the south.

The coast around Lafayette is lined with *filaos*, bent by the winter
winds which are strong between July and August. There are bungalows to rent along this coast, some incorporating abandoned lime
kilns in their structure. The **Coral Beach Bungalows** with self-catering
studios are on this coastal road; *basic* range. Lafayette is named after
one of the surveyors who helped the Abbé de la Caille draw up the
first detailed map of the island. (Another surveyor, d'Esny, has
several points named after him, including one in the bay of Poste de
Flacq.)

Close to the sea on the road into **Poste de Flacq** are some sweetwater ponds fed by underground streams. Poste de Flacq is little
more than a road junction. Don't be surprised to see kiosks selling
oysters; they are farmed on this coast.

Further down are more lime kilns, where coral is burnt over
casuarina wood fires to extract the lime. Vegetables such as onions,
chillies and tomatoes are grown on the land around Belle Mare.

The **Belle Mare** peninsula was for long the preserve of the St Geran
Sun Hotel until the **Sandy Bay Hotel** opened in 1987, right next door
to it. The story is that this spare hectare of land by the beach was
brought unexpectedly by a former employee of the St Geran Sun. He
has created a 60-room, white-washed monolith that offers *basic*-style

accommodation at *medium* price, much less than it costs in the luxury hotel next door.

Sandy Bay provides its clients with free watersports (except diving), free sun loungers, one floodlit tennis court and a freshwater swimming pool. There is a bar and a large, open-sided restaurant. Bedrooms are small with bathroom, air conditioning, radio, telephone and 24-hour room service. Guests have access to the casino of the St Geran Sun.

To welcome guests at the **St Geran Sun Hotel, Casino and Golf Club** a cocktail is served in a coconut shell as they arrive after the 56kms drive from the airport. Excitement is heightened by the glimpse of the slot machines of the casino to the left. These are playable from 10.00 hours, while the casino opens at 20.45, except on Sundays and public holidays, when it opens at 14.30; roulette and blackjack are available. The hotel has a nine-hole, Gary Player-designed golf course with caddies, equipment and golf coach. No green fees for Sun card holders. There are three floodlit tennis courts and a resident tennis coach.

All guest rooms are large with private bath, toilet and shower, radio and TV, mini-bar and electronic safe, telephone, individually controlled air conditioning, and sliding glass doors with view of either sea or lagoon. This is a *grand* category hotel rivalling the Royal Palm but somehow without its cachet, despite working hard on its prestigious, 'exclusive' image.

There is free transport for guests to visit the St Geran's sister hotel, Le Touessrok Sun, further down the coast.

The road there passes through **Belle Mare**, where the prisons and old sugar factory are listed as national monuments. Belle Mare boasts a public beach shaded by *filao* trees, and a hotel, the **Belle Mare Plage Golf Hotel and Casino Resort**. Dedicated to giving guests 'a relaxed and sporty holiday', it sprawls along one of the loveliest sandy beaches in Mauritius, protected by a coral reef, a safe area for watersports (which are free). Also free to guests is use of the new 18-hole championship golf course and the nine-hole course. The casino, at one end of the property, is open every day (21.00–03.00) with access to its one-armed bandits from 11.00.

The hotel has been transformed from its previous lethargy into a dynamic resort, with 86 comfort rooms, 56 prestige rooms, 30 club rooms and six deluxe suites. Fun are the architecturally striking prestige rooms which seem to be part of the swimming pool. This is a *grand* category hotel, independently owned by the Constance Sugar Estate, and offering competition to all the other properties in this price range – especially if you like to play golf.

Two *medium* category hotels at Belle Mare are the 80-room **Le Flamboyant** and the 52-room **Emeraude Beach**. **Le Palmar**, also on the coastal road, is smaller with 40 rooms and a low *medium* price. A

little further south, the listed ruins of **Quatre Cocos Factory**, near
Palmar, have been enlivened by a handicraft centre.

At Palmar Bay, the **Hotel Ambre**, one of the Apavou group which
operates hotels in Réunion, has 226 rooms and 20 suites, with 500
beds, and *grand* prices. The swimming pool is huge (450m²) and the
overall atmosphere is somehow very functional. The small properties
in the low *medium* category are **Le Surcouf Village** (27 rooms, two
suites) and the **Silver Beach** (30 rooms).

Another smaller one, very popular with German guests, is **La
Tropical** at La Pelouse. *Medium* grade, it has 48 rooms and is a cosy
hotel with rooms facing inwards to the pool or out to sea. There is a
twice daily free boat shuttle to Ile aux Cerfs. Rates are halfboard and
include the usual watersports.

The fishing village of **Trou d'Eau Douce** is an early Dutch settlement. The **Puits des Hollandais**, meaning Dutchman's Well, is an
extinct crater well still used for fresh water. Trou d'Eau Douce refers
to this sweetwater spring although, since it is pronounced *Tro do-doo*,
some historians have assumed it is named after the dodo, which lived
in this region.

A few minutes' drive from the village is **Le Touessrok Sun Hotel**.
The reception area is on the mainland; the rooms are on a private
island, reached by a Venetian-style wooden footbridge. The spell is
emphasised by the hamlet of rough white walls, sloping thatched
roofs, palm groves, and gangways hewn out of coloured volcanic
rock. Architect Maurice Giraud has dreamed – and created – a haven
of exclusivity that is relaxing and friendly, with its 100 rooms and 62
suites.

All rooms in these romantic cottages have sea-facing balconies or
patios, and a bathroom/toilet, individually controlled air conditioning, radio, telephone, mini-bar and lounge. Suites are among the
finest in the Indian Ocean region with a jacuzzi and private staircase
to the beach.

Facilities at Le Touessrok include two swimming pools, free sauna,
qualified masseuse, hairdressing salon, babysitting, a nurse and dispensary, three floodlit tennis courts, free watersports at the Ile aux
Cerfs, a poolside a la carte restaurant and a night-time venue for
sophisticated table d'hote dining.

There is a free boat service for holders of the Sun card to the **Ile
aux Cerfs**, which is managed by the hotel. (There are also independent ferry services as the island is open to the public.) With an area
of over 300 hectares, it takes three hours to walk around the island.
Apart from the four hectares of public facilities, the island has been
preserved as nearly as possible to its original state. Deer run wild
(and there is a zoo with tame deer, and giant tortoises), and *filaos*
grow thick down to the unspoiled beaches of golden sand.

But David Sullivan found it 'very touristy, especially around where the boats land', and very expensive for drinks and food. 'They try to say that you can't bring your own picnic. It's pretty but because of the crowds, I would categorise this island as a disappointment to be avoided, unless you find somebody with a boat to take you independently.'

It is a 45-minute drive to the airport from Le Touessrok Hotel, passing through **Bel Air Rivière Sèche**, another of the principal villages of the Flacq district, and crossing the **Grand River Southeast**, a spectacular gorge for photos. At the mouth of the Grande Rivière Sud Est is a charming fishing village and a hotel that is not particularly pretty but has the informal atmosphere and friendly staff that make a good holiday. The **Moonlight Bay** is one of the Protea group of hotels with prices in the low *medium* range. On the opposite bank of the river is the village of **Two Brothers**, with another village, puzzlingly called **Four Sisters**, a little further on. At **Pointe aux Feuilles**, in the foothills of the Bamboo Mountain range, the Flacq district ends.

The heart of the district is **Centre de Flacq**, a town of about 15,000 inhabitants, with a well-maintained, French-style colonial building, listed as a national monument, as the courthouse and post office. Opposite the bus station are some village shops. One of them sells wooden rolling pins and spice mortars which make authentic souvenirs. There are some *basic* category eateries here.

In the entire district, good eating away from the hotels is rare. **Chez Manuel**, a Chinese restaurant in the village of **St Julien**, is recommended by those who know it. I was told that this has grown over the years from a tiny shop serving local clientele into a much larger place for visitors. It is about ten minutes drive from the coast hotels.

A new discovery, which opened late 1993 under new management, is the **Bel Etang Bar Restaurant** (09.30–23.00 daily except Tuesdays) on the main A7 highway from Centre de Flacq to Quartier Militaire. A local-style café owned by Raj, a former Sun hotels employee, we found it by chance and enjoyed a great meal of local dishes and wine at down-to-earth prices.

Grand Port

The district of Grand Port has a little of everything, with low cost, cheerful guesthouses as well as beach resorts for the more affluent and sporty. History buffs have ruins aplenty while nature lovers can marvel at the drama of Le Souffleur water spout, or explore the Domaine du Chasseur forest in the Bamboo Mountains. Mahebourg offers small town nightlife and there is constant activity and ease of communications at the international airport at Plaisance.

The northern boundary of this varied district is formed by the Bamboo Mountains, which rise up to 400 metres in height. The western boundary cuts through the tea plantations behind Nouvelle France, close to the Kanaka Crater at 500 metres. The Post River flows down to L'Escalier, to join the southern coast.

The Bamboo Mountains descend to the sea at the headland of **Devil's Point** (Pointe du Diable), where the ruins of **French batteries** are listed as a national monument. Cannons here date from 1750–80 and were used to guard two wide gaps (North and Danish Passages) in the reef. The devil of this point was said to be responsible for upsetting the magnetic compasses of ships passing the headland.

About 2,350 acres of the Bamboo Mountains form the privately-owned **Domaine du Chasseur** game park and nature reserve. Nature trails wind through the forest which is home to Javanese deer, wild boar, monkeys, hare, and the rare Mauritius kestrel which swoops in to have mice tossed at it by the game warden.

There are six guest cabins, each furnished simply but with hot water showers, with views from their balconies over the hills sweeping down to the distant sea at Vieux Grand Port. They are built on the hillside above the rustic bar and restaurant, where tables are set in *miradors* around a stream; food (venison, hare, wild boar spare ribs) is for trenchermen, with wine for connoisseurs. Owner Alain O'Reilly has created a place that is both sophisticated and informal, blending perfectly with nature. Presidents and royalty have discovered this retreat but it is in the low *medium* price range (at Rs1,750 for two with American breakfast), which makes it remarkable as well as unique and affordable.

The road follows the coast around the edge of the peninsula. An unmanned lighthouse on the **Ile aux Fouquets** marks the rocks at the southern entrance through the reef into Grand Port. This is listed as a

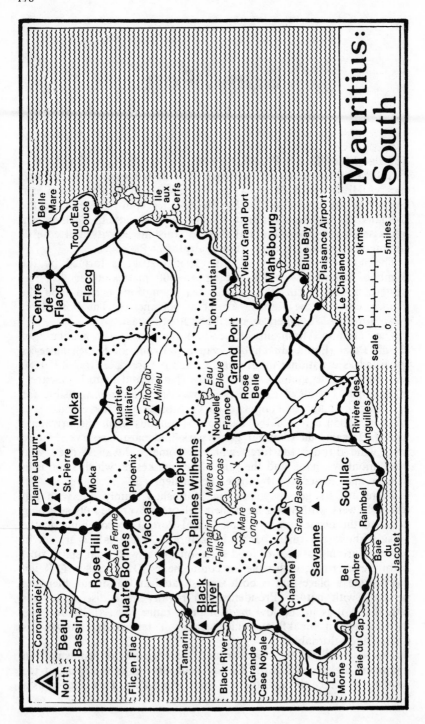

Mauritius:
South

national monument, too, as is the whole of the nearby **Ile de la Passe** with its ruined fortifications. During the battle for Grand Port it was captured by the British, who kept the French flag flying to lure in French vessels.

There are bulk fuel storage tanks, their installation financed by the Russians, close to **Bois des Amourettes** (Young Lovers' Wood). Legend says that French soldiers used to duel over the girls they met here. Swords have been found in the vicinity of the cave and rock known as **Salle d'Armes** down on the sea's edge. The crouching lion of **Lion Mountain** (480m) guards the bay.

Ruins of the Dutch settlement of **Vieux Grand Port** are still to be seen, although they were neglected and plastered with political posters during my last visit. The oldest buildings in Mauritius are in this area, with foundations dating back to the 17th century. The round, topless Dutch tower shows little benefit from having been listed as a national monument.

Grand Port was named Warwyck Bay in 1598 by the Dutch who made two attempts to establish a colony here before they left in 1710. The French named the bay Port Bourbon and planned to have the headquarters of the French East India Company there, although after a feasibility study they chose Port Louis instead.

Port Bourbon then became Port Southeast and slipped into decline. Governor Decaen visited the harbour in 1804 and sensed its vulnerability. He abandoned the manning of the old Dutch posts and built a new town at Colony Point on the opposite side of the bay. Mahebourg, after Mahé de Labourdonnais, was his original name for this new town but he soon changed it for reasons of diplomacy to Port Imperial. He renamed Port Louis at the same time, as Port Napoleon.

When the British tried to take Grand Port in August 1810 they were soundly beaten. Both sides used subterfuge but the French were more successful. They managed to move the buoys marking the passage through the reef, causing British vessels to run aground. The victory of the French is recorded at the Arc de Triomphe in Paris. Four months later, however, the island capitulated and Port Imperial became Mahebourg again.

At **Ferney**, hidden in a grove of palm trees on the coastal side of the road around the bay, is a **monument to the Dutch**. A wall erected in 1953 records the introduction of sugar cane from Java by the Dutch governor, Van Der Stel, in 1639. At the end of a spit of pebbles at the mouth of the Champagne River, an obelisk, erected on September 20 1948, commemorates the landing of the Dutch 350 years before to the day. Bodies of the Dutch settlers are buried at the foot of Lion Mountain.

Mahebourg (pronounced Mayberg by some, Mah-ay-bour by others) is the main town in the south of the island, a laidback community of some 20,000. Its development suffered through the malaria epidemic in 1866 which drove coastal town dwellers to move to the hills.

However, Mahebourg has prospered since it was described in a 1973 guide as 'a down-at-heel town lined with small shops where friendliness of service has to substitute for sophistication of goods'. Its guesthouses are the pleasantest in Mauritius, places where Creole dishes and French wine are consumed with relish by sophisticated visitors who appreciate good value.

Walking along the coastal road (Sivananda Street) from the bus station on the seafront, you will find lots of these guesthouses, each with its own charm. The **Monte Carlo** is a delightful-looking period guesthouse whose seven rooms (common toilet and bathroom) are usually fully booked at Rs150 a night. Also *basic* are the **Aquarelle** with four rooms, and the **St Tropez** with 10 rooms and a bungalow by the beach. **Le Vacancies** bar-restaurant, open 10.00–23.00, is in the same street. The popular *basic* Le Corralie (Chez Joe) restaurant and rooms on the waterfront has been replaced by **La Phare**, not so *basic*.

In the French country mansion, built in 1722 and set in a parkland garden by the River la Chaux, are gathered a collection of relics salvaged from wrecks, some railway models, mouldering prints and photocopies, and some decrepit furniture. Where these items are labelled it is in French. This is the **Mahebourg Naval & Historical Museum**.

Its sorry state is reflected in the condition of the governor's railway carriage, parked in the back garden. This Victorian extravagance, with wooden louvred windows, elegant plush armchairs, and iron-trellised balcony, is being allowed, like the dodo, to disintegrate.

The museum's condition has been known since 1984, when a report noted that the building, which housed the wounded French and English commanders after the Battle of Grand Port, was in need of repair and repainting. The garden was being used as a football field and was 'a place for undesirables at night'. The need was recognised then that this *maison historique* and its contents should be preserved and maintained regularly. As a result, a Village Artisanal of eight wooden huts was created in the garden. Run by the Ministry of Arts, Culture, Leisure and Reform Institutions, the village is open 09.00–16.00, except Tuesdays, Fridays and holidays. Entrance is free to view handicraft production.

At the other side of Mahebourg, on a breezy headland with a public pavilion is **Regatta Point**, there is a **memorial** to the French and English killed 'during the engagement off Ile de la Passe 20–28 August 1810'. This was erected in 1899 and lists the names of the vessels that took part.

The barracks master at Mahebourg from before 1837 and until at least 1858 was a Waterloo veteran called J S Sedley (1794–1867). Mr Sedley was said to be a son of the Duke of Kent and, thus, an elder half-brother of Queen Victoria. Since he lived in Mahebourg so long, it is possible that he left descendants, so there could be distant cousins of the British (and many other) royal families among the town's inhabitants.

There are several islands off Mahebourg. **Mouchoir Rouge** has a small, private bungalow on it. To its south is **Ile aux Aigrettes**, which is popular for excursion visits. It is a protected nature reserve and many of the plants found there grow nowhere else. Endangered species include ebony, orchids and rare palms. Around the headland, in Blue Bay, where there is a well-liked public beach, is another island called **Deux Cocos**.

At **Pointe Jérome**, on the headland, with a view of Grand Port Bay and Mahebourg, is **La Croix du Sud** tropical holiday village. This *medium* category establishment has 70 self-catering, rustic rooms, scattered by the beach. Watersports are free and there is a pool, bar and restaurant, and small grocery store. The hotel is popular as a base for windsurfing, and powerboat trips can be arranged up the coast to Ile aux Cerfs.

The **Blue Lagoon Hotel** is close to the Blue Bay public beach. It has recently expanded from a nine-room guesthouse to a 47-room hotel. The rooms have showers and fans and the hotel caters for family guests. Special evenings include rock 'n' roll and karate nights. Limited watersports are free and there are lots of activities such as volley ball and French bowls. There is a forecourt swimming pool and a bar on the beach. The hotel, which is only 10kms from the airport, also has a day rate. *Medium*.

To get from Mahebourg to what was the island's oldest beach hotel, Le Chaland, involves a drive through **Beau Vallon**, a village that still has some old houses despite cyclones, then alongside the airport runway, and down a road that twists and turns through sugar cane flats. Set in a long established garden of trees and flowers in a 20 hectare estate, Le Chaland has been torn down and replaced by the Beachcomber group's **Shandrani**.

Only superlatives describe this *grand* grade hotel which owes much of its success to its genial general manager, Marcello Giobbe, who previously helped put Le Touessrok on the map. Somehow, Marcello and his public relations team make each guest (and there are 543 of them when it is full) feel special. Shandrani has 173 rooms – furnished like a wealthy friend's luxury apartment – and eight suites. The rooms are in house blocks around mature gardens and face the various beaches. A golf course was being created in 1993. The hotel's breakfast buffet is probably the best in Mauritius with self-service champagne and vodka by the fruit juice counter and a vast range of dishes, including smoked marlin. With all the usual free resort activities, there are plenty of excursions as well, including one to the nature reserve at Ile aux Aigrettes.

The Sir Seewoosagur Ramgoolam International **Airport** at **Plaisance** has had a new passenger terminal since the end of 1987. It was built to a design supplied by China and looks like it. However, at least it's better than the former terminal. It is about 2,000 metres long, with aircraft parking at gates spaced along its length, so passengers have almost a kilometre to walk to immigration if their plane parks at the furthest end. There are two duty free shops on arrival, as well as a good selection of duty free goods to buy on departure.

The public congregate outside the arrivals lobby to meet flights. On the top floor there is a restaurant for passengers and the public, as well as a public viewing terrace with a wonderful view of Lion Mountain and the tarmac. The car park has space for 800 vehicles, shop units and food vendor stalls. VIP government guests have their own separate entrance and a lounge in which to await flights. The public are not allowed to enter the check-in departure area and baggage security screening is done at the entrance to the building.

On the airport site in 1875 an English primary school teacher who worked in Mauritius dug up the bones of a dodo. The teacher, George Clark, had patiently searched for years to find dodo remains and the results of his work are the restored skeletons in museums around the world.

The nearest village to the airport is **Plaine Magnien**, named after a locksmith who settled in Port Louis in 1760 and bought land in the area. The **Tourist Rendezvous** guesthouse, with 10 rooms and common shower and toilet, is located here. *Basic*.

The road from the airport to Curepipe passes through **Mare d'Albert**, where the social centre is in a notable, glass-fronted, wooden cottage. The New Grove industrial area follows, giving way to the double-storey houses of **Rose Belle**, dominated by the government-owned sugar factory of the same name.

To the south of this main road is the town of **L'Escalier** which takes its name from the Baron Daniel l'Escalier, a French officer. There is a road here, through the Savinia plantation, to **Le Souffleur**. A permit must be obtained from the estate office, by the police station, before visiting it.

Le Souffleur is a blow hole formed in the rocks of the coast, through which the sea used to spout spectacularly at high tide. Erosion has deprived it of the power it had 150 years ago when a writer said 'it roared furiously to a height of fully sixty feet'. It still roars a little when the tide is high.

There is an historic château, listed as a national monument, at **Riche en Eau**, on the old road from Mahebourg to Curepipe. As befits its name, there are miles of rivers and streams here, with the main river, Des Creoles, flowing into Grand Port Bay above Mahebourg. Also off this old road is **Le Val**, a country estate which is part of the Rose Belle enterprise. It is surrounded by mountains, with a view down the valley to the distant sea, and has two hectares of palm tree-lined alleys and spring-fed ponds where watercress is cultivated and freshwater prawns are reared. A meal of fresh palm heart salad, grilled giant prawns, watercress and local fruits can be served to visitors by prior arrangement.

Dodo

Savanne

Savanne is the southernmost district of Mauritius, stretching westwards from the sugar-growing village of Savannah along a coast that is the island's most rugged. Yet there is also a golden sand beach, protected by a reef, close to Riambel. The district's western boundary is the Baie du Cap River which flows from the Chamarel waterfall. Its northern boundary is the mountainous forest region of Plaine Champagne, with craters and tea plantations linking up with the cane estates of its eastern limits. Scenically it is breathtaking but, despite its beauty and proximity to the airport, it is not overwhelmed with tourists.

The deep south is plantation country, with the road from **Savannah** winding through the cane fields. An enormous iron bridge alongside the road carries the remains of a railway track across a gorge. An ironic reminder of the railway is a notice barring access to the bridge saying only 'No Passage'.

The **Bel Air** sugar estate was founded by the French in 1804. It is now owned by a wealthy Anglo-Mauritian who maintains it with a devotion apparent from its ingeniously designed water gardens. Two pillars mark the entrance to the estate, then the road passes through a compound of Victorian warehouses (the old mill stopped operating in 1927) and along avenues of Royal Palms which lead through the sugar cane to the cool lushness of the garden, close to the coast.

The estate owner keeps a villa here, a typical Mauritian *campement* of stone walls and thatched roof with exposed beams, from which there is a view of the waves battering the rugged shore. There is no land between there and Antarctica. The atmosphere of the villa is more 1930s than colonial with its flagstone floors, white walls hung with paintings by Mauritian artists, cushioned rattan chairs with glass holders in their armrests, and scattered copies of *Vogue*. It is not normally open to the public but can be visited on the excursion operated by MauriTours, which passes here for tea and biscuits.

Pools in the terraced gardens are fed by an underground spring, which flows from one to another until plunging over the cliff to the sea. There are watercress ponds, prawn pools and a carp lake; vacoas or screwpine (*pandanus*) abound, and there is also a collection of Aldebra tortoises. A cattlegrid stops deer straying along the road from a fenced park. There is a plantation of the palm trees used for heart of palm salad and then come vast fields of cane.

La Vanille Crocodile Farm is located close by, at **Senneville**, south of the town of **Rivière des Anguilles**. The farm was started in 1985 by an Australian biologist with the intention of breeding crocodiles for their skins. It has now become a mini-zoo with monkeys, deer, tortoises, lizards and reptiles, as well as the crocodiles which are the Nile or African variety, imported from Madagascar. The farm is open 09.30–18.00, except Mondays and public holidays, with guided tours on the hour, every hour. Feeding time is at 13.00. The mosquitoes, which are plentiful, feed on visitors at any time. There is a licensed snack bar.

The town of **Rivière des Anguilles** (Eel River), which has the atmosphere of a country village, is reached by crossing a bridge with views down a gorge of sparse countryside and the river. There are plenty of fruit and vegetable stalls and pavement vendors. There is even what could be the smallest discotheque in the world, a room open to the street, only large enough for an old-fashioned juke box and two youths dancing carefully in front of it.

North of the town are the immaculately maintained lands of the **Britannia Sugar Estate** (part of the Lonrho group). In front of the estate factory are neat ornamental gardens and orderly fields of miniature pineapples, part of the estate's diversification programme. The odour of warm sugar pervades the air. Field workers swathed in protective clothing tend the sugar crop.

A knitwear factory at **Tyack** shows how industrialisation has penetrated even this far south.

The **Union (St Aubin) Sugar Estate** lies off the road to Souillac. On it is the **Villa Andrea**, a management bungalow overlooking the sea, where lunches are served by arrangement, through MauriTours. Plantation retainers prepare local dishes such as cold, stewed heart of palm, freshwater prawns with watercress, chicken Creole with rice, and pineapple mousse. A good selection of South African wines is available, too.

The nearby anthurium nursery of Corolla Ltd is open to the public, with tours around its 1.5 hectares of flowers and its packing plant. The anthuriums are of the andreanium type and have been grown in the region for a hundred years. The waxlike leaf (actually the flower spathe) is normally pink although some varieties are blood red and others lime white. These erotic-looking plants, which bloom all year, are grown in humid, warm conditions under vast awnings of green netting.

Each week the nursery, one of a dozen in the island, exports 11,000 flowers to Europe, Réunion and South Africa. Flat boxes of anthuriums can be bought at florists (there is a good one in Quatre Bornes) by departing visitors. The flowers will keep for a week in the box. A box of 24 to 30 blooms can cost from Rs100.

The fishing town of **Souillac** is on the coast, midway between the east and west corners of the island. It is named after the Vicomte de Souillac, governor of Mauritius from 1779 to 1787 who, although he was known for his profligacy, encouraged settlers to develop the south. There is a ponderous Roman Catholic church here, along with a village market and the **Telfair Gardens**.

Charles Telfair was a British planter who arrived with Farquhar in 1810 and took over the sugar factory at Bel Ombre. He published pamphlets on his enlightened treatment of slaves which only won him censure from abolitionists. He was a keen amateur botanist. The garden bearing his name is somewhat windswept and bereft of charm, being mostly lawn, badamier (Indian almond) and banyan (*Ficus benghalensis*) trees. There are pavilions for picnics, but bathing in the sea below the garden is dangerous because of currents. At the mouth of the river, solid grey sugar warehouses have been restored to recall the days when sugar was shipped by boat from Port Souillac to Port Louis.

Le Gris Gris is the name of a drab beach where swimming is also dangerous, despite the apparent shallow lagoon formed by the reef which runs close to the shore. Its name is associated with local witchcraft. There are deep chasms in the cliffs surrounding it which lead to a distinctive headland known as **La Roche Qui Pleure**. A pavilion (and public toilet) overlook the beach. The **Gris Gris Restaurant** (beer and snacks), open 10.00–19.30, has newly built *basic* rooms upstairs for guests.

The house where Robert Edward Hart spent his last years has been turned into an evocative, free **museum**, open daily, except on Tuesdays and public holidays. The house is spartan, with a polished, red cement floor, coral stone walls and a galvanised tin roof. Although the poet died in 1954, he seems to have just popped down to the beach a few yards away and the visitor feels almost embarrassed at wandering around the man's small house while he's out. Belongings such as pith helmet, pens and photographs are as he left them, giving an intensely personal view of this half-French, half-Irish Mauritian writer.

Hart is buried in the cemetery on the point across the bay. He shares it with Baron d'Unienville, the 19th century historian, and with a number of British and French soldiers and drowned seamen whose tombs have been defaced by the fierceness of the elements. Bones were even scattered around the graveyard by the cyclone of 1962.

Rochester Falls are inland from Cemetery Point, reached by following signposts through cane fields. Fed by water flowing down from the Savanne Mountains, they are not high but reveal vertical columns created in the rocks by the constant pounding of the falling water.

The village of **Riambel** is said to derive its name from the Malagasy word for sunny beach. It marks the beginning of a beach that stretches up to Pointe aux Roches. At the western end is the hotel complex of **Villas Pointe Aux Roches**. This has 26 concrete-box bungalow units at *basic* rate.

These bungalow villas, under German management, are only 25 minutes from the airport and on a beautiful and usually deserted beach in a garden of palm trees. There is a good bar and restaurant (*basic* to *medium*) serving meals or snacks all day. Guests welcome being left to their own devices without organised entertainment. The main road runs past the gates and there is a bus service (to Curepipe). The perfect place for people who want to be alone.

There is a two-storey **open air pavilion** on the **Pointe aux Roches** headland. Then, where the River des Galets reaches the sea, there is a beachside **French-style cemetery** close to the St Felix sugar factory. The sea is dangerous, however inviting it looks. A track from the road leads in the direction of **Sancho Islet** in Jacotet Bay.

At low tide it is possible to walk across the pebbles of the beach to this flat-topped coral isle. During the preliminary forages of the British in 1810, the French battery on this island was captured and a French colonist taken hostage in exchange for supplies. Rumours of treasure buried on the island have never been proved. It is covered now in scrub.

Cane fields border the road at **Beau Champ** as it approaches Telfair's old plantation of **Bel Ombre**, actually begun in 1776. There is a wall around the lagoon from which sugar used to be transported in coastal sailing vessels to Port Louis. Sugar cane also grows between the road and the sea until the road emerges opposite the rocky foreshore of **St Martin**, where there are some weekend bungalows.

Close to the **St Martin cemetery** is a cairn monument recalling the landing of survivors from the wreck of the steamer *Travessa*, which foundered in 1923 on its way to Australia. The cigarette tin lid which was the measure for the daily water ration of the survivors during their ordeal at sea is an exhibit at the Mahebourg museum.

Hills roll down to the scruffy beach at **Baie du Cap**. A church on a hillock overlooks the sea here, which is shallow for a long way out. There are also a picnic pavilion, public toilet and a quiet beachside village, whose inhabitants work in the cane fields or fishing. The boundary with the Black River district is the river which reaches the sea at the long inlet of **Maconde**.

On the road to **Choisy**, a village in the hills behind Baie du Cap, there are good views of the sea if you look back before the road gets to **Chamarel**.

Grand Bassin, the Great Lake, is at 702m above sea level. It is regarded as sacred by Hindus, who celebrate the annual pilgrimage of Maha Shivaratree at the many temples nestling in the hills around it. People pay homage here all the year round and birds swoop in and out of the temples, attracted by the fruit left as offerings. It is also

known as **Ganga Talab** (Lake of the Ganges) because of the belief
that it is linked by an underground stream with the Ganges.

Within sight of Grand Bassin is a giant **windmill**, a slim column
with a 'Y' shaped fan at its top. This is a windpowered generator
belonging to the Central Electricity Board, commissioned by the
prime minister in June 1987.

Kanaka Crater, on the northern border of the district, can only be
reached by hiking along a trail off the road that goes beyond Grand
Bassin to **Bois Chéri**. This is tea-growing country, with hills up to
500m above sea level covered with the close-cropped bushes.

Black River

This district is geographically the longest, extending from the south coast by Baie du Cap northwards to the boundary of Port Louis. It is mostly mountainous and sparsely populated, its 32,000 inhabitants employed in fishing, tourism and sugar. It has no towns, only village communities, and is the most 'African' part of the island, with scrub landscape and Creole lifestyle, and is famed for its *séga*. It is also the driest and sunniest of the island's districts. It was called Zwarte River by the Dutch and Rivière Noire by the French, who created the district in 1768. The river itself is not black, so the name probably refers to the black rocks of its bed and banks.

The sheer cliff of the square-shaped **Morne Brabant** (556m) rises out of the southern peninsula, dominating the west coast of the island with its looming presence. The Dutch believed fish caught from the waters around the Morne were poisonous. Runaway slaves took refuge on it. Fearing that the police party sent to tell them slavery was abolished had come to capture them, the runaways threw themselves off the summit to their deaths below. A sadness haunts the mountain still.

At its foot, in a *filao* parkland of 27 hectares, there are two sister hotels, the **Paradis** and the **Brabant**. Both are managed by the Beachcomber group and work in conjunction so they don't duplicate each other's programmes. The facilities of both are available to guests of either. They are in the lower bracket (they use tea bags instead of real tea) of the *grand* category. Both cater for the energetic beach holidaymaker with free watersports, deep sea fishing and diving, a golf course, four tennis courts, two squash courts and horse riding. There is also a casino with slot machines and a nightclub.

The Brabant, which originally opened in 1967, is the quieter and smaller of the two hotels, with 87 rooms and four suites. The Paradis, built in 1972, has 176 rooms and four suites, which use local artefacts and paintings in their decor. All rooms in both hotels, which are built in blocks, have air conditioning, radio, telephone and private bathrooms. There is no room service between midnight and 06.00.

From the village of **La Gaulette** on the coast road heading north, there is a clear view of Morne Brabant. The foothills of **Little Black River Mountain** (Piton de la Petite Rivière Noire), at 828m the island's highest, reach down to the road. There is a turning at **Grande**

Case Noyale, close to the Creole clapboard administration building (dispensary/post office), that leads to **Chamarel**. Two new restaurants are in the vicinity, the **Chamarel** (4km from Case Noyal) and the **Varangue Sur Morne** (10km).

Taxi drivers repeat the words 'seven coloured earths of Chamarel' as a litany that will bring them business. There is, indeed, an exposed heap of clinker at Chamarel: gravel of different shades of burnt umber. Perhaps I was expecting too much after the constant talk about this wonderful tourist attraction. It is stretching the imagination to call it seven coloured earths.

A stall beside the hill road linking Grande Case Noyale with Baie du Cap marks the entrance to a trail leading to the sight of this phenomenon. There is a charge of Rs10 for a permit since this volcanic cinder mound is on land owned by the Bel Ombre estate. There is a token Chamarel coffee bush before the track winds through fields of sugar cane and 'palm heart salad trees'. The **Chamarel Waterfall** can be seen from the track, plunging 100m down a cliff face. It is possible to walk down a path close to it.

There are more coffee bushes and some bedraggled traveller's palms growing wild before the lushness of cane and forest gives way to heaps of denuded earth. The 'seven colours' are best seen with the sun on them. The piles are remarkable for being an exposed part of the stratum under the earth's crust, not to be seen elsewhere on the island. Specimens of the coloured earths in glass tubes are on sale at the entrance stall.

The village of Chamarel has ugly primary health care and post office buildings and makeshift houses. At **Pierre Paul's** shop, there are a few tables and stools in a corrugated iron hut together with a vast selection of grocery supplies, but none of the Chamarel coffee for which the area is famous. All the coffee is packed and sold to hotels or Curepipe supermarkets. However, snacks of succulent wild boar (*cochon marron*) and a thick lentil-based soup called *halim* can be tried instead as samples of Chamarel cuisine.

The Chamarel road continues up to the forest plateau of **Plaine Champagne**, at 737m above sea level. Here there is a fenced-in viewpoint of the Black River Gorge and a panorama of the coast from the Medicine sugar factory in the north to Morne Brabant in the south. Stepping stones lead down to a terrace for a view of **Alexandra Falls**. It is possible to climb in the Black River mountain range, which is rich in bird life. Most of the area is a nature reserve and glimpses of deer, monkeys and mongoose are likely.

A French soldier called Noyale retired to the area on the coast now known as **Case Noyale**. He was renowned for his hospitality and built a rest house at **Petite Case Noyale** further along the road. He was murdered by runaway slaves.

Mountains are the main feature of the landscape on the drive to

Port Louis. Beyond the Black River mountain range is **Simonet** (632m), in the Vacoas Mountain range, overlooking the plain between Rempart Mountain and Yemen to the sea at Tamarin. By the coast is **Tourelle de Tamarin** (548m), but it is the profiles of the upturned udder-like **Trois Mamelles** (667m) and the mini-Matterhorn, **Rempart Mountain** (777m), which are so impressive. They are visible from almost anywhere on the western coast, haunting the visitor with their omnipresence.

Black River Bay is the main starting point for deep sea fishing expeditions. The **Hotel Club Centre de Pêche**, a thatched complex of 34 double rooms, is dedicated to the needs of sports fishermen. There are a score of boats available for charter, the bar walls are hung with stuffed fish trophies, and a ledger recording all the catches made by guests is on display. The International Marlin Championships are held there annually. Room rates, and hotel standard, are *medium* category.

Many of the large marlins caught off the bay finish up (after being photographed on the jetty upside down, alongside their proud captors) in the marlin smoke houses at Black River, to appear on hotel menus as thinly sliced smoked marlin at Rs100 a portion.

La Bonne Chute restaurant, with an unimpressive entrance by a petrol station, is in an equally unimpressive shed-like building. Open for at least ten years, it has a reputation for good food, its specialities being seafood and game. There was an air of nonchalance about it during my visit but at least it's open for dinner as well as lunch. Opposite is the **Shellorama** shell museum and boutique of the commercial Mikado enterprise, which also has showrooms in Port Louis and the plateau towns. Visits can be made to the workshop at the back to see local souvenirs being made.

The region of **Les Salines** has salt ponds. The tomb of Colonel Draper, founder of the Mauritius Turf Club, is at **La Mivoie**, north of the river, and there is a listed monument at **La Preneuse**, a martello tower. **Les Bougainvilliers**, a *basic* category guesthouse, is on the coast near by. Not much of a beach.

The **Black River Aviary** is hidden away near the wooden Creole building which houses the police station. Visitors are not allowed, except by arrangement, as this is a sponsored scientific project to encourage the breeding of rare species of birds which might otherwise become extinct. A restaurant, **Jade Pavilion**, has opened nearby , on the first floor of an isolated store. There is a track into the wilds of the **Yemen** estate opposite, where deer herds roam and rare birds can be spotted. Yemen was formerly an important coffee-growing region.

The road to **Tamarin** runs through salt pans where salt is dried by solar evaporation. The air is despairingly still. The Tamarin peak stands out behind the drying ponds like a giant salt cellar.

On Tamarin, David Sullivan reports: 'This village attracts the young and the hip. Its beach is popular among surfers – it has waves, unlike the northern beaches, though it is probably less ideal for sunbathing'. The **Tamarin Hotel**, *basic* in charm as well as price, has 18 rooms in bungalows.

'Many cheap rooms', adds Sullivan, 'available in guesthouses near the hotel, but we found them all full since the surfers establish long-term residency. Most of those cheap places don't have names or phone numbers. Your best bet might be to get to Tamarin early in the day and plan to return to Quatre Bornes or Curepipe as a fall-back'.

In the **Casela Bird Park** there are 2,500 birds of 42 different species, as well as tigers and monkeys and other zoo favourites. Access is off the Black River road close to the junctions for Quatre Bornes and Flic en Flac. The layout of the park is spacious, giving shaded walks through the 85 aviaries and the chance to see some of the rare pink pigeons (*Nesoenas mayeri*). There is no brochure or guidebook and the atmosphere is laid back. There are toilets, a snack bar, picnic tables and views of the coast and mountains. It is open from 09.00 to 17.00, April to September, and for an hour later in October to March.

I blinked when I saw the outside of the new **Sofitel Imperial Hotel** at **Wolmar**; it looks like a temple in Thailand. There is a serenity within that seems to induce calm and, architecturally, it is unlike the usual beach resorts. There are 136 guest rooms (each 50m^2 in area) and five suites, all with the usual facilities of a *grand* category hotel, including 24-hour room service.

There is a popular public beach at **Flic en Flac**. The odd name of this place is thought to come from old Dutch, an onomatopoeic word for the sound of hands slapping goatskin drums. Say it quickly. There are public toilets, and people sometimes camp by the beach among the *filao* trees. The fenced-off areas are to encourage more trees to grow without interference. Buses serve here from Quatre Bornes.

The distinctive roof over the three-storey public areas of the **Pirogue Sun Hotel**, reminiscent of a pirogue's sail billowing in the wind, is repeated in the thatch over its air-conditioned cottages, set in a nine hectare tropical garden. Its image is that of a family hotel, with day and night entertainment, where guests can do what they like, or nothing at all. There are deep sea fishing and scuba diving centres, free watersports, trimaran cruises, water polo, five floodlit tennis courts, a children's club, video lounge, cabaret shows, a live band each night and a casino.

The hotel was opened in 1976 and has its 250 cottage units grouped in horseshoe shapes, none of them far from the sea and its well-tended beach. All rooms have twin or double beds, private bath/shower/toilet, colour TV, radio, mini-bar, telephone, air conditioning and private terrace. Remarkably in such a sprawling property, there is

24-hour room service to each bungalow, which is good since it takes a while to find your way to the restaurants.

Groups of local schoolchildren are sometimes shown around the hotel to familiarise them with tourism. It is a lively mass market hotel with rates in the *grand* category. Business clients can negotiate special terms according to space available. Most of the rooms are sold through European tour operators.

Near enough for a three-minute walk to the Pirogue casino is the **Pearle Beach (Sunset) Hotel**. This is a small hotel that used its limited space to expand to 50 double air conditioned rooms, all with bathroom and telephone. There is a generous use of concrete and angular walls in the sea-facing bungalows and a solid fence blocking off the beach. *Low medium*.

The **Villas Caroline** at Flic en Flac have expanded, too, from a few self-catering bungalows to 58 double-bedroom units, all with air conditioning and private bathroom, built on a heart-shaped beach that is separated from the main beach strip. There is a fully licensed restaurant with European and Creole dishes and a weekly *séga* show performed by the villagers. *Medium* category. The **Little Acorn** at Flic en Flac is a small guesthouse, not on the beach, *basic* category.

The main road to Port Louis cuts from the coast through cane fields, bypassing the smoking chimney of the Medine factory and the village of **Bambous**, named after the bamboos that once grew there. **La Ferme Reservoir** is below the **Corps de Garde** mountain (719m) on the district border. The **Fisheries Research Centre** is at **Albion** on the coast beyond the cane fields. There are caves at **Pointe aux Caves** and **Trois Cavernes**, which is inland from Flic en Flac. Neither group of caves is commercially exploited.

From **Petit Verger** on the coast, a leafy road with hedges on either side leads down to **Pointe aux Sables**, which has grown into a residential suburb because of its proximity to the city. **Koenig's Tower** on the district boundary overlooking the Grand River Northwest and the road into Port Louis is a national monument.

Plaines Wilhems

Although Plaines Wilhems has had settlers since 1690, officially it only became an inhabited district in 1877. Since then it has burgeoned into the island's most densely populated region, with at least 30% of Mauritius's population living in the plateau towns of Beau Bassin, Rose Hill, Quatre Bornes, Phoenix, Vacoas, Floreal and Curepipe. Historians differ as to how it got its unusual name. Perhaps it came from two Dutchmen, called Wilhelm, who settled there in 1690, or from one Dutchman called William Willemsz, or from a marooned German pirate, Wilhem Leiching, whom the French found there in 1721.

The district begins as a thin wedge between the Port Louis and Black River districts, along the main road through the suburbs of the city to Coromandel. It widens as the road climbs gradually from the 200m elevation of Beau Bassin to the 540m of Curepipe. There are houses and shops all the way until you reach the hills and tea plantations of Midlands, beyond Curepipe, and the forests and reservoirs south of Henrietta.

The upper part of Plaines Wilhems was wild forest for much of the last century. The lower part had a population of 10,112 in 1817, but this had fallen to 7,781 by 1830. The cholera epidemic in 1861 caused the first exodus from Port Louis by people seeking a healthier climate, who swelled the population to 28,020. The malaria epidemic of 1866–68 accelerated the drift.

This migration resulted in ghettos. Whereas Port Louis had been a cosmopolitan mixture, the races divided to form new towns. Those of French origin settled in Curepipe, the upper class of the coloured population chose Rose Hill. The division between social/ethnic groups was emphasised by the trains, which had three separate classes, and were used by the plateau town dwellers to commute every day to Port Louis. Now the settlements from Beau Bassin to Curepipe have merged into a single, built-up area, and people travel by car or classless bus. The divisions remain by tradition.

For the visitor, the district has several *basic* category guesthouses and, oddly, several large hotels that were opened with great enthusiasm, only to degenerate into eyesores on the landscape as guests failed to patronise them, except for a few hours at a time or in occasional groups from Réunion and Madagascar.

On the borders of the district, by the Luna Park fairground, is the **Sunray Hotel**, a huge block built in 1972 with the idea of providing accommodation for visitors to the industrial estate of **Coromandel**, which it overlooks. It has 72 *basic*-category rooms and two enormous halls, popular for wedding receptions.

Buses (from Victoria Square) to Curepipe take either the trunk road or the more interesting main road that leads straight up the hill to **Beau Bassin**, revealing Mauritius' own brand of suburbia. The town takes its name from a pool in the area. It has a small municipal park, **Balfour Gardens**, overlooking the **Plaines Wilhems Gorge**, where there is a waterfall. Across this valley is Le Réduit (see Moka). **La Tour Blanche**, a white manor house built in 1834, lies to the south of the garden. This is where Charles Darwin stayed during his visit in 1836. At the other side of the town are the island prisons, the police training school and the college of education.

Beau Bassin and **Rose Hill** are intertwined, sister towns separated only by a stroke, since they are run with a joint town hall as Beau Bassin/Rose Hill. They are mainly residential without large-scale industries. Taken as one town, it has a larger population (above 90,000) than Curepipe, and is second only to Port Louis.

Although Beau Bassin/Rose Hill was declared a town in 1896, it was not until 1927 that it was decided to build its town hall. This resulted in the series of linked, two-tiered pavilions that lie off the main road just outside the centre of Rose Hill. As well as the town hall, the complex includes the largest theatre in the Indian Ocean region, with an extravagant rococo interior of gold leaf and maroon plush. When it opened in 1933, the first performance was a movie and the theatre became known as **The Plaza**, although from 1934 stage shows and cultural events have taken place frequently. There is also an art gallery in the complex.

The **British Council** office and library is in Rose Hill, with a director appointed in 1987 to revive the Council's work after a period of reduced activity.

A number of solid Victorian buildings have been preserved amidst the lock-up shops and apartment blocks of this bustling town. Some say its name comes from the rosy glow of sunset on the Corps de Garde mountain behind it, while others claim the town, being on a hill, was named after Rose, the mistress of the landowner. The **Corps de Garde** mountain (719m) won its name because a French military post was established on it to control the bands of runaway slaves.

The **Auberge de Rose Hill** is close to the Plaza Theatre, down an alley off the main road, 500m from the town centre. There are 25 *basic* category rooms (at Rs150 a night) with shower and toilet.

Rose Hill has several eateries, all low in price and service. Don't be confused into thinking the **Café de France** is a charming French restaurant. Whatever it was once, it is now *basic* Chinese. The

Veeramunder Restaurant has an old-fashioned frontage with bottles in glass cabinets. I was attracted to the **Blue Dahlia** bar-restaurant by its blue and white checked tablecloths but was put off by prices which rose as I sat down. The **Blue Mauritius** nightclub is above a shopping arcade and has a notice saying it is a tourist residence. Another notice says: 'Persons without partners not admitted'.

While the **Riverside Hotel** at Belle Rose is indeed beside a river, it is unattractive and stagnant-looking. The hotel is a guesthouse-type block of 15 rooms, each with telephone, fan and shower/toilet. By the main road, it is *basic* category.

The main road links up with the highway of Phoenix and Curepipe at the St Jean's Church roundabout. Buses turn there to **Quatre Bornes**, where four former sugar estates (Bassin, La Louise, Palma and Beau Séjour) shared a common four-point boundary. With a population of some 55,000 this town has developed on either side of the main road as the centre of five residential communities. The emergence of a large middle class in the area is apparent from the attractive modern shops, two bookshops, supermarkets and the quality restaurants and snack bars. It aspires to resemble High Street, UK or Main Street, USA.

The island's top business-class hotel is located here, above a shopping complex in the Georgetown Building, opposite the town hall, taxi stand and bus-stop. The **Gold Crest Hotel**, opened in 1986, has a lift up to the wood-panelled bar and reception lobby on the third floor where a small fountain lends it a tranquil atmosphere.

There are 43 bedrooms and five suites, all with individual air conditioning, private bathroom/toilet, TV, radio and direct-dial telephone. All rooms have lots of cupboard space, two armchairs, and a long desk/vanity unit. Suites have a separate sitting area and a telephone extension in the bathroom. The rooms are on one side of a corridor with floor-to-ceiling windows overlooking the central plaza, so the ambience is bright and spacious.

This is a *grand* hotel in style and service, with rates unbelievably in the *basic* category, inclusive of breakfast and tax. With special facilities for business visitors (discount on rack rate, 24-hour telex, room service, efficient switchboard, photocopy and typist service and conference/banquet hall), it is also popular with tourists and long-stay visitors, especially because of its midway location within easy reach of any part of the island.

Lying back from the main road is **El Monaco**, a hotel that is a warren of 94 rooms of different vintages (the hotel was begun in 1971), with shower/toilet and fans. Brightly decorated in green and white, this is a *basic* category hotel catering for tour groups from Réunion.

Quatre Bornes has an open air market on Wednesday and Saturday, the exotic jewellers **Bijouterie Ravior** (tel: 454 3229), and such diversions as a Yoga Meditation Centre and a Unisex Gym.

It has an odd selection of eateries. The main one is **Rolly's Steak & Seafood House** (*medium*) on the first floor of the building next to the Gold Crest. Open daily 11.30–13.30 and 18.30–22.00, it serves steaks imported from Australia. On the opposite side of the road is the **Happy Valley Seafood and Sharkfin Restaurant**, open daily 12.00–14.30 and 18.30–23.00, where there is also a takeaway counter with such delicacies as suckling pig. *Medium.*

Bread and cake fanatics are well served in Quatre Bornes. **Le Croissant Pastry Shop** is open 05.00–21.00, and freshly baked bread is also available from **La Baguette Magique**. For Indian specialities, look for **Le Piment Rouge** at the Port Louis entrance to the town with a terrace overlooking the main road. **Le Top**, a new disco, is in the town centre while upstairs above an office complex (you'll spot its mauve neon sign) is **Le Snooker**, open 14.00–02.00, with a smart bar serving snacks, a restaurant and three pool tables (the craze in Mauritius). The Skills Training Centre is a video game joint.

Southwards beyond the Candos Mountains, the main road leads to **Vacoas** (pronounced Vak-wa), named Les Vacoas in the last century after the pandanus trees that grew in the region. A sister town of Phoenix, with which it shares a population of 55,000, it obtained municipal status in 1968. Residential and agricultural, it produces mainly vegetables with some light industry. The heart of the town is a crossroads with a taxi park and a public toilet on one side and the Savoy Cinema near the municipality building.

Overlooking the taxi park is the **Café National**, open for lunch and dinner in a *basic* grade snack bar atmosphere. More overtly Chinese is the **Mandarin Restaurant** around the corner, with a vivid red door and scrolls at the street entrance. The first floor restaurant has tables around a dance floor and tiny stage that are never used. It is something of an institution for the expatriate diplomats and Franco-Mauritians residing nearby and is open for lunch and dinner every day.

The British presence in Mauritius lingered on at Vacoas after independence with **HMS Mauritius**, a land-based communications station at St Paul's Avenue, and with British instructors training the men of the Special Mobile Force, which has its HQ in Vacoas.

The **Gymkhana Club** (tel: 696 1404) nearby originally opened in 1844 as a polo club for officers. It now has an 18-hole golf course, tennis courts, swimming pool, snooker room and a modern clubhouse with a view of the golf course, a restaurant with a stage, a lounge bar, changing rooms, and the atmosphere of a well-run establishment with dedicated, long-serving staff. Temporary membership is available to visitors on a daily or monthly basis.

Phoenix is an industrial area, with Mauritius Breweries producing their Phoenix and Stella beers at **Pont Fer**. Maurifoods is also there, and the colonial house close to its factory complex is the Phoenix

Youth Training Centre. The Margarine Industries factory is at Trianon. The old Trianon labourers' quarters is on the list of protected buildings.

Members of the diplomatic corps live in **Floreal**, in country houses set in large gardens on leafy lanes, which give the English stranger the impression of being in Haslemere. The **British High Commission** is at King George V Avenue in Floreal. The consular section is open 09.00–12.30, Monday to Friday. (If you don't have a car, the best way to get to the consulate is by bus to Vacoas, from where a taxi costs Rs40.) The **Madagascar Embassy** is in Queen Mary Street, Floreal, and visas are obtainable from its consulate for visits to Madagascar. Floreal is a comparatively new community, having been begun by Governor Hesketh Bell during his tenure, 1916–1924.

Two places in Floreal of interest to visitors are the **Floreal Knitwear Factory** and the **Diamond Duty Free Boutique** (tel: 686 5246, fax: 686 6243, telex: 4441 DIAMAUR IW), both at Mangalkhan, Floreal. The diamond show room is open 09.00–16.00, Monday to Friday and 09.00–12.00 on Saturdays, and has been selling diamonds direct to visitors since 1983. It is attached to a workshop operating under the EPZ laws, importing rough diamonds which are then cut and polished and exported. The enterprise employs 450 people.

Diamonds are on sale at prices upwards from US$100, with several worth $40,000 on display. Video cameras watch the shopper's every move. Any visitor who brings along a valid air ticket and passport can buy either diamonds or diamond and gold jewellery and duty free watches, but only with foreign currency (travellers cheques and credit cards are accepted). It must be done at least 48 hours before the purchaser's intended departure. When the customer has chosen a diamond and paid for it, it is sealed and placed in the safe and a receipt given. Delivery is made to the purchaser discreetly at the airport after check in and before Immigration. No duty is payable in Mauritius on the purchase, so the saving can be considerable.

There is an extraordinary hotel in the Floreal area, built like a castle with battlements around its roof and two cannons in front of it. It is called the **Mandarin** and is Chinese run, *basic* category, with 98 rooms. It is next to a private clinic.

Many writers in the past have seen **Curepipe** as a dismal place. Mark Twain described it as 'the nastiest spot on earth'. Michael Malim writing in the 1950s book *Island of the Swan*, which caused a stir in Mauritius when it was published, said 'it seems drowned in some immemorial woe ... stricken and inconsolable'. Mauritians themselves say there are two seasons in Curepipe: 'the rainy season and the season of rains'. Its annual rainfall matches London's. It can be humid ('God – the dankness of it all', wrote Malim) and temperatures as low as 7C have been known there.

Perhaps its off-putting publicity is a campaign by residents to keep

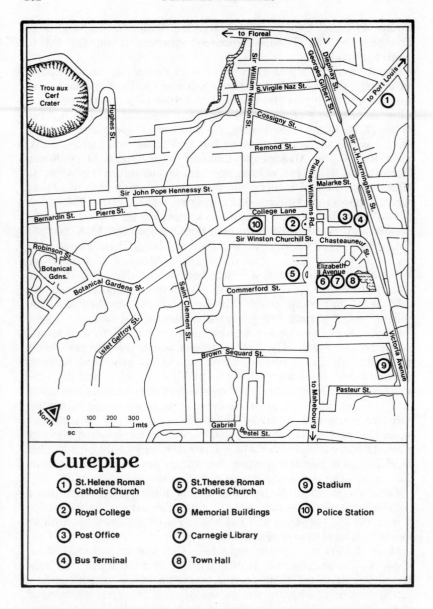

Curepipe

① St.Helene Roman Catholic Church
② Royal College
③ Post Office
④ Bus Terminal
⑤ St.Therese Roman Catholic Church
⑥ Memorial Buildings
⑦ Carnegie Library
⑧ Town Hall
⑨ Stadium
⑩ Police Station

visitors away. They like their privacy. The avenues of the residential areas are lined with tall bamboo hedges, hiding the old, French-style, verandaed villas, wooden cottages and concrete, cyclone-proof houses. Streets have no names displayed, nor numbers on the houses, so only those familiar with the town will find their way around. It is not a welcoming place, with its grim market building of upturned culverts. The town seems to have no heart, either geographically or spiritually.

Its origins go back to the 18th century when it was a halt for travellers from one side of the island to the other. The usual story is that travellers stopped to smoke there, after which they would clean (cure) their pipes. Its name is more likely to have come from a village in France. It was a military post in the 1830s and has a small hotel. In 1858, the population was 200. An invasion of new residents began in the 1860s and now the population is above 60,000.

From Curepipe to Port Louis is 22.04kms and to the airport is 21.72kms. It is at the highest elevation of any town in the island, 540m. Sometimes Curepipe is recommended for shopping but prices of the same goods will be lower in Port Louis. The only hotel of charm, a colonial mansion, the Park, opened to cater for the first air travellers, has now closed. It houses the headquarters of the Beachcomber group.

The best hotel in Curepipe is the **Continental**, above the busy Currimjee Arcade in the main shopping centre. There are 48 rooms (and two suites), all with air conditioning, bathroom, radio, telephone and TV, with two channels for in-house videos. The complex was built in 1972 yet the hotel, with its long entrance lounge and muted decor, manages to convey a tired 1950s ambience. There is a wealth of plastic upholstery. The bar is through a door at one end of the lounge and the public area toilet is locked so people who want to use it have to look for someone with a key. There are a restaurant, conference room and facilities for business visitors, but no atmosphere for work. In the arcade downstairs is a snack bar and a fish and chip shop, both belonging to the hotel. *Basic.*

The **town hall** overlooks a large compound of open square and gardens with the **Carnegie Library** and the former railway station, now used by the Central Water Authority, close to it. On the other side of the municipal compound are the Roman Catholic church of St Thérèse, the Prisunic supermarket and the casino. This is open every evening and from 14.00 on Sundays.

The formal **gardens**, with lawns, flower beds and pathways, softens the administrative square and provides relief from the chaos of the open air market nearby. The gardens include a memorial to Abbé de la Caille, the 18th century surveyor of the island, and a romantic statue of Paul and Virginie, which is a bronze replica of Mauritian sculptor Prosper d'Epinay's original. There are other listed national monuments in Curepipe, notably the grim stone building of **Royal College** and the **war memorial** in front of it.

It is tempting to wonder if the **market** building will ever be declared a national monument; it is certainly a unique feature of Curepipe's skyline, with its concrete pipes pointing upwards. In its foyer are kiosks selling local dishes, with eating booths behind the partitions.

The public toilets are closed for cleaning every day, 06.00–06.30, 10.30–10.45, 15.00–15.15 and 17.15–17.30. Be warned. The **bus station** adjoins the market and also has several *basic* category eating places. Buses from here go to all parts of the island.

Eating in Curepipe fits all pockets. As well as the basic places there are a few medium grade ones, such as **Asterix** (formerly Nobby's), a ground floor restaurant reached along a passageway through shops. Descended from 'the first steak house of Mauritius established in 1975' the restaurant has a lot of cutely named dishes on its menu, such as 'Hors d'oeuvrix' and 'Soupsix'. It is open for lunch and dinner, except on Sundays, and tries to ape European quick steak food bars. There is a **Kentucky Fried Chicken** outlet, too, in Curepipe, to show it is keeping up with the times.

The **Tropicana**, a first floor Chinese restaurant, opened in 1964 and is showing its age. A restaurant with lots of stairs to climb is the **Chinese Wok**, which specialises in seafood.

Le Gaulois is a corner cafe with a streetside terrace for watching the passing parade of shoppers. It is open daily, except Sunday, for lunch and has a selection of table d'hote menus as well as a la carte, *medium* range. With a few tables covered in check cloths and a photograph of James Dean by the bar, it has an upmarket ambience, popular with tourists and locals, and run with quiet charm since 1979 by its owner, Alain Maderbocus.

For fine cooking, served in a summery atmosphere, there is **La Nouvelle Potinière**, with a waiting area of comfortable sofas, rustic walls, and a proper bar. Standards have remained constant over the years in this *medium* category restaurant, popular with lunchtime tourists.

Dining in a *grand* style is possible at **Au Gourmet Restaurant**. A house built in 1888 is given over to the splendour of this restaurant set in a landscaped garden, which boasts a scaled-down 1889 replica of the Eiffel Tower in one corner. The restaurant is open daily, except on Sundays and public holidays, for lunch (when customers are mostly tourists) and dinner (when they are locals).

The **Botanical Gardens** are not far from this restaurant, and its well-kept lawns enhance the charm of this miniature Pamplemousses. There is a small lake in which *nandia* palms can be seen growing. Entrance is free and it is a pleasant place in which to recover from the cacophony of Curepipe. Lovers like to linger there. The Forestry Department offices next door are where permission can be sought to visit the nature reserves of the interior.

The unsightly spread of Curepipe can be seen from the hills around the extinct volcanic crater of **Trou aux Cerfs**, at 650m above sea level. The panoramic view takes in the plateau towns and the mountains to the north and northwest, including the three cones of **Trois Mamelles**. The inside of the crater is wooded and it is possible to climb down the 85m to its bottom. The rim measures 335m across. There is a meteorological station of futuristic design poised by the crater, as though mooning for its architectural soulmate, the market complex.

On the Brasserie road from the residential enclave of **Forest Side** to Mare aux Vacoas is one of the model ship workshops, **Comajora** (tel: 676 5345, fax: 675 1644). The model shipbuilding industry started small but became so successful the original craftsmen split up and developed rival workshops. There are now several all over the island. Comajora employs 300 people, making models of historical vessels based on plans used to build the original ships.

The 60 different models include famous ships such as the *Golden Hind, Victory, Mayflower, USS Constitution* and the *Cutty Sark*. Each model is made by hand exactly to scale, using camphor or teak: camphor for the keel, hard *bois de natté* for the masts, yards and pully blocks, soft lilac for the helm and capstan. The sails are 'weathered' by being soaked in tea. Copies of period naval furniture, such as sea chests and wardrobes with brass fittings, are also made here. Some models, like the *Bounty*, take six months to make. Prices are high, but there are models as low as Rs400 and some more than Rs20,000. Model ships can be sent worldwide, or packed for taking in the hold, as checked baggage, on the plane home.

Mare aux Vacoas is the largest reservoir in Mauritius, a mountain lake at 600m above sea level, surrounded by forest. Unlike many of the reservoirs it can be visited by road. At **La Marie**, on the road from Curepipe, there is a memorial erected to the hapless Matthew Flinders who, having helped discover and map Australia and circumnavigated it in stages, was confined to this region of Mauritius for six years by the French after landing at Baie du Cap.

An aqueduct runs alongside the road, flowing to filter beds at La Marie. The Mare aux Vacoas reservoir can be seen by climbing up 62 steps set into its side from the road. There are two observation shafts built into the water about 15m out from the bank, and it is possible to descend the spiral staircase to where the water roars through the intake. The lake is surrounded by pine forest and traveller's palms, and ripples with waves as the wind ruffles it.

Further on through the forest, where deer abound, there is a motorable track leading to **Mare Longue**, another reservoir. The track passes through the shorn terrain of tea plantations and through woods where monkeys leap excitedly out of the way of the occasional car. It is possible to hike from the main road on forest trails to reach the seven cascades of **Tamarind Falls**. This is a restricted area so permission is required from the Forestry Department. The main road continues southwards, to turn off at **Le Pétrin** (where there is a noticeboard showing forest walks) to Grand Bassin in the Savanne District.

Moka

This central district is part of a plateau of scrub, sugar cane and, in the Midlands area, tea. It caters for the educational overspill of Port Louis, with the University of Mauritius and the Mahatma Gandhi Institute, and also has the governor's official residence at Le Réduit. Its population is about 55,000.

Coffee was planted here when it was introduced from Al Makha in Yemen, hence the name Moka. Its boundary runs along the mountains ringing the south of Port Louis to Pieter Both, then skirts below La Nicolière Reservoir, across Nouvelle Découverte plateau, embracing the agricultural centre of the island, to the outskirts of Curepipe and Rose Hill.

The approach to Moka is by the two-lane motorway that links Port Louis with the residential plateau towns. Landscaped with oleanders, this is a pleasant contrast to the garbage-littered main road which provides access to it from Port Louis. The road to Moka was originally built by Labourdonnais and the highway was begun in 1960.

After crossing the St Louis Stream, the road passes through **Pailles**, a suburban community with church, temple and mosque overshadowed by **Pailles Hill** (225m) and the peaks of the **Moka mountain range**. The countryside opens up as the road begins to climb, with hills on the left and the flats of Coromandel on the right. The western boundary is the Grand River Northwest, into which flows the **Terre Rouge River** which forms the southern boundary.

Pailles has become widely known with the recent opening of **Domaine Les Pailles** (tel: 212 4225, fax: 212 4226), an extraordinary creation by a Mauritian who has converted previously unutilised land into a kind of theme park. A whole day can be spent there discovering 'the old ways of living in an environment surrounded by nature with old traditions carefully revived'. It is only 10 minutes' drive from Port Louis and visitors stay a few hours touring in a horse-drawn carriage, visiting a sugar mill and a rum distillery (with tasting of the products) watching *séga* dancing, or going by Land Rover into the surrounding forested hills, trying trekking, horse riding or taking a 1.5km tour by 'ti-train'.

There are four *grand* restaurants: the **Canelle Rouge** for lunch parties and, for lunch or dinner, the **Clos St Louis** with Mauritian and French cuisine, the **Indra** for impressive Indian dishes and the **Fu**

Xiao for Chinese specialities. The **Grand Casino du Domaine** is open from 13.00 for slot machine playing, and from 21.00 to 03.00 for the tables; on Sundays it opens at 15.00.

The road branches off to the left beneath **Junction Peak** to the residential sprawl of **Moka**, **St Pierre** and **Constance**. The highway continues, skirting around the University and leaving the Moka district at the Cascade Bridge. The range of hills between Moka, St Pierre and Port Louis consists of the bush-covered **Guiby**, **Berthelot**, **Junction** and **Mount Ory** peaks, rising to 500m.

Off to the right, just after the road to Moka crosses the rubbish-clogged Moka River, is a lane leading to the commercial museum enterprise known as **Eureka**. Although it has the appearance of a fine French colonial house with its many dormer windows and encircling veranda, it was built by an Englishman, with the help of a French carpenter, at the beginning of English colonisation. The layout of the garden is English. It gained its name when Eugène Leclézio, a wealthy lawyer and planter, cried 'Eureka' as his bid to buy the house at auction was accepted. There are guided tours of the house, and in the garden small pavilions offer 'made in Mauritius' products and quality souvenirs.

The **University of Mauritius** is situated in front of the governor's residence at Réduit. Rose Hill is only 3kms away and Port Louis, down the highway, can be reached by car in ten minutes. The university was created in 1965 with the help of a £3 million grant from the British Government, with the College of Agriculture, established in 1924, as its nucleus. It provides training facilities on an in-service, non-graduate basis in technology, administration, and agriculture to support the government's policy of industrialisation and improved agricultural productivity.

The student population varies from year to year, according to financing, and once reached 1,500. Together with the school of agriculture, there are a centre for medical studies, a school of administration and a department of law, as well as a school for industrial technology and a computer centre. In the same area are the Sugar Research Institute, the Institute of Education, the Examinations Syndicate, the College of the Air, and the Ministry of Agriculture. The **Mahatma Gandhi Institute**, for the study of Indian and African cultures, is within walking distance of the Réduit campus.

In 1748, the French governor, David, built a small wooden fort, surrounded by a ditch and stone walls, on a 290m high bluff between two rivers. It was to serve as a redoubt (*Réduit*) for women, children and valuables of the French East India Company if ever the island was invaded.

La Brillane, who was governor from 1776–1779, added a central block with two wings and the date of his addition (1778) is carved on a plaque above the front door. **Le Réduit** became the official residence of the governors from then on, with Government House in Port Louis used as a residence only during the winter theatre, racing and social season.

Part of the house was destroyed by a cyclone in 1868 and it was extensively added to during the 19th century, particularly when Napier Broome was governor (1880–83). During his tenure of office, the first telephone line in Mauritius was installed, to connect Government House with Le Réduit. A special stop was made at Le Réduit by trains bearing officials when the governor was working at home. Governor Bell (1916–24) erected a small, stylised white temple in the grounds, dedicated to the creator of Le Réduit, from 'his grateful successors'.

Camphor and badamier trees line the drive that curves up to the entrance of the two-storied mansion, with its columns, verandas and mix of Victorian and French architecture draped in bougainvillaea. The gardens in the 132 hectare estate are overlooked by a wide terrace joining the two wings of the house.

The French botanist, Aublet, laid out the original gardens, which were later gradually anglicised by British governors and their wives. One British governor called the house 'our prison between the ravines' and the point between the gorges is called **Le Bout du Monde** (end of the world). The gardens, but not the house, are open most mornings according to government usage, and with security permission obtained at the gate.

Tea plantations thrive in the Moka district, their clipped bushes giving an orderly air to the landscape. Almost the whole of Mauritius can be seen from the summit of **Piton du Milieu**, a tower of rock rising to 585m in the middle of the island. It looks unscaleable if viewed from the pumping station in the valley below the dam of the Piton du Milieu reservoir. There is a path leading to it behind the station, but the actual climb is steeply precarious and a rope is necessary for the vertical sections.

In the early days of the French occupation, the path from Vieux Grand Port to Port Louis passed through the district. The settlement at **Quartier Militaire** remains from the days when it was a military post offering protection to the travellers against attacks by runaway slaves. Moka is the only district of Mauritius with no hotels, although the villages all have shops where beer and supplies can be obtained.

210

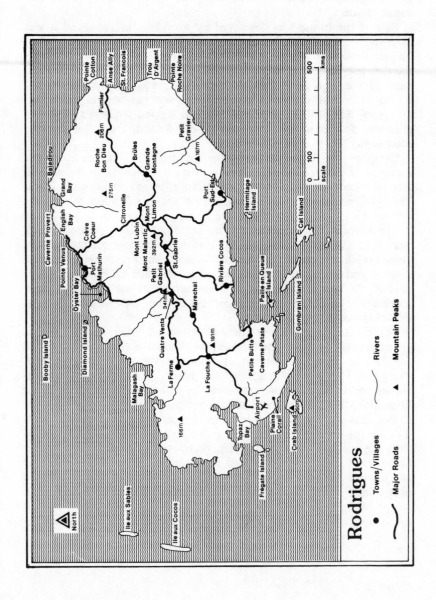

Rodrigues

• Towns/Villages

⌒ Major Roads

~ Rivers

▲ Mountain Peaks

THE ISLANDS

Rodrigues and Island Dependencies of Mauritius

RODRIGUES

Rodrigues is an island alone, part of the Mauritius nation but 500kms further east. It has a mostly Roman Catholic Creole population who, in their isolation, sometimes feel close to the Creoles of the Seychelles than to Indo-Mauritian dominated Mauritius. That's a contention visitors are made aware of as Rodriguans speak their mind about what they see as neglect of their island.

Rodrigues is mountainous and stark, a tough place in which to earn a living. It is not a tropical paradise but the adventurous will find it a fascinating, peaceful place to explore, with a people whose shy friendliness is genuine. Since there are few places in which to stay and not much transport to get around, camping and hiking are probably the best way to enjoy the island.

It is 108km^2 in area, about the size of the British Channel Island of Jersey. It is shaped like a fish, is 18km long (west to east) and 8km wide (north to south), and has a population of 36,000 Creoles of African, Malagasy and French stock. Of volcanic origin, Rodrigues has a mountainous profile of steep hills and narrow valleys, the highest points being **Mounts Limon** at 393m and **Malartic** at 326m. Its climate is relatively warm, with a temperature varying from 15°C in winter to a maximum of 32°C in summer.

History

Rodrigues shares its history with Mauritius although it was discovered later, in 1528, and retained the name of its Portuguese discoverer, Diego Rodrigues, throughout Dutch, French and British colonisation. The Dutch paid little attention to Rodrigues and the first known settlers were French, although they came during the Dutch period. These were nine French protestants fleeing from France, led by François Leguat. They arrived in 1691 to find the island covered in luxuriant vegetation, with an abundance of birds and tortoises. After two years, the settlement broke up and Leguat was arrested on the orders of the Dutch governor of Mauritius.

In 1725, France decided to colonise Rodrigues in the name of Louis XV and sent eight soldiers, 13 planters and 15 slaves. The colonisation was unsuccessful, although some of the slaves remained when the French left. The French noted that Rodrigues suffered from more cyclones and higher winds than the Ile de French, and had a difficult approach through rocks and shoals to the harbour they called Port Mathurin.

The first settler who stayed permanently was a master mariner, Germain le Gros, who arrived in September 1792, to engage in fishing and trading. He was followed in 1793 by Michel Gorry and Philibert Marragon, who had earlier visited in 1791. Marragon and his wife lived at L'Orangerie until both died on Rodrigues in 1826.

In the time-honoured manner of expatriates living on a small island, the three French settlers distrusted each other and soon fell out. Marragon was civil agent for the French government, a position that did not deter him from entertaining and victualling the crews of British ships when they put in for water and food, much to Le Gros' annoyance.

The fraternisation of the settlers on Rodrigues with the British made the new governor of the Ile de France, General Decaen, keen to replace Marragon and the others with his own island's unwanted lepers. The plan failed. Marragon remained and the lepers went to Diego Garcia.

Marragon conducted a census in 1804 which shows the island's population as 22 whites (about half of them actually mulattoes) and 82 slaves. The majority of the slaves were from Mozambique, yet nearly a third (24) were born in Rodrigues.

In 1794, Britain decided to capture the Ile de France, but their attempts were limited to foraging expeditions to Rodrigues. They wanted to take Rodrigues, too, and concentrated on building up good relations with the settlers and paying for their supplies instead of looting. By August 1809, they had no qualms about making their intentions known and landed the first of the forces being assembled to capture the Ile de France, 200 infantry and 200 sepoys.

The occupation of Rodrigues began enthusiastically, with Colonel Keating, who was in command, writing home: 'These are some of the most delightful valleys I ever saw and the soil naturally rich in one of the finest climates in the world capable of producing every sort of vegetation and there is a sufficient quantity of land already cleared for cultivation and the feeding of cattle'. Keating imported cattle and slaves from Madagascar as more British troops assembled.

In July 1810, a force of 4,000 left Rodrigues and went on to capture Bourbon (Réunion) from the French. Following their unexpected defeat at Vieux Grand Port in August, the British gathered a large force in Rodrigues for their successful assault on the Ile de France in December 1810. After that, the British occupied Rodrigues until April 1812 when they withdrew, leaving behind most of the 300 slaves they had imported. British rule of Rodrigues was confirmed by the Treaty of Paris in May 1814.

The first British settler was a young man called Thomas Robert Pye, a lieutenant of the Marines at a loose end, who was sent by Governor Farquhar in 1821. He only stayed two years. When slavery was abolished, those slaves who had not emancipated themselves already promptly left their owners and squatted on crown land. They finally settled in the mountains where their descendants still live today, farming the cattle which were, by now, roaming freely.

In the mid-19th century, several Europeans or near-Europeans settled in Rodrigues, mostly in the lowlands. They included ship-wrecked sailors and minor British functionaries, such as policemen, who liked the island. Some of the British married Rodriguan women while others had affairs with them and, as the saying goes in Rodrigues, 'left one or two portraits behind'.

The portraits and the mixed-blood population were centred around Port Mathurin, Oyster Bay, Grand Bay and Le Ferme. When the first steamer arrived in the 1890s, so did more settlers, including Indian and Chinese traders. By 1970 the Chinese owned 90% of all the shops on the island.

The growth of the population was rapid. Because there were more men than women at first, most women had several partners, their children being raised as the children of the man of the moment. At the end of the 19th century, the population was 3,000. Twenty years later this had become 6,573. The population almost doubled itself in subsequent 20-year periods, becoming 11,385 in 1944, 18,587 in 1963 and 32,000 in 1981.

Rodrigues was administered as a dependency of Mauritius during the 158 years of British rule. Like a poor relation, it was mostly forgotten or neglected, with occasional official reports warning of the consequences of too large a population.

Since 1968, it has been an integral part of Mauritius. The chief government official is now an administrative secretary, appointed by the prime minister, and working under the aegis of the Ministry of Rodrigues, which has its office and civil servants located in Port Louis. The island elects two members to parliament.

Besides Port Mathurin, there are agglomerations such as Oyster Bay, English Bay, La Ferme and Mont Lubin. However, most of the inhabitants are scattered, living either on hillsides or in valleys and dependant on farming. The export of agricultural products (livestock, maize, onions) to Mauritius, and fishing, are the main income sources.

Getting there

The sense of going somewhere 'off the beaten track' begins when you try to get to Rodrigues. Neither of the two options (sea or air) is simple.

By sea

Sailings by scheduled ferry service from Port Louis are irregular, at intervals of 16 to 20 days. Sea travel is really only suitable if you are in Mauritius, with time to spare to wait for the next sailing. All fares include meals and the fares are the same for tourists and residents.

The voyage takes about 36 hours (two nights). The vessel spends about seven nights in Rodrigues before making the return journey, giving time to explore. For the latest information, contact Rogers & Co, Shipping Department, 5 Kennedy Street, PO Box 60, Port Louis, tel: 208 6801, fax: 208 5045, telex: 4312 FINSHIP IW.

By air

Flights to and from Rodrigues are by the 46-seat ATR42 aircraft of Air Mauritius. There are daily flights with an extra one on Tuesdays, Wednesdays and Saturdays. Demand seems great and reservations need to be made well in advance, and reconfirmed. Rodrigues is linked by air only with Mauritius; it has no international air services of its own.

As well as the one-way fares, there are two official fares available: the 30-day domestic excursion round trip far at Rs1,593, saleable only to Mauritian citizens and residents of either Mauritius or Rodrigues; and the 30-day round trip fare at Rs3,046 (almost double) for non-residents. Tourists can soften the blow by buying the air ticket from a travel agent in Mauritius (instead of from Air Mauritius or overseas), when it comes lower as part of a package that includes accommodation.

The check-in procedure at Sir Seewoosagur Ramgoolam Airport for flights to Rodrigues is informal and involves sorting out standby passengers from those with confirmed reservations. It is advisable to check in early in case your seat is given to one of the standbys. Each passenger as well as luggage (maximum is 15kgs) is weighed on the scales. Foreigners have to fill in an embarkation card and show passport at Immigration, even though this is a domestic flight. The ATR42 has 46 seats and not much leg or arm space, so keep your hand baggage small.

The first sight of Rodrigues, in the dry season, is of parched hillsides with cactus-like vegetation and box-type houses dotted all over an inhospitable landscape. The airport is at the opposite end of the island to the main town.

The terminal is a small, one-storey building, with spectators waiting obediently behind the perimeter fence where jeeps and buses are parked on the hard coral sand. There are more policemen in uniform on duty than one usually sees in one place in Mauritius. An Air Mauritius clerk is at a desk in the baggage reclaim hall (shed) to reconfirm the departure reservations of all arriving passengers.

If you haven't prearranged transport you can take a bus or one of the jeeps or vans that come to pick up hotel guests. When it's time to leave Rodrigues, remember neither food nor drink is available at the airport and, since you must check in with enough time to make sure you have your seat, take refreshments with you. The flight may be late so a good book helps, too, as there is nothing to do during the wait. There is a toilet in the airport building.

Getting around

The name to remember is **Henri Meunier**. Henri's card says: '*Organisateur de vos excursions – Plongeur Professionnel – L'Homme à tout faire*'. He can be found in Mann Road, Port Mathurin, where he runs the Lagon Bleu restaurant and bar (tel: 831 1635). At the airport, look for a tough, fair-skinned man with a broad smile and the swagger of a pirate. His slogan is '*Sans Henri, vous n'êtes pas a Rodrigues*', and it's true. He has one of the island's only taxi-jeeps and whether you want to go touring by land or sea, he is the man who'll take you. You couldn't be in better hands.

Henri has various tour programmes for visitors that include trips by jeep and boat, with packed lunch, excursions to the nature reserves of the islands of Cocos and Sables, visits to the caves, diving and hiking. His prices are not excessive and his ability to arrange things seems limitless. Henri once found a message in a champagne bottle that had been dropped from the *SS Oriana* and drifted 4,000kms from the coast of Australia to the uninhabited Ile aux Cocos.

Excursions are also organised by Ebony Tourist Service (tel: 831 1540) whose proprietor, Willie Auguiste, also has a restaurant/bar, Ebony, in Jenner Street, Port Mathurin.

Getting around Rodrigues independently is difficult. There are buses that begin running at 05.30 and finish operating at 15.00. Most of them go into Port Mathurin, the island's main town, in the morning and out again in the afternoon, so a round trip to a particular beach in a day isn't possible unless you go out by bus and walk back, hitchhike, or hire Henri or a hotel van.

Beaches

Rodrigues is completely surrounded by a reef, with negotiable channels by the harbour and other points. There are sandy beaches although few of them are easily accessible by road. The best is **Pointe Cotton** in the east, but **Baladirou** on the northern cost is also recommended. To get to the beach at **St François** takes 30 minutes' walk from the nearest motorable point. **Petit Gravier** is a good beach in the south.

The **Ile aux Cocos** and the **Ile aux Sables**, which are pure beach islands, can only be reached by government boat from Port Mathurin. A permit (cost Rs250) is required for visiting Ile aux Cocos as it is a nature reserve (see Henri to arrange a trip). Excursions can also be made to **Diamond Island** and **Booby Island**, where there is a lighthouse, from Port Mathurin. In the summer, sailing competitions are held at **Pointe l'Herbe** (by the airport) with races around Frégate and Destinée Islands to Crab Island.

Caves
In the southern tail of the island, in an area of rugged views across a coral landscape, is a cave, its entrance hidden some way from where the jeeps park. A permit (which costs Rs50) has to be obtained to visit it and a guide is necessary. He waits for visitors only until 10.00, so don't be late. Best to go on an organised excursion. The **Caverne Patate**, near **Petite Butte**, is 600m long, a wondrous walk through a maze of stalactites and stalagmites of weird shapes.

The guide carries a *flambeau* (a flaming sack fuelled with kerosene on the end of an iron stake) to light the depths of the cave. The mud floor is damp and the cave floods when it rains. The exit has steps built into the rocks, emerging near the jeep park.

Souvenirs
Lots of dried squid and octopus. Also an amazing range of containers made out of *vacoas* (screwpine) reed, including some novelty brief-cases. There are several shops in Port Mathurin with a bewildering assortment of different baskets hanging from their ceilings. Prices are about Rs60 for the briefcase-size baskets, less for the *tente* individual lunch carriers. A Muslim shop sells T-shirts overprinted with Rodrigues slogans in badly spelled French and a Cocos Island T-shirt that has copied the Coca-Cola logo.

Economy
Fishing and agriculture provide the livelihood of Rodriguans although the young hanker for employment either with government or in commerce, not as independent entrepreneurs. There is no vibrant private sector as in Mauritius. Onions and garlic are grown for export to Mauritius and maize (the staple) and chicken are produced for home consumption. Livestock (cattle, pigs, sheep) are also reared for the Mauritian market. Octopus is dried and fish salted for export.

The old system, with farmers growing maize and beans and helping each other with harvesting and existing on a barter basis, has died out. People have become money and subsidy-minded. As a district of

Mauritius, social benefits filter through to the island from central government and international aid agencies.

Fishing

The island's fishing industry is organised on a cooperative basis under the auspices of the Rodriguan Fishermen's Cooperative Federation. Fish, when caught, is delivered to the area cooperative for distribution and sale in the island or for cold storage at the plant in Port Mathurin. Considerable training in fishing methods, assistance with boat and equipment purchase, catch monitoring and marketing, and also foreign aid funding, are provided under various schemes to sustain a viable fishing industry.

Banking

There are five banks, the main one being Barclays Bank. There are also branches of the State Commercial Bank, the Indian Ocean International Bank (IOIB), the Mauritius Commercial Bank, and of the Development Bank of Mauritius. Hours are 09.30–14.30, Saturdays 09.30–11.30, although the IOIB is open to 12.30.

Post office

The main post office is in Port Mathurin, part of the administration complex. It is open Monday to Friday, 08.00–11.15 and 12.00–16.00, and on Saturdays 08.00–11.45.

Telephone

Mauritius Telecom has a public call office with a spectacular view out to sea at **Mount Venus**, a 15-minute walk out of Port Mathurin. It is open Monday to Saturday, 07.00–22.00, and on Sundays and public holidays, 07.00–20.00. Collect calls can be made. There is IDD outgoing, and incoming IDD calls are possible. An international telex link was established in 1987 and there is a fax service, too.

IDD calls can be made worldwide, starting with 00 followed by the country code and the number being called. The number for national directory information is 90 and 10090 for international directory enquiries. To book calls to Mauritius and abroad, dial 10091. For weather information, dial 96; for police emergency, 999. The area code for Rodrigues is 8311 followed by three digits. From other countries, and from Mauritius, the country code is 010 230.

Entertainment

Séga is the traditional dance of Rodriguans but the older generation can cut a dash in formation dancing such as *le scottish rodriguais* and *la polka bébé*. *Séga* in Rodrigues is said to be more authentic (wilder?) than the stereotyped version danced for tourists in Mauritius. For the youth of the island, disco music is more popular, at informal functions or in dives in Oyster Bay.

There are 25 cultural groups in the island, linked together through the 500-member Rodriguan Artistes Association.

Language

Creole is the everyday language but educated Rodriguans will also speak French. English has been neglected, with the result that young Rodriguans' aspirations to work in government service (for which a credit in English is compulsory) are thwarted. Efforts are being made to improve the standard of teaching of English in the schools.

The main school in Port Mathurin is a joint venture between the Roman Catholic and the Anglican churches. There is a large state secondary school at Maréchal in the centre of the island, which is attended by pupils from all over Rodrigues.

Religion

The Roman Catholic faith is very strong and the religion of the vast majority, although perhaps less than 97% which is the figure usually quoted. Other active religions are Anglican, Adventist, Muslim and Hindu. Witchcraft is also practised, in the traditional Afro Creole manner of believing in the efficacy of certain potions, charms, herbs, fortune-telling and the warding off of evil.

Creoles and Chinese form the Roman Catholic community, although some Chinese are members of the Anglican church. There are no Buddhists. The Muslim community is small, mostly traders, but supports a mosque in Port Mathurin. There are a few Rastafarians to be seen in the interior village communities.

Where to stay

So far there are only a few places to stay. The official response to tourism is to encourage it as long as it remains simple and compatible with the island. At present, the attractions are seen as independent exploring, hill walking and isolated beach swimming.

There is one hotel, the new **Cotton Bay Hotel**, built on a white sand beach at Pointe Cotton, on the east coast. It is managed by Air Mauritius. There are 46 rooms and two suites all with air conditioning, mini-bar, telephone, music system, private bathroom with shower and toilet. The public rate quoted for 1994 is Rs3,500 for a double, Rs2,350 single, superior room with breakfast and dinner, so it is in the *medium* category. It is bound to be quiet.

There are guesthouses closer to activities in Port Mathurin and accommodation can be arranged in them in advance through a Mauritius tour operator (such as MTTB) or on arrival. Since the situation changes (new places opening, others closing) the best method is to leave everything to a local contact, such as Henri

Meunier, or the driver of the bus that takes you from the airport. All guesthouses are in the *basic* category, as are meals in the local snack bars and grocery shops.

AROUND RODRIGUES

The island's fish shape has its head in the east and its forked tail in the west. The bay at **St François** is its mouth. The road from the airport at the western corner of Rodrigues to Port Mathurin winds over the spine of mountains in the island's centre. The spines run north to south with deep ravines between them.

The airport is at **Plaine Corail**, aptly named for the coral plain on which the airstrip is built. The road passes through **La Ferme** where a school and church serve scattered dwellings. The crossroads at **Quatre Vents**, with Chinese grocery stores on opposite corners, reveals views down the valleys to the sea on both sides. A building proclaiming itself to be a 'nightclub' is isolated on the road to **Malartic**. It's sometimes open on Saturday nights. **St Gabriel**, with its enormous church, is located to the south of the main road. The area around **Mont Lubin** has a compound of government workshops and offices.

There is a kiosk as a viewing pavilion by a double bend after **Citronelle**. Red-fruited aloes, with their cactus-like leaves, grow with the mango trees and scrub where the road descends into **Crève Coeur**. The Queen Elizabeth Hospital is on the right and the meteorological station and a Hindu temple are on the left. The road divides when it reaches the coast at **Lascar Bay**, the right fork leading to **English Bay** and the left fork to **Port Mathurin**.

This is a pretty, well-ordered town with the access road (Jenner Street) running its length (1,700 metres) and emerging to cross over reclaimed land and on to the residential village at **Oyster Bay**. Parallel to Jenner Street is Fisherman Lane on the waterfront, where there are a small market, the customs office and a jetty. There are three other streets also running parallel northeast to southwest: Duncan, Douglas and Victoria Streets, giving the town a depth of about 300 metres. The streets linking them at right angles are leafy lanes lined with neat houses, many of them colonial wooden bungalows behind well-trimmed hedges.

A popular guesthouse in Port Mathurin is the **Beau Soleil** (Victoria Street, tel: 831 1637). This is a bright and airy building with one shower and toilet for the rooms downstairs and six rooms sharing one shower and toilet upstairs. Continental breakfast is served in the rooms or there is a small dining room on the ground floor with a view over the street. Meals there by arrangement. The atmosphere is polite and friendly; rates from Rs350 for two people.

In the same street is the **Victoria Restaurant**, with a thatched roof, red-painted, wrought iron frontage, and a view of a vacant lot. Although it is said to be open until 22.00 every night, it is often closed when there are no customers. It is a good spot for drinks. There are some taverns in the town which serve drinks and snacks but they are very *basic*. Lunch is taken from 11.30.

In Mann Street is Henri's restaurant, **Lagon Bleu**, family run and not cheap but lots of food and good fun. In Jenner Street is the **Ebony**, also *medium* in price, with seafood specialities and Rodrigues cuisine in a bamboo-enclosed patio, and also a disco.

The **Restaurant du Port** is to be found where Duncan Street divides into two at the eastern end of the town (Johnston Street). It is open from 10.00 to 23.00 daily and is a lively local café where the cook will prepare whatever you request from his fridge. Fish is served either as a main course or chopped up for snacks. Wine, spirits and beer are sold and all drinks have the prices marked on their bottles. There is an outside patio and an inside, shed-type dining room with loud music. If any customers get too friendly, the others will intervene. *Basic* and good.

There is *basic* accommodation at **Ciel d'Été**, in rooms above a Chinese general store at the Jenner Street entrance to the town. The cost is Rs150 per person with breakfast. Shared shower/toilet. There are six small bungalow units, part of the Ciel d'été establishment, a minute's walk away over the bayfront river bridge. These have brightly furnished rooms with attached shower/toilet (and hot water), available for rent by the day, with breakfast.

A walk down Jenner Street leads past the colonial house of the administrator (built in 1873), with a cannon outside the gates and the gardener acting as security guard. The new administrative offices are opposite. Police headquarters and the post office are in Mann Street. At the approach to the jetty is a **war memorial** with three rifles forming a tripod and two cannon shafts beside them. The inscription reads: '*Aux engagés volontaires Rodriguais 1914-18, 1939-45*'.

In Jenner Street, opposite Barclays Bank and almost hidden by one-storey houses, are the six miniature minarets of the **Noor-ud-Deen Mosque**, rebuilt in 1979–81. Fisherman Lane is behind it with a public toilet on the bayfront and the slaughterhouse, where the white-painted buildings are marked PORC, CABRIS and BOEUF. The **St Barnabas Anglican Church** and school complex is at the eastern end of Jenner Street. The church is contemporary in style (built in 1977) with an interior tower. There is a gym in the compound, too. The **Roman Catholic Church** is in Ricard Street, in the same block as the colonial building which houses the fire station.

The **bus park** is at the top of Gordon Street, where the town is being expanded and developed on reclaimed land. There are kiosks selling snacks open in the mornings and early afternoons. In Duncan

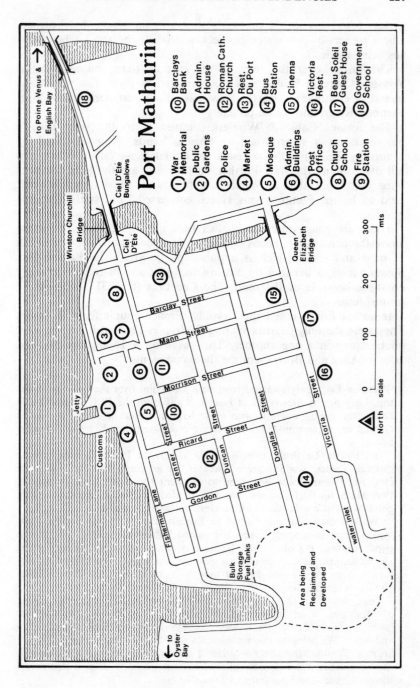

Port Mathurin

1 War Memorial
2 Public Gardens
3 Police
4 Market
5 Mosque
6 Admin. Buildings
7 Post Office
8 Church School
9 Fire Station
10 Barclays Bank
11 Admin. House
12 Roman Cath. Church
13 Rest. Du Port
14 Bus Station
15 Cinema
16 Victoria Rest.
17 Beau Soleil Guest House
18 Government School

to Pointe Venus & English Bay →

Winston Churchill Bridge

Ciel D'Été Bungalows

Ciel D'Été

Queen Elizabeth Bridge

Barclay Street

Mann Street

Morrison Street

Ricard Street

Gordon Street

Fisherman Lane

Jenner Street

Duncan Street

Douglas Street

Victoria Street

Jetty

Customs

Bulk Storage Fuel Tanks

Area being Reclaimed and Developed

water inlet

to Oyster Bay

0   100   200   300   mts
scale

North

Street close by, there is a tinker's shed and showroom by the road, where passers-by can watch buckets, watering cans and kitchen utensils being made.

The bridge over the river at the east of town, officially called **Winston Churchill Bridge**, was reconstructed in 1980. The road turns inland or continues along the coast past the government school, over Bamboo River, and past a cemetery.

The former Cable & Wireless complex is to the right (there's no sign), up a steep road to Mount Venus. Now operated by Mauritius Telecom, the **overseas public telephone** office is on this hill overlooking the bay. Further up the road are the long barracks once used by Cable & Wireless staffers and above them is what used to be the Pointe Venus Hotel, converted from staff bungalow quarters.

There are guesthouses in English Bay, a kilometre's walk further along the coast road. **Filaos** is close to (but not actually on) a beach of mud and rocks which is a public picnic area. The **English Bay Sports Club** is a bar in a tin hut in front of it and there is a cemetery on the other side of the road. The **Cocotiers** (tel: 831 1800) has 12 rooms, *basic*.

It was at Filaos that I met a young French couple from Réunion. They were the only tourists visiting Rodrigues that week and we kept on bumping into one another. They were on a 14-day holiday and after it, Alice and Bruno sent me these comments.

'**Port Sud-Est**, newly surfaced road with viewpoint over the coast from the top. Ugly new houses (kind of boxes), a gift from the EEC. **Mount Lubin** has a craft centre where women make bags in *vacoas* or aloes for sale. **St Gabriel** has an enormous but not very nice-looking church; tropical vegetation.

'By bus to **Le Brulé**, then one hour's walk to **Pointe Cotton**, passing through **Trèfles**, a windy place where an air generator (windmill) is to be established near **Roche Bon Dieu** to augment the diesel power supply of Port Mathurin. Ugly houses here, too, funded by EEC. Pointe Cotton is a good beach in a wild place, with a clear but shallow lagoon.

'Walked back along the coast to English Bay, very easy and pleasant walk that took us three hours. We passed **Baladirou**, which is not such a good beach as P Cotton, and **Grand Bay**, where the surfaced road starts again. Beaches here quite isolated and we saw only a few fishermen who waved to us. At **Caverne Provert** there is a small public beach with grass and filaos surrounding it.

'Inauguration of the TV station and the arrival of the Governor General of Mauritius in an Indian warship. The ship was too big to enter the harbour. The military parade was accompanied by folkloric music, polka and waltz. Waited with two male nurses who told us about a court divorce hearing. The husband told the judge: 'I am a farmer. When I sow onions, I harvest onions. When I sow maize, I harvest maize ... But in this case I sowed 'Creole' and I harvested 'Chinese'.

'Feast at **Fumier** (Ally Bay) with the Governor and ministers present. We sat on benches in the back of a lorry watching families and young children on the beach. It was very quiet. Walked across to **St François**, beautiful wide and wild beach, and on to **Trou d'Argent**, small deserted cove beyond *filao* plantation fenced to keep out cattle. Big waves.

'By bus to **La Ferme**, more ugly EEC houses. Women's centre, no crafts, only cooking, knitting and sewing instruction. Library and a few shops here as well as a new (ugly!) church. Returned on foot to Port Mathurin (four hours) along the coast, no beaches nor vegetation and only a few houses in each bay. Invited for tea inside a small house at **Malagash Bay** where the daughters wanted addresses in Réunion as they hope to go there. Bigger houses, but not pretty, in **Oyster Bay** where the wealthy people of Port Mathurin live. Passed the prison with three men and one woman inmates.

'Bus to **Petit Gabriel** (Rs2.5), by taking bus to La Ferme and stopping at P Gabriel. From there by food to **Rivière Cocos** (one hour; we had to ask people the way.) From the top, superb viewpoint to the lagoon and islands inside it: Gombrani, Paille en Queue, Hermitage and Cat. By boat with fishermen to **Gombrani Island** (Rs25 each, two people in a boat). Very windy, we tore a sail and kept on with a paddle (45 minutes). Rodriguan fishing boats look like Egyptian boats.

'**Gombrani Island** is the largest in the lagoon. One house for the caretaker, who has two dogs as company. Small acacias and *filaos* everywhere, and a small beach. On the way back by boat in rough sea a turtle swam in front of us. There are still a few turtles but people keep on killing them although it is forbidden by law. We hitched a car ride to La Ferme and then returned by bus to Port Mathurin.

'By car (a lift) to Port Sud-Est, then on foot to **Gravier**, good beaches along the coast. Nice view of Hermitage Island. From Gravier went on to a small creek with two names: **Anse Vacoas** or **Anse Bouteille**. Good swimming in clear blue water with big fishes. Hiked along a path which took us to **Grande Montagne**, an easy two-hour climb, then hitched a ride to Port Mathurin.

'Dinner with a Rodriguan family in town and, at 23.00, we had a beer in the Victoria Restaurant which was still open! Next day got a lift to the airport and went on foot to **Baie Topaze**, arid landscape, very hot, no wind. Returned to **La Fouche** by food and then by bus to Port Mathurin.

'Some hints for seeing Rodrigues: catch the bus either outside **Ciel d'été** (but it's usually full then) or from the bus station. Buses only go to Rivière Cocos on Saturdays. New asphalted roads to Fumier, Port Sud-Est, La Fouche, Quatre Vents and Rivière Cocos.'

From an article I wrote for *The Sunday Telegraph*:

'Buses are privately owned and wistfully named: Air Jumbo Jet was typical. Buses go to the beach only on Sundays.

'At **Mangue** Village, I found the only restaurant in Rodrigues open on Sunday, **Chez Jean**. Raw, mottled red sausages, traditional to Rodrigues, hung from a wrought-iron fence to cure among the scarlet leaves of poinsettias. There were no prices on the menu as Jean, the proprietor, charges according to his mood. My bill was the equivalent of £3.70 for a spicy sausage starter, fish with ginger, and a beer. As I left, Jean must have felt he had charged too much for I was presented with a bottle of his own, bilious green chilli sauce as a souvenir.

'At the road junction where the Ho Tu Nam store, Chez Ah Kong, Mrs Wong Tong's grocery and Jameson Begue's bar and bakery constitute the village centre, I waited for a bus back to town. Mr Begue, the baker, sold me a hot sponge cake and advised me to walk.

'The breeze tempered the heat of the sun and the climb was gentle to **Quatre Vents**, a hilltop village with views of both north and south coasts and the constant, reassuring blue where sea and sky merge. I asked a group of farmers sitting on the steps of the grocer's shop when the next bus was due.

' "No bus", one of them said cheerfully. "You'll have to walk."

' "There's a short cut to Oyster Bay", said a boy when he saw my look of despair. "You can get a lift to town from there. I'll show you."

'We set out through an avenue of trees along a grass path that opened up to a hillside of green sloping down to the coast. **Oyster Bay** seemed a long way off. At an isolated house where tanned, flaxen-haired children played in the garden, the boy invited me to meet his family. I gave them the cake and they presented me with another bottle of chilli sauce, brimful with whole chillies and garlic.

'It took us an hour to reach Oyster Bay. A bus pulled up on the main road. It was the one that had taken me to the town from the airport a week before. The driver smilingly refused payment.

'The next day, on the plane back to Mauritius, the pilot warned us before take-off: "It is strictly forbidden to carry fish on flights from Rodrigues." I looked at my bag. All I had from Rodrigues were two bottles of chilli sauce.'

AGALEGA

Agalega is situated between the Seychelles and Mauritius, west of the Mascarene Ridge, about 1,206kms north of Mauritius and 563kms south of the Seychelles. There are actually two islands (North and South), separated by a sandbank which can be forded at low tide. Taken as one, the island is 24kms long but not more than 3.25kms wide.

North Island is elongated and has the main coconut mill on it; pear-shaped South Island is used as the administrative centre. There are nearly 300 people living on Agalega, which is administered by the Outer Islands Development Corporation as an island plantation producing coconut oil. It is almost entirely covered with coconut palms and some *filaos*. The highest points are sand dunes of 15m: **Grand Mountain** on South Island and **Emmerez Mountain** on North Island.

The islands were named by the Portuguese after the nationality of their discoverer, Juan de Nova, who was a Spanish Galician serving the King of Portugal. Galega or A'galega means Galician. At the time of the British takeover they were occupied by the captain of a French privateer, licensed by General Decaen to cultivate and harvest coconuts, using slaves from Madagascar. The importance of coconut oil to Mauritius resulted in the island being left alone to continue production by various French concession holders.

From the 1930s, exploitation of Agalega was by Mauritian/Seychellois companies until the government of Mauritius took over control in 1975, paying Rs13.2 million in compensation. In 1982, the Outer Islands Development Corporation was formed, with responsibility for all the islands of the State of Mauritius, except for Mauritius and Rodrigues. A board of government officials and knowledgeable citizens was set up with a general manager to run the corporation.

In Agalega, the resident manager is responsible for a working population of 180 to 200 including administration staff, police, meteorologists, teachers, medical personnel, and approximately 150 labourers. These include carpenters, masons, gardeners, and the coconut cultivators employed on contract. Wives and children make up the additional population.

The majority of labourers work from 06.00 to 11.00 every day except Sunday on a task basis. They are paid partly in cash and partly in supplies. After work they fish, attend to chores or relax. This idyllic existence is ruled by a bell. It is rung to wake them up at 05.00, then again at 06.00 to call them for work, and at 06.15 for work to commence. At 11.00 it sounds the lunch break. At 12.00 the bell rings for those not on tasks to recommence work, and at 18.00 it sounds again to warn people that work areas are from then out of bounds. Lights out is rung at 21.00 hours. On Mondays and Fridays the bell rings at 13.00 to announce the opening of the shop. It is also rung to summon people to special occasions such as pay or ration distribution, funerals and religious services.

The entire population is Roman Catholic and Creole. Culturally they have been much influenced by the Seychelles connection and Radio Seychelles is better received than MBC. Consequently, their language is a mix of Mauritian and Seychelles Creole. *Séga* and sport (there are two football clubs) are their main diversions. Staple diet is rice and fish, with a liberal amount of coconut milk in curries and sweet preparations.

Permission to visit Agalega and other islands has to be sought in writing from the Outer Islands Development Corporation (4th Floor, Jade House, cnr Jummah Mosque and Remy Ollier Streets, Port Louis, tel: 240 4061). The OIDC is the only authority to give security clearance, and also controls the sale of tickets on the irregular (twice a year?) ferry service.

ST BRANDON

In Mauritius, reference to '**Les Iles**' means the St Brandon archipelago, also known as the Cargados Garayos Islands. These lie 395kms northwest of Mauritius, forming an arc from south to north, its convex facing towards the east. There are 22 low-lying islands, parts of which are sometimes submerged, as well as numerous reefs and sandbanks. Eight of the islands are in the south of the arc, where the biggest (at 12.2 hectares) is **Cocos Island**. **Albatros** is 48kms to its north. Between the two is **Raphael Island** (10.1 hectares), which is the administrative centre, also sometimes known as Establishment Island.

From 1546, the islands were shown on Portuguese charts as Sao Brandao, puzzling since St Brandon is an Irish saint. The Portuguese also called them Cargados Garayos, deriving the name from Coroa dos Garajaos, meaning reef of seabirds.

The islands abound with birds and guano was the main export. In 1862, cotton was tried, without success. Cyclones, problems with fresh water, and the harsh conditions of life (no women) also affected the islands' development. Since the 1830s, the richness of the fishing grounds has been exploited and in 1910, there were a hundred fishermen based in the islands.

Fish is still king, salted and dried for export to Mauritius. Fishermen are engaged by the Outer Islands Development Corporation, which manages St Brandon, on a four to six months' contract. Their work day begins at dawn and by 07.00 they are at sea. After they have returned with their catch, the fish have to be gutted, cleaned and put in the salt beds.

The fishermen, several dozens of them from Mauritius, Rodrigues and the Seychelles, lodge in barracks. Raphael (Establishment) Island has a modest chapel, a house for the administrator and his staff, a hanger for the salt fish, a community hall and a shop.

Beaches of soft, white, powdery sand, waving palm trees, and translucent lagoons with thousands of seabirds living undisturbed, make St Brandon seem a tropical island paradise. Perhaps it is, but not for the fishermen who have to work there in isolation from family and girlfriends.

TROMELIN

Mauritius claims sovereignty over Tromelin but France occupies it and Madagascar wants it. It is a flat, sandy, barren place, less than two kms long and about 640m wide. It is located between the St Brandon archipelago and Madagascar, actually closer to Madagascar than Port Louis, which is 482kms away.

It was known in the 18th century as Ile aux Sable or Sandy Island.

In 1761, a French vessel was shipwrecked on the reef which extends from its southern point. The whites in the crew built a boat and reached Madagascar safely. They left 80 blacks on the island, promising to return. It was 15 years before a French chevalier, M Tromelin, landed and found seven women living there. They were the only survivors, having existed on shellfish, turtle and brackish water. He took them to Mauritius.

The French cultivate turtles on the island and export them to Réunion. There is also a weather station. Mauritius' claim to ownership is based on the capitulation terms of 1810, as Tromelin was regarded then as a dependency of Mauritius. Also, there are guano gathering permits granted by the British colonial government in 1902. Fishing rights were claimed in 1980 by an act of the Mauritius parliament.

THE CHAGOS ARCHIPELAGO

The Chagos Archipelago, together with Desroches, Farquhar and Aldabra, formerly part of the Seychelles group, now constitute the British Indian Ocean Territory (BIOT). They lie 1,930kms northeast of Mauritius, south of Gan in the Maldives. Visits by individuals are difficult to arrange.

Six Islands
Six low islands arranged in a horseshoe shape, these are 109kms distant from Diego Garcia. When they were dependencies of Mauritius, they were harvested for coconuts as well as supplying pigs, poultry and fat-tailed land crabs. They are connected by shoals and access is difficult due to the reefs and breakers.

Peros Banhos
A cluster of a score of small islands which form the largest group of the Chagos archipelago, the islands form a basin of 29kms in length, north to south, and 19kms breadth from east to west. The main one is about 3kms long. They were also known as the Iles Bourdés after a M de Bourdé, who is credited with discovering them after the Portuguese had named them.

In the mid-19th century, these islands were a flourishing fishing station and establishment for the manufacture of coconut oil, under Mauritian ownership and employing 125 people.

Salomon Islands
Known as Les Onze Iles, being 11 in number, the Salomons were named after a ship called *Salomon*. They form a basin with a safe

anchorage for vessels of small draught. Their soil is rich in coconut trees, which used to be harvested by resident Mauritians.

In the last century, these islands were noted for a rare tree called *faux gaiac*, which grew to a height of 40 metres, and was a deep chocolate colour, with sound wood when old. Fresh water could be obtained from wells. Turtles used to be found there but not so many fish, due to the presence of seals.

Trois Frères

Actually four small islands, connected by shoals. Coconuts grow on all of them and fish and turtle and fresh water are to be found. Nearby, between this group and Six Islands, are **Eagle** and **Danger** Islands. All used to provide coconut oil for the Mauritius market.

Diego Garcia

The name of the archipelago used to be Bassas de Chagos, after the largest island of the group, which was known as Chagos, or Gratiosa, as well as by the name which has survived today, Diego Garcia.

The island is in the form of a serpent bent double, its interior forming a broad, steep, coral wall standing in the ocean. This encompasses a lagoon which is itself a large national harbour and safe anchorage. The island is $28.5km^2$ in area with a steep coral reef all around, except at the entrance to the lagoon.

The French exiled leprous slaves to Diego Garcia from Mauritius claiming that the turtle, which would be their sole diet, would restore them to good health. In 1792, an English merchant ship sent two Lascar crew members ashore for water and some of the leper residents – women as well as men – met them and showed them to a well. When the master of the brig learned of the encounter, he made the Indian seamen stay on the island and sailed away as fast as he could.

After the British takeover in 1810, the exiling of leprosy sufferers was discontinued and some 300 migrants, including Europeans, went voluntarily from Mauritius to set up a saltfish trading company and to plant and harvest coconuts. The settlement flourished peacefully for 150 years, with produce being ferried to Mauritius, from whence came the imported goods the settlers needed to live.

By 1965, the population of the entire Chagos archipelago had grown to some 900 families, representing 2,000 inhabitants. The islands were dependencies of Mauritius and the *îlois* – the Creole term for the Chagos islanders – conducted trade with Mauritius through an irregular ferry link. They were content with their simple and presumably happy existence.

In the countdown to independence, Britain decided to detach Diego Garcia and the nearby islands from Mauritius, virtually taking them over a second time. The politicians in Mauritius were obliged to agree because, being a colony, they had little choice and gaining independence was their priority.

Three million pounds in development aid was the reward while Mauritius stipulated two conditions for letting Britain keep Diego Garcia: it would be used for communication purposes only, and the atoll would be returned to Mauritius if Britain no longer needed it.

Having signed the agreement, Britain created a new colony: the British Indian Ocean Island Territory, BIOT. The Chagos islanders were bemused but they did not have long to wait. The ferry service linking them to Mauritius was stopped, the sole employer of labour was bought out by the British and the copra plantation was closed down. Work ceased, and so did food imports. To survive, the *îlois* had to leave.

Less than a year later, the BIOT was leased to the United States of America for 'defence purposes'. By then it was nominally uninhabited and both the British and North American public were kept in the dark about the real situation. The lease to the USA is for 50 years, with an option for a further 20.

Now Diego Garcia is the main US military base in the Indian Ocean, with superb port facilities, the latest in communications systems and a 3,600m runway capable of handling, and fuelling, B52 bombers. The coconuts have been replaced with a nuclear arsenal.

When politicians in Mauritius realised what had happened, a cyclone of protest and controversy raged. After years of angry negotiations, Britain acknowledged that the Chagos islanders, who had been forcibly displaced from their homes, were entitled to better treatment than being abandoned in the backstreets of Port Louis. Compensation was paid in 1982.

While the *îlois* no longer seem to be an issue, the question of sovereignty over the Chagos Archipelago remains. In the meantime, the BIOT is a blot on the peaceful waters of the Indian Ocean.

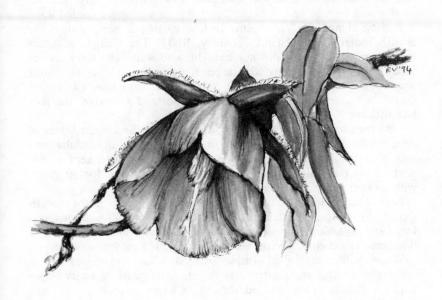

Appendices

MAURITIUS: HOTELS

A selection of hotels grouped according to price range. A stay at a hotel in the *medium* or *grand* category would work out at less than the public rate per night if booked through a travel agent as part of a package including flights.

Basic Hotels
(In 1994, a single room cost between Rs100 and Rs800.)

Hotel/Address	Telephone	Fax
Aquarelle Guesthouse		
Mahebourg	631 9479	631 9991
Arc en Ciel		
Baie du Tombeau	247 2616	247 2772
Bourbon Tourist		
J Mosque St, Port Louis	240 4407	
Capri		
Baie du Tombeau	247 2533	247 1071
City Hotel		
Port Louis	208 5340	208 7882
Coin de Mire Village		
Cap Malheureux	263 7302	212 1361
Continental		
Curepipe	675 3434	675 3437
Etoile de Mer		
Trou aux Biches	261 6561	261 6178
Etoile du Nord		
Pereybere	263 8303	
Gold Crest		
Quatre Bornes	454 5945	454 9599
Little Acorn		
Flic en Flac	453 8431	453 8828
Mandarin		
Floreal	696 5031	686 6858
Mascareignes		
Cap Malheureux	262 7373	263 7372

Monaco
Quatre Bornes   425 2608   425 1072
Monte Carlo Guesthouse
Mahebourg   631 9514
Notre Dame Guesthouse
Mahebourg   631 9582
Riverside
Belle Rose   464 4957   464 5553
St Tropez
Mahebourg   631 9646
Sunray
Coromandel   233 4777
Sylvilla
Pereybere   263 7424
Seapoint Beach Bungalows
Pointe aux Canonniers   263 8604   686 7380
Tamarin
Tamarin Bay   683 6581   683 6927
Tandoori Tourist Hotel
Port Louis   212 2131
Tourist Rendezvous
Plaine Magnien   637 3516
Rose Hill (Auberge de)
Rose Hill   464 1793   464 6997
Villas Pointe aux Roches
Chemin Grenier   625 5112   626 2507

Medium Hotels

(In 1994, the public rate for a single room ranged from Rs800 to Rs2,500.)

Hotel/Address	Telephone	Fax
Blue Lagoon Beach		
Mahebourg	631 9045	631 9046
Calamar		
Balaclava	261 5187	261 5247
Casuarina Village		
Trou aux Biches	261 5653	261 6111
Centre de Pêche		
Black River	683 6522	683 6318
Colonial Coconut		
Grand Bay	263 8720	263 7116
Croix du Sud		
Mahebourg	631 9505	631 9603

Domaine du Chasseur
  Vieux Grand Port   631 9261   631 9261
Emeraude Beach
  Belle Mare   415 1122   415 1109
Flamboyant
  Belle Mare   415 1036   415 1035
Island View
  Grand Gaube   283 9544   283 9233
Kuxville
  Cap Malheureux   263 7913   263 7407
Moonlight Bay Protea
  Grand River Southeast   419 2106   419 2106
Mauricia
  Grand Bay   263 7800   263 7888
Palmar
  Belle Mare   415 1041   415 1043
Paradise Cove
  Cap Malheureux   263 7983   263 7736
Pearle Beach Sunset
  Flic en Flac   453 8428   453 8405
PLM Azur
  Mont Choisy   261 6070   261 6749
Sandy Bay
  Belle Mare   413 2880   413 2054
Silver Beach
  Trou d'Eau Douce   419 2600   419 2604
Surcouf Village
  Palmar   415 1800   212 1361
Tropical
  Trou d'Eau Douce   419 2300   419 2302
Veranda Bungalow Village
  Grand Bay   263 8015   263 7369
Villas Caroline
  Flic en Flac   453 8411   453 8144
Villas Pointe Aux Biches
  Pointe aux Piments   261 5901   261 5904

Grand Hotels
(In 1994, the public rate for a single room ranged from Rs2,500 to as much as Rs12,000.)

Hotel/Address	Telephone	Fax
Ambre		
Belle Mare	415 1544	415 1594
Bella Mare Plage		
Belle Mare	415 1515	415 1082
Brabant		
Morne	683 6775	683 6786
Canonnier		
Pointe aux Canonniers	263 7997	263 7864
Grand Gaube		
Grand Gaube	283 9350	283 9420
Maritim		
Balaclava	261 5600	261 5904
Merville Beach		
Grand Bay	263 8621	263 8146
Paradis		
Morne	683 6775	683 6786
Pirogue Sun		
Flic en Flac	453 8441	453 8449
Royal Palm		
Grand Bay	263 8353	263 8455
St Geran Sun		
Poste de Flacq	415 1825	415 1983
Shandrani		
Blue Bay	631 9301	631 9313
Sofitel Imperial		
Flic en Flac	453 8700	453 8320
Touessrok Sun		
Trou d'Eau Douce	419 2451	419 2025
Trou aux Biches Village		
Trou aux Biches	261 6561	261 6611

MAURITIUS: RESTAURANTS

In this selection of various restaurants in different price ranges, those I have particularly enjoyed because of their good food are marked with *. Further details about them are under the different location headings.

Amigo	
Cap Malheureux	263 8418
***Assiette du Pêcheur**	
Grand Bay	263 8589
***Au Gourmet**	
Curepipe	676 1871
Bateau Ivre	
Pointe aux Canonniers	263 8766
***Bel Etang**	
Bel Etang	435 5148
Bonne Chute	
Black River	683 6552
Bonne Marmite	
Port Louis	212 2403
Café de la Plage	
Grand Bay	263 7081
***Café du Vieux Conseil**	
Port Louis	211 0393
Canelle Rouge	
Pailles	212 4225
Carnivore	
Pointe aux Canonniers	263 7020
Carri Poule	
Port Louis	212 1295
Chamarel	
Chamarel	683 6421
Chez Manuel	
St Julien	418 3599
Chinese Wok	
Curepipe	676 1548
Clos St Louis	
Pailles	212 4225
***Domaine du Chasseur**	
Vieux Grand Port	631 9261
Domino	
Morne	683 6675
Flore Mauricienne	
Port Louis	212 2200

Flore Orientale
Port Louis   240 3017
Fu Xiao
Pailles   212 4225
*****Gaulois**
Curepipe
Happy Valley Seafood & Sharkfin
Quatre Bornes   454 9208
Kentucky Fried Chicken
Curepipe   676 6394
*****Kwang Chow**
Port Louis   240 9735
Indra
Pailles   212 4225
*****Lai Min**
Port Louis   242 0042
Mandarin
Vacoas   696 4551
*****Namaste**
Port Louis
*****National Hotel**
Port Louis   212 0453
*****Nouvelle Potinère**
Curepipe   676 2648
ONU (Bar)
Port Louis
Palmeraie
Port Louis   212 2597
Paloma
Port Louis   208 5861
Pizza Hut
Port Louis
Piment Rouge
Quatre Bornes   464 4444
*****Providence**
Port Louis   212 2427
Rolly's Steak House
Quatre Bornes   464 8267
Shamrock
Port Louis   212 5271
*****Snooker**
Quatre Bornes   464 2432
Snow White
Port Louis   208 3528
*****Tandoori**
Port Louis   212 0031

*Tan Yan (Bar)
   Port Louis   240 0228
Underground
   Port Louis   212 0064
Val
   Cluny
Varangue sur Morne
   Plaine Champagne   423 7810

TOUR OPERATORS IN UK & IRELAND FEATURING MAURITIUS

Abercrombie & Kent, tel: 071 730 9600; fax: 071 730 9376
Airwaves, tel: 081 875 1188; fax: 081 871 4668 (*w*)
Beachcomber Tours, tel: 0483 33008; fax: 0483 32820 (*w*)
British Airways Holidays, tel: 0293 611611; fax: 0293 552319 (*w*)
Carrier, tel: 0625 582006; fax: 0625 586818 (*bh, w*)
Cosmos Distant Dreams, tel: 061 480 5799; fax: 061 480 0833 (*w*)
Elegant Resort, tel: 0244 325620; fax: 0244 341084 (*w*)
Elite Vacations Ltd, tel: 081 864 9818; fax: 081 426 9178 (*w*)
Grenadier Travel, tel: 0206 549585; fax: 0206 561337
Hayes & Jarvis, tel: 081 748 0088; fax: 081 741 0299
Inghams Travel, tel: 081 789 6555; fax: 081 785 2045 (*w*)
Kuoni Travel, tel: 0306 743000; fax: 0306 740719 (*w*)
Okavango Tours & Safaris, tel: 081 341 9442; fax: 081 348 9983
Silk Cut Travel, tel: 0730 268 511; fax: 0730 260263 (*w*)
Somak Travel Ltd, tel: 081 903 8166; fax: 081 903 3464
Southern Africa Travel, tel: 081 892 3637; fax: 081 891 5027
Sunset Travel, tel: 071 498 9922; fax: 071 978 1337 (*sc, bh, w*)
Tana Specialist Travel, tel: 0789 414200; fax: 0789 414420 (*sc, bh, w*)
Thomas Cook Faraway, tel: 0733 332255; fax: 0733 505784 (*w*)
Thomson Worldwide, tel: 081 200 8733. 21 (*w*)
Tropical Places, tel: 0342 825123; fax: 0342 822364. ITV Teletext p259
(*sc, bh, w*)
Tropix, tel: 081 875 1777; fax: 081 875 9111 (*w*)
Twickers World, tel: 081 892 8164; fax: 081 892 8061
Twin Towers, tel: 0532 754721; fax: 0532 784667 (*sc, bh, w*)
VFB Holidays, tel; 0242 240338 (reservations) 240310 (brochures)
Fax: 0242 570340 (*bh*)
World Travel Ltd, tel: 071 636 4141; fax: 071 637 2418 (*sc, bh*)
Mauritian Connections, tel: 061 865 7275; fax: 061 865 2501
Union-Castle Travel, tel: 071 584 0001; fax: 071 581 8122
John Cassidy Travel, Dublin, Ireland, tel: 8 735 000; fax: 8 735 015
Ultimate Horizons, Belfast, Ireland, tel: 0232 439 399; fax: 0232 331
007

---

sc   Self-catering accommodation available
bh   Includes good standard budget hotels
w   Organises weddings

USEFUL PHRASES – HOW TO SAY THEM IN CREOLE

To speak Creole, the slightest knowledge of French will be useful for the formalities; for instance, 'Good Morning' is 'Bon-zoor'. Here are some useful phrases that differ from the French.

I want to go to...	*Mwa oo-lay al...*
How much is it?	*Kumien sa?*
It's too expensive	*Li tro ser*
Good/That's fine	*Li bon*
Take me to the hotel	*Amen mwa lotel*
What is your name?	*Ki oo non?*
How are you?	*Ki man yeah?*
Very well, and you?	*Mwa bee-en, eh oo?*
What are you doing?	*Ki toe pay fare?*
I don't understand	*Mwa pa kompran*
Speak slowly	*Pa coz tro veet*
Would you like a drink?	*Oo poo bwah keek soz?*
I'd like wine	*Mwa oo-lay do van*
How old are you?	*Ki arje too en?*
Where are you going?	*Kot oo pay allay?*
I want to stay	*Mwa pay restay*
What's this?	*Ki etay sa?*
Goodbye	*Sallaam*

How to say places

Baie du Tombeau	*Beige-tom-bo*
Beau Bassin	*Bo Bassa*
Belle Mare	*Bell-mar*
Case Noyale	*Kaz noy-al*
Curepipe	*Kew-peep*
Grand Bassin	*Gra Bassa*
Gris Gris	*Gree-gree*
Ile aux Cerfs	*Eel-oh-sair*
Ile aux Aigrettes	*Eel-oh-saygrett*
Mahebourg	*Mayberg or Mah-ay-bour*
Morne Brabant	*Morn Brabon*
Port Louis	*Por(t) Loo-ee*
Quatre Bornes	*Katr born*
Réduit	*Raydwee*
Rodrigues	*Rodreegs*
Rose Hill	*Rohzill*
Souillac	*Soo-ee-yak*
Triolet	*Tree-oh-lay*
Trou aux Biches	*Tro' beesh*
Trou d'Eau Douce	*Tro'do-doo*
Vacoas	*Vak-wa*

FURTHER READING

Atachia, Michael: *Sea Fishes of Mauritius*. Mauritius 1984

Baker, Philip: *Kreole – A Description of Mauritian Creole*. Seahurst & Co, London 1972 (OP)

Durrell, Gerald: *Golden Bats and Pink Pigeons*. Fountain, 1979

Goswami-Sewtohul, K: *A Mauritian Phrase Book*. Mauritius 1981

Hildebrand: *Travel Guide to Mauritius*. Frankfurt/London 1985

Macmillan, Allister: *Mauritius Illustrated* (1914). Editions du Pacifique, 1991

Marsh, R V R: *Mountains of Mauritius: A Climber's Guide*. Mauritius.

Michel, Claude: *Birds of Mauritius*. Mauritius 1986

Michel, Claude: *Marine Molluscs of Mauritius*. Mauritius 1985

Michel, Claude and Owadally, A W: *Our Environment, Mauritius*. Mauritius 1975

Owadally, A W: *A Guide to the Royal Botanical Gardens, Pamplemousses*. Mauritius 1978

Sookhee, Lalita: *Mauritian Delights*. Mauritius 1985

Riviere, Lindsay: *Historical Dictionary of Mauritius*. Scarecrow Press, London 1982

Vaisse, Christian: *Living in Mauritius*. Editions du Pacifique, 1989

Ventor, A J: *Underwater Mauritius*. Media House Publications, South Africa 1988

Index